ROUTLEDGE LIBRARY EDITIONS:
INDUSTRIAL ECONOMICS

Volume 23

PRICING IN BUSINESS

PRICING IN BUSINESS

D. C. HAGUE

Routledge
Taylor & Francis Group
LONDON AND NEW YORK

First published in 1971 by George Allen & Unwin Ltd

This edition first published in 2018
by Routledge
2 Park Square, Milton Park, Abingdon, Oxon OX14 4RN

and by Routledge
711 Third Avenue, New York, NY 10017

Routledge is an imprint of the Taylor & Francis Group, an informa business

British Library Cataloguing in Publication Data
A catalogue record for this book is available from the British Library

ISBN: 978-1-138-30830-5 (Set)
ISBN: 978-1-351-21102-4 (Set) (ebk)
ISBN: 978-0-8153-7030-7 (Volume 23) (hbk)
ISBN: 978-1-351-24970-6 (Volume 23) (ebk)

Publisher's Note
The publisher has gone to great lengths to ensure the quality of this reprint but points out that some imperfections in the original copies may be apparent.

Disclaimer
The publisher has made every effort to trace copyright holders and would welcome correspondence from those they have been unable to trace.

Pricing in Business

by D. C. HAGUE

London

GEORGE ALLEN & UNWIN LTD

RUSKIN HOUSE MUSEUM STREET

First published in 1971

ISBN 0 04 658040 9

Printed in Great Britain
in 10 point Times Roman
by Alden & Mowbray Ltd
at the Alden Press, Oxford

Foreword

The research described in this book was mainly carried out between 1964 and 1968, when prices in the U.K. were rising, but not more quickly than they had done during much of the post-war period. It is only during 1970 and the first half of 1971 that the rate of price increase in the U.K. has become really rapid. It therefore seems worthwhile to add to the suggestions we have made at various points in the book about how prices should be set. In this Foreword, we look at the questions which firms should ask themselves during periods of rapid inflation, if they are to ensure that increasing costs do not reduce profits to intolerably low levels.

One can only hope that, in some way, the rapid increase in U.K. prices and costs which is taking place as these pages are being written will soon be halted. If it is not, then it is essential that firms should pay serious attention to the points raised in this Foreword. Otherwise, they will not be able to operate profitably or maintain the capital value of their assets. Even if the rate of price and cost increases returns to around the 3–5 per cent level that has been commonplace since 1945, these questions are well worth asking. Firms which pay careful attention to the issues listed below will avoid the slow erosion of their profits and the values of their assets that can only too easily happen when inflation is fast enough to cause damage, but not fast enough to be treated as a really important problem.

We consider three aspects of inflation. First, its general impact; second, its impact on producers of consumer and intermediate goods; third, its impact on producers of capital goods.

1. GENERAL PROBLEMS OF INFLATION

One effect of inflation which affects *all* firms is that it is almost impossible for financial accounts not to overstate profitability. This can be very serious if inflation is rapid. It is well known that Merrett and Sykes have calculated that in the past the overall rate of return on equities in the U.K. (including capital gains as well as dividends) has been around 8 per cent per annum. After tax, and after allowing for the rate of inflation experienced in 1970 and 1971, such a return would give a 'real' rate of return near zero. The issues that have to be considered if the firm is to offer its shareholders more satisfactory returns fall under a number of heads, but most of them are concerned with one part or another of the firm's accounting system.

1.1. CONTROL ACCOUNTS

Should firms take account of inflation in setting their *internal* objectives and budgets and in evaluating the performance of individual departments and managers? For example, should budgeted figures for turnover or profit be deflated to cancel out the effects of price increases? Again, should higher turnover and profit objectives be set than in the past to allow for inflation? If this is not done, will some parts of the firm appear to be increasing their turnover or profitability when they are actually slipping backwards in real terms?

1.2. DECISION ACCOUNTS

Should inflation be allowed for in DCF calculations, or other kinds of investment appraisal? If so, when and how? Should cash flow projections and capital budgets make more allowance for inflation? Whatever the period of time (or purpose) for which funds are invested it is important to get back the amount originally invested, plus enough to cancel out the effects of inflation during that period of time. The *real* value of the capital invested must be maintained.

1.3. STEWARDSHIP ACCOUNTS

Is it good enough to give investors near-zero real rates of return, even if investors are prepared to accept them? Does the rate of return the firm is trying to give to its shareholders (whether via dividends or capital appreciation) take enough account of inflation? In the U.K., have businesses and those who invest in them done enough to maintain the real value of dividends and share prices in recent years?

2.1. PROBLEMS WITH CONSUMER GOODS

2.1.1. Costs

What is the effect of inflation on costs? How much detail about inflationary increases should cost information give? To whom should it go? In what forms? How far should wages be given special treatment? Or other items?

How far can one use different and/or imported raw materials, components, etc. to reduce the effects of inflation on profits?

What about inventories? Are inventories sufficiently often valued at replacement cost, especially for pricing purposes? Or are inventories never held long enough for it to matter?

How should one handle capital costs in setting prices? Is enough account taken of replacement costs rather than of book values? Is the firm allowing inflation to reduce the real value of its capital assets?

2.1.2. Demand

What information is needed about the effects of inflation on demand conditions? Is enough effort being devoted to judging when increases in prices and/or incomes elsewhere in the economy have made it profitable to increase one's own prices?

2.1.3. Prices

When should prices be increased because of inflation? How much? How often? How far should price increases allow for rises in the replacement value of assets? Can one take advantage of the seasonal introduction of new fashions or styles to raise prices? Or can one introduce 'differentiated' products aimed at different market segments and selling at different prices? Or can one raise prices by changing the models one is selling and effectively increasing prices when new models are introduced? Can 'contribution' pricing, if not used already, improve the flexibility of pricing in inflationary periods? How far should the individual firm take 'the public interest' into account when setting prices during inflation? What does 'the public interest' require of the firm?

2.2. PROBLEMS OF INTERMEDIATE GOODS

What are the special problems of intermediate-good producers? How far are they 'squeezed' between suppliers and customers? Is this pressure correctly perceived? Does the firm exaggerate it? If so, how can it be more accurately judged? Is there any way of reducing it?

3. PROBLEMS OF CAPITAL GOODS

All British firms which contract to sell goods or services at fixed prices have been in difficulties because of cost inflation in recent years. The longer the period of time during which the contract ran the greater the problems.

Capital goods producers are particularly likely to run into difficulties during inflation because a long time often elapses between the receipt of an order and the delivery of the capital good.

Some of the key questions which capital goods firms must therefore ask are: How long a period elapses between the price being quoted and delivery taking place? How far can the firm predict cost increases over this period? What rate of return should it be aiming at in these circumstances?

How far can the firm allow for inflation in its contracts? Can an allowance to cover inflation be added on when the capital good is delivered? For example, can the firm introduce some kind of U.K. price or cost index number into the contract, so that the price ultimately received allows for inflation? Or can some allowance for inflation be included in the price quoted at the beginning?

If not, why is it not possible to set prices at a level high enough to cover likely future cost increases? Is it the problem that one's competitors allow too little for future cost increases in the prices they quote? Are there any ways to persuade or induce them to charge more?

Can one find ways of reducing uncertainty over future rates of inflation? For example, should one try to take smaller orders at more frequent intervals?

Individual readers of this book may well find that they need to ask additional questions or different questions to fit in with their own particular circumstances. However, this basic list of questions is intended to help anyone who is meeting the challenges which businesses face in a world where inflation appears to be a permanent problem.

May 1971

Contents

Acknowledgements

Although this book appears under my name, it is the result of a major collaborative effort over a period of six years, during which four researchers have done a great deal of the underlying work.

From 1964–6, Chris Troughton and David Taylor worked on the project. They are responsible for several of the case studies. David Taylor has also commented on the manuscript. In 1966, Dick Cripps and Bob Vause took over the field work and completed the cases. Bob Vause has since commented on the manuscript and wrote a first draft of Chapter 8. Peter Chew wrote the detailed report lying behind one of the cases.

My biggest debt is to Dick Cripps. Apart from his fieldwork, he has helped considerably in writing the book. He provided early drafts of Chapters 4 and 7 and parts of Chapters 1 and 5. He has made detailed comments and criticisms on the final manuscript. I am very grateful to him.

The Check List, written at an earlier stage and reproduced in Chapter 3, was a joint effort in which Bob Vause, Dick Cripps, Roger Morris (at the time General Manager of the Centre for Business Research) and I collaborated.

I also thank my colleagues Grigor McClelland and Baxter English for commenting on the manuscript. To all these, and to those in member firms who helped by providing case material, comment and research effort, I express my sincere thanks. However, since I wrote the whole of the final draft, I take the entire blame for any mistakes that remain.

One possible criticism may arise from the fact that the book is aimed simultaneously at three rather different groups of people. First, there are businessmen engaged in or interested in pricing. Second, there are students in business schools, colleges and universities. Third, there are students and teachers of economics.

This book is aimed especially at business. Although we hope it will be useful to economists as well we have made little attempt to relate the discussion to academic issues, like the debate over the relevance of the economic theory of the firm. However, we hope that the book will prove valuable to all who, for any reason, want a thorough and detailed analysis of how a number of British firms set their prices in the late 1960s.

D. C. HAGUE

November
1970

CHAPTER 1

What the Book is About

1.1 OUR AIMS

This book contains the findings from a study of pricing carried out in a number of member firms of the Centre for Business Research, which is linked to Manchester University. The subject was chosen because of the interest of member firms in pricing and because the Centre had some expertise in the field.

We must emphasize at once that we realize that pricing is only part of the much broader activity of marketing. We shall therefore have a good deal to report about these broader issues as well, but we do not pretend that our comments about marketing are systematic. Our real interest is in pricing. It is an important enough business problem to be worth looking at for its own sake, quite apart from any light that we may be able to throw on the related problems of marketing. In particular, a study of pricing tells us a great deal about the internal information system of the firm; about human and organizational relationships within the firm; and about problems in analysing the firm's external environment, present and future. Pricing decisions are among the most demanding ones that a manager has to take, not least because they require an understanding of the uncertain and changing external environment. This is why pricing is so well worth studying.

The main aim of this study was to add to our knowledge of how prices are fixed and so increase our understanding of the practical and theoretical problems of pricing. We feel that the study will do this in two ways. First, it will help those (whether they are practising managers, consultants or business-school teachers) who are actively engaged in pricing or in helping business to improve its pricing procedures. By seeing what was done in a number of firms, we were able to see where their approaches to pricing were similar, and where they differed. Because we were not directly involved in pricing in these firms, we were able to take a dispassionate view, to pinpoint weaknesses in their pricing procedures and to suggest ways of dealing with them. We acknowledge that because we did not have continuous, detailed contact with these firms and their markets over a long period of time, we may have been tempted to over-simplify a number of complex situations. However, we have tried not to let this happen.

Business-school teachers and consultants are involved in prescription—in explaining what businessmen *should* do in setting prices if they are to improve their pricing methods. To say this is not to condemn British industry. In every firm, there is always scope for learning, room for improvement. However, there are good reasons why this may be a time when more firms than usual are interested in improving their pricing methods. First, large sections of British industry, including some of the firms we studied, have until recently been protected by collective pricing agreements from the full effects of price competition within their home markets. Most of these agreements have been outlawed by the Restrictive Practices Court since 1958. The result is that many British firms have effectively been 'learning' to price again in the home market at some time during the period since 1958. Second, bodies like the Prices and Incomes Board have been forcing firms to look afresh at their pricing practices.

Apart from helping teachers, consultants and businessmen, we think that this book can also help economists to improve their theories about the role which prices play in individual firms, industries or in the economy as a whole. We shall leave most of what we have to say to economists for articles in the learned journals. However, it will pay us to spend a little time now giving a brief outline of those concepts from the economic theory of pricing that will be useful to us.

1.2 PRICING DECISIONS

In this section, we do not pretend to give a complete account even of the parts of economic theory that are relevant to pricing. We simply describe those economic concepts which will help us in this book. It must be emphasized, at the outset, that some of these concepts are also used by operational researchers and others studying these problems. The fact that the concepts we shall describe are used by economists certainly does not mean that economists have an exclusive right to them.

Perhaps the most convenient way of putting what we have to say into a conceptual context will be to look first at the broad characteristics of pricing problems. Indeed, the main elements of every pricing problem are the same, in principle, as the main elements of all business decision problems.

First, there are the objectives. Unless the firm knows what objectives it is pursuing, no rational pricing decision is possible. Second, there is the structure of the pricing problem. Every pricing decision affects a number of variables, some or all of which will be related to each other in some way. Indeed, both economists and operational researchers often set out the relationships between relevant variables by constructing a 'model'. Such a model isolates the key variables in in the problem and ignores the remainder. The model goes on to specify the broad character of the relationships between these key variables, expressing them in equations or diagrams. For example, in most pricing problems one needs to know what kind of relationship there is between the prices that might be charged and the quantity of product which would be sold at each of those prices. All this is done in the model-building stage.

This leads at once to the estimation stage. One has to discover the actual size of the variables in the specific problem and the precise nature of the relationships between them.

Third, the decision must be taken. In some cases this may be very easy. Given the particular pricing problem set out in the model, and the firm's objectives, it simply tries to find which course of action will best achieve those objectives. However, it may not be as simple as that. Firms may not want to take optimal decisions—those which come closest to achieving the firm's objectives. Even if they do, they may lack the necessary information; or human and organizational factors may impede optimal decision taking. Nor, of course, may firms use models of this kind at all. These are issues we shall have to consider as we proceed.

Our immediate task is to look a little more fully at the main elements in pricing problems, in order to introduce the concepts that we shall need in the remainder of the book. We must emphasize that, at this stage, we are not necessarily implying that firms do, or should, use 'models' in pricing.

1.2.1 Objectives

Economic theory has concerned itself very largely with the problems of what we shall describe as a 'competitive industry', where large numbers of smallish firms compete with each other. Indeed, a good deal of jargon has been developed to describe such industries, much of which we shall ignore because it is too esoteric. In this chapter we shall use the simple words 'competition' and 'competitive industry' to describe a situation where large numbers of firms compete in a market. It is essential to remember that we are using these words in a special sense.

The first assumption that economists have made in looking at 'competitive industries' is that each firm seeks to maximize profits. The reason why economists began to make this assumption was that it enabled them to predict what firms would do if economic conditions changed. They could then assume that the firm would react to any change in such a way that it would continue to earn maximum profits. Fortunately or unfortunately, the idea of profit maximization has spilt over into everyday discussions of business objectives, despite the fact that ours is a world where many industries contain only small numbers of firms. One difficulty which results is that profit maximization usually becomes a 'non-operational' objective. By a non-operational objective we mean one which does not tell a businessman precisely what action to take in given circumstances in pursuing an objective. This is a concept we shall look at in more detail in Chapter 4. The reason why the profit maximization is usually a non-operational objective in real-world industry is largely that the businessman does not know enough about the alternative courses of action between which he is choosing to be able to say which of those alternatives would give him maximum profit.

More precisely, there are four main reasons why firms find it hard to maximize profit. First, this is a world where 'competitive industries' rarely, if ever, exist. The result is ignorance about the present position of the firm. Especially if firms are large and complex, they will lack information about what their competitors are doing; even about what prices they are charging. Second, there is uncertainty about how the firm's position will change as a result of taking any given decision. Third, there are problems in organizing complex organizations to take good decisions, even where decision takers have the necessary information. Fourth, most human beings find it difficult to understand problems which involve relationships between a number of variables. The human brain works efficiently in two dimensions at most.

Our aim in this study is therefore to try to answer a number of questions about how ignorance, uncertainty and complexity of both organizations and pricing problems are overcome in practice. Are routines developed which eliminate some alternatives and so simplify the decision? Do organizations, and human beings, devise ways of using two-dimensional brains to solve multi-dimensional problems? Does the organization set itself the objective of reaching satisfactory rather than maximum solutions? Does the fact that the firm is a coalition of individuals, rather than a unitary organism affect the kind of objective that is set? Can one say anything about how far away from the optimal solution one reached by these methods is?

In recent years, a good deal of work has been done on these problems in the USA, especially at Carnegie Tech. under the influence of Professors Simon, Cyert and March. These last two have recently given an explicit description of what they term 'satisficing behaviour', where firms set a less demanding objective than maximizing profit. Cyert and March do this in their book *A Behavioral Theory of the Firm.*[1] As we shall see later, Cyert and March introduce other concepts which are extremely helpful in describing and understanding how firms operate, but the notion of satisficing underlies the whole of their analysis. Satisficing is an extreme form of choosing not to maximize profits. One cannot predict what results satisficing behaviour will have without a detailed understanding of how the firm takes its decisions. This means that no general theory of the satisficing firm yet exists, and that perhaps none ever will. However, the only way in which economists will be able to learn more about whether such a theory can be devised at all is by learning more about how firms do behave. We hope that the research described in this book will make a small contribution to this.

The second assumption made by the traditional economic theory of the 'competitive industry' is that the profit-maximizing firm is run by 'the entrepreneur'. The attraction of this second assumption has been that it has enabled economists to assume away all the complications which arise where there are differences of opinion between members of boards of directors, or other groups of managers, over what pricing (and other) decisions should be. Of course, the ideas of 'competition' and 'the entrepreneur' go together. In industries where competition is keen, it can be assumed that there is little scope for choosing any action other than the profit-maximizing one, even if the firm is run by a number of managers, each with his own

[1] Prentice Hall, Englewood Cliffs, New Jersey, USA, 1963.

solutions to its problems, rather than by a single entrepreneur. The assumption that 'the entrepreneur' runs the firm is then a reasonable one. Choosing any other course of action than the profit-maximizing one sooner or later leads to bankruptcy. Of course, in an industry with a large number of small firms, some of these really will be one-man firms. There, at least, such conflicts are impossible.

In reality, there will be many situations where small numbers of firms, or even one firm, are selling in a given market. The firm can then choose whether or not it will try to maximize profits. If it is the only firm in its market—if it is a 'monopolist'—it can make this decision for itself, though it may have to take into account anti-monopoly laws or the reactions of the Government. The biggest problems for economic analysis and prediction arise where there are several firms in the industry, but not so many that there is 'competition'. In these circumstances, the firm's freedom of choice is limited because it has to take into account what its competitors—or at least the biggest of them—are doing. Nevertheless, choices still have to be made, not only about whether to maximize profits but also about how the firm should seek to maintain or improve its competitive position by using various price, or other, weapons. The greater the room for choice, the greater will be the room for disagreement between managers about what choices to make, particularly since there will be few 'one-man' businesses in industries with small numbers of firms.

Cyert and March have contributed a good deal to our understanding of all this. They emphasize that the modern firm is typically run by a collection of individuals. They go on to argue that while individuals have goals, collections of individuals do not. They therefore see the firm as a 'coalition' of managers, workers, shareholders and others. The various members of the coalition have their own individual objectives and play changing roles in the coalition. Our study will throw a little more light on these issues. We shall find that the firms we have studied are best seen as organizations where managers have to act both as individuals and as members of the coalition.

1.2.2 The Structure of the Problem

We have seen that economists (and indeed business school teachers) assume that the best way of looking at business decision problems is to build models of them. To do this, one has to consider relevant relationships within those models. With pricing problems, these relationships will be between variables like cost, revenue and output. Obviously, it will not always be easy to calculate relevant costs or revenues, especially if the firm is producing many products, each of them in competition with the products of fairly small numbers of other firms. It will then be very difficult for the firm to calculate what effect a change in its own price will have on its competitors' prices, and so on its own revenues and profits. What happens to the sales of its own products when their prices alter will depend very largely on how the competitors react to its own price changes, whether by changing their prices or in other ways.

On the cost side, too, it will often be difficult for a multi-product firm to discover exactly what effect a change in output and sales will have on the costs of any one product. Even where it is not too difficult to obtain this information, the firm may not trouble to obtain it. Even where it is obtained, it may not be passed on to decision takers in the most useful form.

Perhaps, at this stage, we should define more explicitly the terms which economists use to describe different kinds of market situation. We have seen that, at one extreme, economists have spent a good deal of time dealing with situations where there are large numbers of firms competing keenly within the same market. Obviously, if competition is keen, firms must be producing identical, or similar, products. The terminology and ideas economists have developed to describe such situations are complex, but the word 'competition' is as good as any to describe this type of market situation.

At the other extreme, there will be 'monopoly' where, for the product we are studying, the firm apparently does not meet competition from any other firm. In fact, this is misleading. All firms must be competing with each other to some extent, if only because all have to achieve their sales, in the end, out of given consumer incomes. If no close substitute for the product of one firm is made by any other firm, we can describe the firm as a 'monopolist' for the product. It must be understood that the word 'monopolist' is used with no pejorative overtones at all. We do not imply that any blame or criticism attaches to a 'monopolist'.

Finally, there is the market situation where small numbers of firms compete with each other. Economists describe such a competitive situation as 'oligopoly', a term derived by analogy from the better-known word 'monopoly'. Oligopoly is important because, in developed countries, it is the dominant market form, certainly if one looks at the percentage of total output which is produced by oligopolistic firms. It must be remembered that even if the industry, defined in technical or organizational terms, contains a large number of firms, they may not all be competing with each other. In some markets, only small numbers of firms may be competing, though some or all of them will be operating in more than one sub-market.

We have already seen that one complication which arises in oligopoly is that it is not necessary for firms to seek maximum profits. We have also seen that what attracted economists to the idea of 'competition' was that the firm had little choice in deciding what action to take in each decision situation. Unless it chose the profit-maximizing course of action, it would relatively soon find itself bankrupt. Economists could therefore predict how the firm would react when changes in, say, taxes, wages or technology occurred. Such prediction is often very difficult in oligopoly. Nor can one ignore the fact that disagreements between managers may impair the efficiency of decision taking. For the oligopolistic firm can choose whether or not to maximize profit. It can do so individually, if it is very strong, or by tacit agreement with its competitors, if it is weaker, though its freedom of choice will be limited, to the extent that it has to take account of the actions of its competitors.

A major characteristic of 'competition' between a large number of small firms is that it is impersonal. If one firm cuts prices, it takes only a small amount of business away from any one of its competitors. So, while competition is keen in one sense, there is an absence of acrimony and criticism. It is accepted that price cutting is inevitable. To take an example from a field other than manufacturing, jobbers on the stock exchange do not criticize each other for marking down the price of a share if demand for it falls off. In such a situation, price competition is accepted as an inevitable part of the established order of things. It simply represents the way that impersonal market forces work.

With oligopoly, matters are quite different. One might expect that, with fewer firms, competition would be less fierce. So in a sense it is. Explicit or tacit agreements to limit competition can be made; price wars can be avoided; competitive advertising expenditure can be collectively restricted. Yet, at the same time, because competition becomes more personal it often becomes more acrimonious as well. If an oligopolist cuts his price, or takes some other competitive action, his rivals feel the effects very obviously and directly. What is more, they know who the initiator of the particular change was and will often feel that their response to that change is directed personally against the managers of the rival firm, whom they are likely to see as a set of misguided individuals. With only a few competing firms, a change in policy by one must affect the others both directly and substantially. The fact that there are fewer rather than more competitors increases the intensity of competition in oligopoly, and makes it less impersonal than in a 'competitive industry'.

Not surprisingly, it turns out that a large proportion of the decisions studied in this book are in oligopolistic firms. This is therefore an opportunity to study pricing in oligopoly. Some of the questions we shall need to ask are these: Is it possible, in oligopoly, for firms to make reasonably scientific assessments of the way in which competitors will react to given price changes on their part? More important, is it possible to say more about the problem, ignored in traditional economics, of how much it is (a) necessary to pay and (b) worth paying in order to obtain extra information about the reactions of competitors? Can one do anything to devise ways of calculating the costs and benefits of obtaining extra information about markets, costs, etc.? In other words, can one put a value on cost accountancy and market research in oligopoly?

1.2.3 Decision Taking

If one bases one's pricing on the use of 'models', using concepts like those we have just described, the factors which have to be considered are likely to be interrelated in complex ways. This will be especially true if one is concerned (as one often is in practice) with other marketing variables as well as price. Yet it is not easy, even with pure pricing decisions, to handle all the relevant variables simultaneously.

There are therefore two broad issues which we must consider as we proceed. First, what is done at present in taking pricing decisions? How do those who take them deal with the complexity of pricing problems? Do they simplify these problems and so obtain tolerably good solutions? If so, how do they do it? Second, what *ought* they to do? Should they use complex interrelated models, perhaps with computers? Or should they use simpler methods? If so, are the existing 'simpler' methods good enough?

One way to simplify pricing decisions is obviously to look at various parts of the problem 'sequentially' rather than 'simultaneously.' Indeed, this is how human beings always have tackled difficult problems. Where this happens, how far are the results less satisfactory because the elements in the problem are not looked at simultaneously? Could one design computer programmes to reproduce what human beings do when they use these sequential methods? Would this be better than doing what most economists and operational researchers would advise—namely, building a complex interrelated model which looks at all aspects of the problem simultaneously.

The attraction of using a computer to simulate what human beings do when they take pricing decisions is that one might then be able to understand what happens well enough either to make the decision process more routine or to computerize it altogether. Some management time would then be free for other activities. Moreover, one could work out how sensitive any pricing process was to changes in the type or accuracy of the data used. This would make it possible to improve that pricing process in a pragmatic and realistic way. In doing so, of course, one would want to allow for the fact that pricing takes place in a dynamic, not a static, world.

1.3 THE CASE STUDIES

In our research, we looked in detail at the way thirteen different products had been priced initially or re-priced later. We did not study the pricing of services, and looked only very briefly at the 'transfer prices' charged where goods were sold, or transferred, between different parts of the same organization. We mainly considered the pricing of manufactured products sold to third parties.

Surprising though this may sound, we find it hard to say how large the units whose pricing we studied really were. In one sense, we studied only pricing in large firms, because it is mainly large, oligopolistic concerns which have provided the Centre for Business Research with its membership and so with its case material. The divisions or subsidiaries we actually studied were usually medium-sized, or even small ones, which had been given considerable autonomy to set their own prices. Despite this, we feel we were mainly concerned with pricing in oligopoly: with large—rather than small—firm pricing. In particular, while the individual units were small, the ethos of the firms we studied and the pricing practices they used, was that of big rather than small businesses.

We think this is valuable. We do not deny the importance of small firms; they produce a sizeable proportion of industrial output. Nevertheless, as we suggested in introducing the economic concepts we need, it may be easier to describe how prices are set in small firms than in large ones. The former find their choices much more constrained by competition. It is in oligopoly, especially, that we lack facts about pricing practices, and eleven of our thirteen case studies are concerned with pricing in oligopoly.

The thirteen cases could be classified in a number of ways. The two most useful are probably those in Tables 1.1 and 1.2.

Table 1.1

Classification by Types of Product	*Number of Cases*	
	Established Products	*New Products*
(a) Mass Consumer Goods	2	2
(b) Raw Materials and Components	3	1
(c) Capital Goods	4	1
Total	9	4
Grand Total:	13	

Table 1.1 shows that four of the firms produced consumer goods. All of them were manufactured on a large scale. The nine remaining firms produced industrial goods—five making capital goods and the rest semi-manufactured materials and components. It can be seen from Table 1.1 that about a third of the case studies were concerned with the pricing of new products.

We have already suggested that when looking at pricing it is often useful to classify firms by the nature of the market in which they are selling. Table 1.2 shows that, for the products we studied, all our firms were operating in one of two broad types of market situation. The first was where there was competition between large numbers of firms, not necessarily all small; two cases deal with such situations. The second kind of market was oligopolistic; eleven case studies deal with oligopolistic firms. In two cases there were only two firms selling in the market. This is a limiting case of oligopoly, which economists describe as duopoly. Our classification of the oligopolists can be elaborated in two ways. Like the two 'competitive' firms in Table 1.2, nine of the eleven oligopolists sold to large numbers of customers. The latter therefore could not use any kind of monopoly pressure to keep down the prices they paid to our oligopolists in the way a very large individual purchaser might be able to do.

Two of the oligopolists each sold most of their UK output to one very large customer. Their pricing policies had to take into account the fact that such a customer could, if it wished, use its market power to play one supplier off against another and so keep prices down.

The other way in which our classification of oligopolistic firms can be elaborated is this. Two of the oligopolists were innovators; when they introduced new products it was frequently a considerable time before their competitors were able to offer close substitutes. Until these other firms had time to enter the market for these new products,

TABLE 1.2

Classification by the Type of Market in which the Products we Studied were being Sold

Type of Market in which Firms were Selling	*Number of Cases*	*Number of Buyers*	
		One Dominant Firm	*Many Competing Firms (or Individuals)*
Duopoly	2	—	2
Oligopoly	9	2	7
'Competition'	2	—	2
Total	13 cases		

our firms were monopolists rather than oligopolists so far as these particular products were concerned. Only later, when the competitors had introduced similar products, could one strictly describe the two firms as oligopolists for the products in question.

From the material we collected in our researches, we have produced thirteen case studies. They represent the raw material for this book. However, we have been given permission to publish only nine of the cases, though we have drawn on all of them in writing the book. The studies have been disguised in order to avoid giving confidential information to the firms' competitors, but we do not think that the disguises we have used have distorted any significant factors affecting pricing.

However, the reader should not be misled into believing that the case studies say anything valid about the products which have been selected as disguises. For instance, the case of the Surgical Instrument

Company appears to discuss the pricing of scalpels with disposable blades. It actually describes the pricing of a quite different product and is valueless as the discussion of the surgical instrument industry, although this industry and the actual industry have enough in common for the disguise to be reasonably apt. All the case material in the book must be read with this proviso in mind. It is also essential to remember that the material was collected between 1964 and 1968; the present marketing and pricing practices of the firms may be different from those described.

1.4 INTRODUCTION TO THE CASE STUDIES

In this section, we give a short description of each of the firms which provided a case study. In brackets, after each description, we classify the firm in terms of the type of competition met with in the market where the product or products were being sold.

Alpha Ltd is the producer of 'Alpha', a long-established consumer good. It is a subsidiary of a large concern and sells a number of similar products throughout the United Kingdom. (Duopoly.)

The Surgical Instrument Company Ltd is one of the largest subsidiaries of a very large concern. The Surgical Instrument Company produces a wide range of surgical instruments. The case study is concerned with the introduction of a metal scalpel with disposable steel blades. (Oligopoly.)

Gamma Products Ltd. This company is a subsidiary of a well-known manufacturer of consumer goods. The study describes Gamma Products' attempts to expand the market for one of its existing products (batteries for battery-operated razors) by introducing its first line of razors. (Oligopoly.)

Dee Plastics Ltd is one of the smaller subsidiaries of a larger concern. It specializes in the production of plastic slats for venetian blinds, together with a number of related products. (Duopoly.)

Wensum Engineering Ltd. This firm manufactures a range of specialist engineering products. It is a comparatively small subsidiary of one of the largest engineering concerns in the United Kingdom. The study is of the annual price review for Wensum's main product line. (Oligopoly: monopoly with new products.)

Fourways Manufacturing Ltd. The subsidiary of a major engineering concern, Fourways Manufacturing produces a range of highly-technical products. The study concerns the introduction of a new product. (Oligopoly: monopoly during the early life of a product.)

Basic Foods Ltd. Basic Foods manufactures and markets a range of foodstuffs, all made from the same basic ingredient. The company is a subsidiary of a large group. (Oligopoly.)

Heavy Technology Ltd. This is a large concern making products of an advanced kind, in the heavy engineering field. The product we studied is a capital good, for which individual contracts are negotiated. One very important customer takes a large proportion of the firm's output. (Oligopoly: a predominant customer.)

Epsilon Ltd. 'Epsilon' is a new, branded consumer good, based on a new production method, and produced by Epsilon Ltd, a large subsidiary of a major manufacturer of consumer goods. The study is concerned with the introduction of 'Epsilon' to the market. (Oligopoly.)

Medlock Engineering Ltd. This firm is a substantial manufacturer of capital goods for the United Kingdom and overseas markets. The study concerns the pricing of the capital good in very competitive export markets. (Competition.)

Wessex Timber Industries Ltd. One of the largest companies in the United Kingdom timber trade, Wessex Timber Industries imports, processes and sells a wide range of timber. The study is of the pricing of a major type of imported timber after it has been processed by the company. (Competition.)

The Clean Engineering Ltd. Clean Engineering is a well-established engineering firm supplying water-purification equipment to public authorities in the United Kingdom. The case study describes the pricing of this equipment. (Oligopoly: a predominant buyer.)

Universal Corporation. Universal Corporation is a major division of a very large industrial group in the UK. It produces and distributes, on a very large scale, a product whose production requires very advanced equipment and techniques. We studied the way the firm prepared its annual price list. A new way of doing this was being used for the first time. (Oligopoly.)

1.5 THE ARRANGEMENT OF THE BOOK

In this book we do four things.

1. Explain what it is thought firms ought to do in pricing (Chapters 2, 3 and 9 and parts of Chapters 7, 8 and 11).
2. Explain what we found firms doing (Chapters 4 and 5 and parts of Chapters 7, 8, 9 and 10).
3. Discuss how actual behaviour seems to differ from what 'should' be done (Chapter 6 and parts of Chapters 7, 8 and 11).
4. Summarize our recommendations on how pricing procedures could be improved (Chapter 12).

CHAPTER 2

The Check List Analysed

2.1 INTRODUCTION

The case studies underlying this book each took a great deal of time and effort to construct. In each case, we visited the firm on several occasions—usually staying for one or two days at a time. We began by collecting information about the firm generally and about the product we were studying and its markets. In later visits, we interviewed those mainly concerned with particular pricing decisions and checked and cross-checked our information. We then presented the firm with a detailed report on what we had learned. When this had been agreed by the firm, it was used as a basis for a disguised case study like those presented at the end of the book.

It will be obvious that by working in this way we collected a vast amount of data. The task of drawing conclusions from it was almost overwhelming. We therefore wanted to be quite clear in our own minds about what were the essential elements in any pricing decision. We felt that besides making a number of generalizations about the way our group of firms set prices, we ought to be going on to suggest how current pricing procedures could be improved. It was in thinking about this problem that we were attracted by the idea of building up a check list, showing the essential elements in any pricing decision. Our check list is reproduced in Chapter 3. Although we originally saw this as a list which would help us to clear our own minds on exactly what the stages of each pricing decision were, we soon saw that it could also be useful to businessmen in reminding them of the essential steps in any pricing decision. The check list was first published separately.[1] We also found that the check list could help us by providing a framework for this book—which follows the check list quite closely in its general layout. We therefore begin this chapter by commenting on the check list in a general way.

[1] Readers of this book who want extra copies can obtain them at a price of 35p each from the Centre for Business Research, Booth Street West, Manchester, M15 6PB.

We confess that we were not entirely happy about producing a detailed check list of this kind. Like most of those who teach in business schools, and an increasing number of practising managers, we feel that businessmen should learn to analyse problems for themselves. The analysis they need to use in looking at pricing problems is basically the same as that needed for all other business problems. It requires a good understanding of the objectives; a clear analysis of the situation within which the decision has to be taken; and a logical procedure for deciding what should be done. We cannot help feeling that a check list will be used as a crutch to lean on. We may be actively helping price setters to avoid working out pricing principles and procedures to suit their own situations. Consequently, we hope that the detailed analysis of this book will encourage those who are responsible for taking pricing decisions to go beyond our fairly brief check list to work out their own detailed pricing processes and methods.

Having said this, we must now spend a little time explaining how the check list is intended to be used. It is aimed at those who take or recommend pricing decisions, and those whose job it is to see that these decisions are taken correctly by others. Those who take part in pricing will find the check list a useful device for reviewing the steps they should take and of making sure that none of these steps is left out. This can easily happen when familiarity with the pricing process breeds carelessness, if not contempt. Changes in conditions in the market, or indeed inside the firm, may be overlooked. Those who have to supervise the pricing activities of others may use the check list to ensure that the organization of their firms, and their control procedures, are designed to encourage effective pricing.

Two major problems faced us as we constructed the check list. First, it was clear that all pricing decisions would not contain exactly the same steps. Second, it seemed that we should want a separate check list for each different class of pricing decision. There would be one for new products; one for existing products; one for capital goods; one for consumer goods, and so on.

As it turned out, the second problem was more easily solved than the first. Having tried to draw up two separate check lists—one for pricing a new product and one for re-pricing an existing product—we found that there was an enormous amount of duplication. So we decided that a single check list, covering every kind of pricing decision, would give us all that we needed, and would avoid the confusion arising from having several separate but overlapping documents.

However, there was no way of devising a general pricing check list that included only those steps which were required in any particular pricing decision. Anyone using the check list will therefore have to decide for himself how relevant each item is to him. We realize this means that the check list will not be tailor-made for all price setters, or even for any individual. We hope that anyone who uses the check list will appreciate this problem and will be prepared to work out for himself which parts of it are relevant to his own firm, his own products or his particular decision.

This was devised as a check list, not as a text book on pricing. It sets out the questions which price setters need to answer in taking pricing decisions. In the remainder of the book we go in detail into all the points covered by the check list. Briefly, it asks managers first to define what objectives are being pursued in the particular pricing decision being taken. It then asks them to consider what information they require for this decision, including information about the market; about government policy; about costs, revenue and profit; and so on.

Proceeding to the pricing decision itself, the check list stresses the need to look at alternatives. All business decisions require those who take them to choose between alternative courses of action. (Doing nothing is always one alternative.) The questions asked inevitably reflect the fact that every pricing decision requires the decision taker to weigh various costs, revenues and benefits against each other. He can then see which decision comes closest to achieving the firm's objectives. Since the human brain finds it difficult to consider more than one or two variables simultaneously, it is likely that computers will increasingly be used to work out which of a set of possible solutions will be most likely to achieve the firm's objectives in particular market conditions. In many cases, this computer work is likely to involve some simulation.

Finally, the check list shows that pricing must be a continuous, feedback process. The extent to which objectives are being met should be continuously studied. The price setter should analyse the firm's performance before and after the given price changes were made. He should see this analysis as a major source of information. Our researches suggest that there is a weakness here in member firms. The procedures they follow do not always ensure that sufficient effort is given to studying the effects of pricing decisions previously made, and to comparing these with the results that were expected. Firms may well not be adequately equipped to take the steps necessary to set prices more successfully in the future; or indeed to review their pricing objectives, or their entire arrangements for price setting, if this is necessary.

We have referred throughout this section to 'pricing decisions', almost as though pricing were an isolated business function. We must emphasize that we have treated pricing in the check list as part of the whole activity of marketing; this includes product design and presentation, as well as advertising and other forms of sales promotion.

We prepared the check list with some humility. It says nothing which an efficient price setter does not know already. What it does do is to set out the steps in the pricing procedure explicitly, providing an easy and quick way of checking that no step in the process has been left out. We feel that the pricing check list is sufficiently important to be given a chapter of its own. It is therefore reproduced, in full and without further comment, in Chapter 3.

2.2 TERMINOLOGY

While long discussions on terminology are usually extremely frustrating, we must briefly clear the ground by defining a few of our terms. Indeed, provided that too much time is not spent on it, there is much to be said for making certain that everyone in a firm knows what the important words used in his job really mean. This is because firms often give special meanings to everyday words. Every manager needs to know what these special meanings are for the words used in his own part of his firm.

Scientific and technical terms usually have a clear meaning for all concerned; business terms often do not. It is no accident that modern philosophers spend so much of their time discussing the meanings of words. Words are the most important means of communication between human beings, and much misunderstanding is caused in all spheres of life because the same word means different things to different people. This is just as true of business as of any other activity, and this is why we believe that a clear understanding of the key words is so important.

2.2.1 What Is Price?

One might well suppose that a simple word like price could be quickly defined. In fact, it cannot. One meets with prices at many different stages in each economic process. The first question which arises is whether price means ex-factory, wholesale or retail price. Since this book is concerned with the prices of manufactured goods, we shall usually be concerned with ex-factory prices, and not with wholesale prices.

However, in a few firms, especially Alpha Ltd and Epsilon Ltd, the manufacturer needed to know what actual retail prices were in order to be able to assess his markets correctly. Otherwise he could not, for example, calculate what total expenditure on his product was, or what were the prices at which his products and those of competitors really were being sold. In Alpha Ltd, for example, resale price maintenance had not been used for several years and many of the larger firms retailing 'Alpha' had been cutting prices. The actual price at which Alpha Ltd sold its product to retailers was relatively easily defined and calculated, because rebates and discounts were offered only on terms formally laid down by the board of Alpha Ltd, though they were altered from time to time. Alpha Ltd's salesmen were not allowed to offer special terms on their own initiative. At the retail level, however, Alpha Ltd had actually encouraged its retailers to cut the price of 'Alpha' in order to compete with 'Omega'. Although Alpha Ltd officially defined 'price' as recommended retail selling price, actual retail selling prices varied considerably. By the time of our study they were hardly subject to control by Alpha at all. Decisions on pricing within Alpha Ltd therefore had to begin from a clear understanding of what was the relevant price for any given decision.

This is a common problem for consumer goods firms in Britain now that resale price maintenance has been abolished for most products. In our study, the situation facing Epsilon Ltd, Basic Foods Ltd and Gamma Ltd, was similar to that for Alpha Ltd. This reinforces our plea for a clear definition of what price is for any particular decision.

The firms we studied that were selling industrial goods did not meet these problems, since they were rarely selling to wholesalers or retailers; 'price' was usually ex-factory price. A few firms, especially Wensum and Fourways, were selling standard products on a large enough scale for a price list to be published annually. In Wensum, prices were reviewed towards the end of each year, though if the profitability of an individual product altered significantly during the year, its price could be changed at any time. List prices were charged to all customers though standard, aggregated rebates were given to individual customers in proportion to their total annual purchases from Wensum. It was therefore important to distinguish between list price and actual price for any sale. Wensum also sold a sizeable proportion of its output, at considerable discounts, to other firms within its own group. We shall see later that the low level of these 'transfer' prices gave rise to a good deal of dissension both within Wensum and between Wensum and its parent firm. This meant that Wensum was very often concerned with a third kind of price—'transfer price'.

The situation in Dee Plastics was quite different. Individual prices were negotiated for each contract (usually for a year). Price was therefore easily defined; for each customer it was the selling price set out in his contract. However, depending on the terms of any contract, the level of price could vary between customers. Price could also vary between slats that represented 'base load' production and for those that represented incremental quantities over and above this 'base load'.

With firms like Medlock and Heavy Technology, the relevant prices were those tendered for particular orders. Clean Engineering was in a similar position, though it usually tendered for contracts covering more than one piece of equipment. For Clean Engineering, the important variable was the size of the discount offered in each case. 'Price' was the price charged to an individual customer for a particular tender.

We must also distinguish 'price' and 'cost'. We found some confusion between the two, because one man's price is another man's cost; and unguarded references to 'price' and 'cost' seem frequently to confuse the two. Whether this failure to distinguish them is a cause or an effect of the notion of 'cost-plus' pricing is not relevant. The point is simply that blurring the distinction frequently leads to confusion in pricing.

2.2.2 Quantities of Output Concerned

It may sound too obvious to mention but, in defining what 'price' means in any context, it is important to be quite sure which products are being priced and what the exact product specification is. The price setter should then go on to consider what quantity of the product is involved. Is the decision about the price for the whole of the firm's output of this product? Or for only a part? If it is price for a part of output only, which part of output is it? And over what time period?

This was an important issue for several of the firms we studied. For example, Heavy Technology and Medlock Engineering were very short of business at the time of our study. It was therefore very important for them to know how much of their capacity a given order would employ, and for how long. Only then could they decide how important it was to obtain the order.

Dee Plastics was in a similar situation. Once all its plant was employed on one-shift working for a given period of time, it could accept a lower level of price for further business, provided only that different prices could be charged to some customers. Once again, it was important to know which part of the firm's output was being priced.

2.2.3 The Firms Studied

One of the difficulties in writing a book like this is that one tends to repeat the same phrases too often. We therefore feel that to avoid trying the patience of our readers, and indeed to save words, we should not continually use the phrase 'the firms studied'. We have often used the rather ambiguous phrase 'our firms' instead. We hope that no confusion will be caused.

2.2.4 Price Fixers

A similar problem arises over the phrase we should use to describe those who take pricing decisions. We shall often use the words 'price fixer' or 'price setter'. Two things must be understood about this. First, the 'price fixer' may be a group of people, not an individual. Second, the word 'fix' or 'set' is not intended to mean that the firm has any monopoly power to set whatever price it wishes, however high. We simply mean that the person or group who 'fixes' or 'sets' prices is deciding what price the firm should charge for its particular product, given the freedom (or lack of freedom) it has in doing so.

2.3 CONCLUDING COMMENTS

We are now in a position to look in detail at what we have learned about pricing from our field work. After reproducing the pricing check list in Chapter 3, we shall begin to do so in Chapters 4–6, by looking at the firm's objectives.

CHAPTER 3

The Pricing Check List

A. PRELIMINARY

A.1 *Terminology*

Ensure that all terms and concepts are clearly and adequately defined and understood.

A.2 *Product Specification*

What products are involved?

A.3 *Will this decision set the price for all or part of output? What part?*

A.4 *Objectives of the Firm*

What are the objectives of the firm as a whole?

For example:

Consolidation or Expansion?
Profit or Growth?
Market and/or Technological Development?
(NB. None of these alternatives necessarily excludes any other.)

B. PRICING OBJECTIVES

Find out the objectives of this pricing decision; ensure that they are understood by all concerned with the decision.

B.1 *Time Span*

What time periods are relevant to this decision?

B.2 *Profit Objectives*

How are profit objectives set?
What levels of profitability are desired?

B.3 *Market Objectives*

On what basis are market objectives set?

For example:

Sales (value, volume, growth).
Market share.
Reaction to competitors.

B.4 *Other Objectives*

Are other objectives relevant to this decision?

For example:

Capacity utilization.

Production and inventory goals.

Adjustment to national policy.

Public image of the firm.

B.5 *Consistency of Objectives*

Are pricing objectives consistent with the firm's overall objectives?

Are they consistent among themselves?

If not—what are the priorities between them for this decision?

C. INFORMATION REQUIRED FOR PRICING DECISION

C.1 *Information on pricing objectives listed under* B *above*

C.2 *External Information*

Information about conditions outside the firm.

C.2.1. *Information on the Total Market*

What are the markets in which this product is sold?

Is the market national or international?

Who are the significant competitors—now and in the future?

What is the size of the market? What are its growth prospects, allowing for expected product developments?

How do different sectors of the total market interact?

C.2.2 *Competitive Market Information*

Products:

What are the competing products?

What do buyers require? What are their attitudes towards the competing products?

How much room is there for price changes?

Market Growth, Market Share and Marketing Plans:

Trends and projections, for own firm and for competitors.

The financial situation, and the implications of planned investment, for own firm and for competitors.

Expected competitive reactions to change.

Price:

Prices of competing products.

Is there a price leader? Who? Why?

Can price differences be related to differences in the specification of each product? How?

Price and volume relationships (Elasticity of Demand).

Pricing practices and price structures—for example:

Discounts and rebates.

Associated charges (extras, packing, delivery, etc.).

Price maintenance and price cutting.

Credit policies.

Advertising and sales promotion.

C.2.3 *Government Policies*

How is the market influenced by Government?

How are individual firms influenced by Government?

For example:

Government as customer.

Tax policies.

Money and credit controls.

Import, tariff and quota policies.

Monopolies and Restrictive Practices legislation.

C.3 *Internal Information*

Information about factors inside the firm (and equivalent information about competitors).

C.3.1 Cost Information

What costs are relevant for this decision—e.g. within the firm what costs will be incurred for the first time, or altered, by this decision? (Bear in mind the time period relevant to this decision—see item B.1.)

For example: Manufacturing, Distribution, Selling and Promotional costs:

Own and competitors' methods.

Own and competitors' costs.

Volume, capacity and cost relationships.

Joint and Overhead Costs, etc.

Are the methods of cost allocation between products understood?

If methods of cost allocation are not appropriate for pricing decisions, is it possible to obtain different cost information which *is* relevant?

Production and Inventory Levels:

What are present levels of production? Of inventory?

How were they determined? Are they appropriate?

What are the costs associated with these levels?

What effects would production and inventory changes have upon these costs?

C.3.2 Revenue and Profit Information

Revenue, cost and profit relationships:

For the product.

Effects on other products.

Effects of volume, cost and price changes on revenue, cost and profit relationships.

Effects of advertising and sales promotion on revenue and profit.

Own and competitors' profit margins.

D. AVAILABILITY OF INFORMATION

D.1 *Availability*

Consider what information is now available.

For information which is not available:

Can it be made available?

How soon? At what cost?

From what sources can information be made available?

Inside the firm—for example:

Market research.

Management accounting.

Competitor analysis.

Outside the firm—for example:

Specialist agencies.

Trade associations.

Information agreements.

D.2 *Reliability*

How recent is the information?

Is it quantitative or qualitative?

How reliable is it?

Is it about the relevant *future* time period?
Can estimates and forecasts be improved?

D.3 *Priorities*

What are the most important needs for information, given the costs of acquiring it?

E. PRICING DECISIONS

E.1 *The Alternatives*

What will be the effects of alternative levels of price, revenue, sales volume, selling and promotional expenditure on the following?

Within the firm:
- Costs.
- Utilization of plant, labour force, etc.
- Production and inventory levels.
- Other products and/or total sales.
- Sources of finance, and cash flow.

Outside the firm:
- Market growth.
- Market shares.
- Competitors' performance.
- Competitors' reactions.

What alternative levels of price, revenue, sales volume, selling and promotional expenditure contribute most towards achieving:
- The overall objectives of the firm?
- Profit objectives?
- Other objectives?

E.2 *The Decision*

Choose the best alternative.

If none of the alternatives contributes towards the achievement of objectives, then reconsider the following:
- Product specification and design.
- Revenue, cost and profit variables.
- Objectives.

E.3 *Recording the Decision*

Record which alternative is chosen, and why, together with the assumptions and expectations upon which the choice was based.

F. THE RESULTS OF PRICING DECISION

Establish procedures for reviewing regularly the results of pricing decisions.

Review results in the light of the details recorded when the decision was made.

Initiate remedial action if results are unsatisfactory.

Review pricing objectives in the light of operating results.

Review procedures for making pricing decisions.

CHAPTER 4

The Firm's Objectives

4.1 INTRODUCTION

Business objectives are a vast subject, not least because they are important for every conceivable kind of business activity. No manager, at any level in any firm, can do his job without having some sort of objective. But discussion of objectives can, and often does, create a tremendous amount of confusion. Most people in business are reasonably clear what an objective is, but one is less sure how far firms define objectives precisely and pursue them consistently. In this book, we shall see examples of the problems that arise. Moreover, the confusion of terminology is undeniable. Words like aims, aspiration levels, goals, objectives, plans and targets are sometimes used as synonymous with each other and sometimes not.

The word 'objectives' is a good one because it covers the whole field and is widely accepted. There is no point in adding further confusion by trying to introduce a new term. We shall therefore use the word 'objectives' to describe the whole range of firms' plans, intentions and wishes. In this chapter, we discuss some of the general characteristics of business objectives in the firms we studied. In Chapter 5, we shall look at the objectives which these firms pursued in pricing. In Chapter 6, we shall draw some conclusions about objectives.

4.2 NON-OPERATIONAL OBJECTIVES

An important distinction must be made at the beginning of any study of objectives. This is between operational and non-operational objectives. The simplest and most traditional of all statements of objectives is probably that: 'We are in business to make money'. Alternatively, a firm may say: 'We are in business to make motor cars', or 'to sell transport'. Similarly, a firm may set itself the objective of striving for product or process innovation, of serving the community, or merely of perpetuating itself. Statements like this are very vague indeed. They describe objectives which are 'non-operational.'

They do not say, or even imply, exactly what action the firm should take to achieve them. At any moment, a number of different courses of action will often be perfectly compatible with each non-operational objective. Indeed, the reason why firms set themselves non-operational objectives is often precisely this. No specific action is prescribed for the manager responsible for day-to-day activities. This vagueness enables individual managers in the firm to work together with a sense of unity and of common purpose, while none of them is committed to any precise action in any particular set of circumstances. Disputes over whether specific objectives are realistic or acceptable are avoided.

We found that all the firms we studied had some non-operational objectives. Indeed, in two firms they were written down and circulated to managers. In a few firms, what seemed to be operational objectives were treated effectively as non-operational ones. Managers who had been set to earn a particular rate of return on capital did not expect to be criticized by their supervisors if they did not attain it.

Another kind of objective we found was one which laid down the results the firm as a whole was expected to achieve in a general way. It set out the levels of turnover, profit, etc. to be reached by the whole firm but it did not explain in detail how any individual product, or department, was expected to contribute to those results. Nor did it provide a plan of action for those responsible for individual products. These objectives were again non-operational ones for managers concerned with particular products, even though for the whole firm they were less vague than the non-operational objectives discussed in the previous paragraph. Indeed, they were often quite precise. This second kind of non-operational objective is important because it helps to determine the atmosphere within which managers have to set and to achieve specific targets for individual products. All the firms we studied had non-operational objectives of the second kind, whether they were implicit or explicit, or worked out in more or less detail.

4.3 OPERATIONAL OBJECTIVES

All the firms also had operational objectives. The distinguishing characteristics of operational objectives are:

1. They set specific tasks for the firm or for particular individuals or groups.

2. They enable the firm to discover whether or not these tasks have been performed.
3. They state clearly the way the firm will judge whether or not the tasks have been achieved, both in terms of what will be judged and how.
4. They set a time limit for carrying out each task.

It is because they are precise that operational objectives *are* operational.

If they are to achieve their targets, firms must have arrangements for stating at least their key objectives in operational terms and for comparing performance with these operational objectives. Only in this way can they discover how far their objectives have been achieved. Firms should go on to study any differences between results and objectives and take whatever remedial action is necessary to bring the two back into line. However, this leads us beyond objectives to control systems. We shall discuss these briefly in Chapter 11.

Some idea of the scope for disagreement over terminology where business objectives are being discussed was given in section 4.1. It seems to us that such disagreement is the one thing to avoid. It does not much matter which words are used within a company to describe its objectives. What matters is that each word which *is* used should have a precise meaning for everyone who is expected to use it. We believe that, wherever possible, the firm should choose and define the terms it uses so as to emphasize the distinction between operational and non-operational objectives. It should ensure that its important objectives, at least, are stated in operational terms.

We accept that there is a difficult problem here both for managers and for management scientists. The problem is how to reconcile different objectives and to state them in ways that provide the firm with a sense of direction and purpose. Cyert and March have only pointed the way for future discussion and research. They do not yet tell us enough about how conflicts between objectives (and managers) are reconciled. Work is now needed to make the process more constructive for the manager. We hope that we shall provide some insights into the problem in this book.

4.4 PRICING AND MARKETING OBJECTIVES

This is mainly a study of pricing, but we have seen that pricing and marketing are—or should be—inseparable. This is consequently to some extent a study of marketing as well. In Chapters 4 and 5, we shall be especially concerned with the operational objectives that firms pursue in their marketing (including pricing) operations. We believe that marketing is best defined as including all the activities of the firm that are concerned with the assessment, stimulation and meeting of demand. However, using this definition, one immediately faces a problem. The definition makes virtually every business activity a part of marketing, and almost every business objective a marketing objective. On this definition, marketing seems to become synonymous with business.

Perhaps the best way of sorting things out is to realize that businessmen use the term 'marketing' to describe three different activities, and that this is a major reason why there is so much confusion. First, at the policy-making level, the firm will be setting its corporate strategy; marketing strategy is an important element within the overall business strategy. At this policy-making level, marketing is, if not the whole of business, at least one of the key elements that the firm has to consider in formulating its corporate strategy. Second, marketing is, at the same time, an important functional activity within the firm. Those concerned with marketing as an everyday operational job have to ensure that the task of stimulating the market through pricing, advertising, and other forms of sales promotion, is well done. They also have to supply the market, using efficient transport and distribution systems. We believe that the most important source of confusion over the meaning of marketing is that marketing in the first and second senses—as an element of policy and as an operational activity—is not carefully separated out in managers' thinking.

The third activity covered by the word 'marketing' is that of market assessment or market research. This will often be performed by the marketing section of the firm, but it may well be a quite separate task. Once again, confusion can be caused if it is not remembered that market assessment is another functional job, though now one which precedes rather than follows a decision about what marketing strategy and marketing policy should be. It is also a research task. One would therefore expect it to be the job of a specialist department, though one that ought to be carefully briefed, used and controlled, by operational management. However, outside the consumer goods industries market research is frequently not the job of a specialist department. This is a major reason why market research is often badly done; it is too often attempted by operational staff or salesmen.

Within the objectives which make up the firm's overall strategy, one can always identify a number of separate marketing, including pricing, objectives. At the same time, however market-oriented a firm may be, it is bound to find that it cannot run efficiently unless it sets up specialist research and operational groups and departments with specialized skills. The result is that these groups and departments have to be given their own objcctives, which are not always immediately or obviously related to pricing, marketing or any other objectives. A department's objectives are bound to define its job in terms of its own specialism. However much it may contribute to achieving the firm's overall marketing objectives by making it possible, say, to sell a particular type of goods, the department is most immediately concerned with its own activity. For instance, a production department will be trying to turn out goods in quantities and at costs which have been laid down in its operational objectives. A scheduling department will be trying to ensure that, given the production department's operational objectives and demand in the market as defined by the sales and marketing departments, the production department is using the available raw materials, machinery and buildings in the best way; and so on. If the marketing objective for the company as a whole is to earn a given level of profit, the operational objectives of the production and scheduling departments will rarely be linked in any obvious way to this marketing objective. It is important that they *should* be so linked.

The operational objectives of a marketing department will determine how the specialists in that department operate, just as production objectives will determine what is done in a production department. However, there are two points to remember. First, we have seen that there is a good deal of confusion over the meaning of the word 'marketing'. Some of this arises because the marketing department is not merely concerned with marketing as its own functional activity but also—and in a sense more than any other department—with seeing that the firm's whole marketing strategy is carried out. It is because of this that marketing men often claim that they are more important to a market-oriented firm than are their colleagues. Yet one can argue that, in their role as functional specialists, they are doing no more to put the firm's marketing strategy into effect than are other departments. It is because their functional role keeps them so closely in touch with the market that marketing men tend, more than anyone else, to see themselves as the acknowledged, self-appointed guardians of the firm's whole marketing strategy. In fairness, however, one must add that a marketing director may well have a somewhat bigger contribution to make when a strongly market-oriented firm's board is setting its overall strategy than he would in a less market-oriented firm.

The second point is this. Pricing and marketing objectives, like target rates of profit, and, particularly among consumer goods manufacturers, target market shares, are not objectives for the marketing department only. They are often also the measures that top management uses in judging the degree of success achieved by the whole firm. The qualifying word 'often' is necessary. Rather too frequently for comfort, one finds that a high (or maximum) value and volume of sales, or of market share, becomes the main objective of the marketing department or of individuals within it. If this happens, it will usually happen at the expense of profit.

A final distinction turned out to be important in our study. It was the distinction between the profit and marketing objectives of the firm as a whole, and these objectives, not for individual departments, but for individual products and product lines. As we shall see, the operational objectives pursued in most of our firms were for single products or product lines, though they were not always linked clearly with overall objectives. The reason why this distinction was important is that most firms, and certainly all the firms we studied, are multi-product firms. Pricing and marketing decisions usually have to be made for individual products, not for the whole firm, and separate operational objectives have to be pursued for each product.

4.5 OPTIMIZING AND SATISFICING

Two words are continually met with in business-school discussions of the way in which business decisions are taken. They are the words 'optimizing' and 'satisficing'.

'Optimizing' means, first, that the firm must set objectives, or criteria, by which performance in any activity is to be judged. Second, it means that the alternative courses of action open to the firm must be examined to see how well they meet these criteria. Third, the best, the optimal, alternative must then be chosen.

Although there is a good deal of discussion of optimal decision taking in the management literature, most of this is really concerned with the extreme case where an optimal result is defined as one which maximizes something—usually profit. This is important, because we explained in Chapter 1 that we are interested in seeing how far our research provides evidence to support the idea that firms maximize profits in the way that economists have long assumed that they do. Of course, the definition of optimizing given above means that an optimal solution to a problem need not require the firm to maximize anything. If the firm's objective is to earn a 15 per cent return on capital, and not to maximize profit, then an optimal decision in any situation will be one which allows the firm to earn 15 per cent on capital. Maximization is simply a special case of optimization, where an optimal solution requires alternative courses of action to be judged by how well they satisfy the criterion that the firm wishes to maximize a given variable, perhaps profit. Indeed, in the literature it is difficult to find examples of optimal decisions or decision techniques, where the objective is *not* to maximize or minimize some variable. The same was true of our firms.

However, we still have to suggest what firms which do not attempt to maximize profit are trying to do. One possibility is that they are still optimizing. We have seen that a firm which does not attempt to maximize profits may nevertheless still be trying to take optimal decisions. It may simply be setting out to earn a particular absolute amount, or percentage rate, of profit, but an amount less than the maximum one. It may still be taking whatever decisions will bring it as close as possible to earning that amount. If it does this, of course, then the fact that its objectives are less demanding than maximizing objectives will mean that more than one solution to a particular problem can be optimal. However, this is not very important in practice. Optimizing almost always means maximizing or minimizing.

In practice, too, as we shall see, even when firms attempt to maximize, they usually do so subject to various constraints. Prices may be set so as to maximize profits, subject to the constraint that the overall level of employment in the firm must not be reduced significantly below the current level; or that the level of inventories must not be increased. We should perhaps emphasize that where individual managers or departments are setting prices (or indeed taking other decisions) they are bound to be doing so subject to such constraints. For the constraints within which individual departments operate will usually have been set for them at higher levels in the firm.

If firms do not seek to maximize profit, the likelihood is that they will not optimize at all but that they will 'satisfice'. Writers like

Simon, Cyert and March have spent a great deal of time emphasizing that firms often satisfice.[1] What we do not know is just how common 'satisficing' behaviour really is. When they 'satisfice', firms do not try to find that course of action which brings them as close as possible to a particular objective. Instead, they set minimum levels of performance in each of a number of different fields—say, a return of 10 per cent on capital employed, a market share of 25 per cent and production running at 90 per cent of existing capacity. These minimum levels of performance are often described as 'aspiration levels'.

Two things then usually seem to happen. First, the firm takes no non-routine decisions at all so long as the aspiration levels set for a product, department or indeed for the whole firm are being achieved. Only if the firm fails to earn the required rate of return on capital employed, or to reach the required market share, will special action be taken. So long as all aspiration levels are being met, it will seem unnecessary. The firm may or may not be exceeding the minimum level of achievement which it has set itself but, so long as it is not achieving less, managers will be content to leave things as they are. Second, if any aspiration level does cease to be met, the firm will then take some remedial action. In taking this action it will not seek to optimize anything. Those responsible for ensuring that a particular aspiration level is reached once more will accept the first solution they find which they think will enable them to meet this aspiration level again—even if the solution is inferior to the optimal one. They will make no attempt to find a still better solution. Very often, the way of discovering a satisfactory solution to a problem will be to ask what was done on the last occasion that the problem arose. Provided what was done was successful last time, it will be done again.

Of course, aspiration levels will not necessarily remain unchanged. At the least, negative precedents seem to be accepted. Firms often seem to argue in this way. 'We earned 15 per cent on capital last year. We must therefore earn at least as much this year.' They say this, even when external conditions will make it harder to earn 15 per cent this year than last. Where external conditions give them more freedom, firms appear to raise aspiration levels over time; unfortunately our evidence does not allow us to say how this was done in our firms.

The fact that they do 'satisfice' in this way seems to explain most

[1] See for example, R. M. Cyert and J. G. March, *A Behavioral Theory of the Firm*, (Prentice Hall, Englewood Cliffs, N.J., 1963) pp. 26–43.

satisfactorily how firms can tolerate inconsistencies among their objectives. Cyert and March, in particular, argue that where a satisficing firm ceases to reach one of its aspiration levels it will proceed to search for a solution which will enable it to meet, or exceed, the aspiration level once again. Cyert and March go on to argue that each of these decisions is taken in isolation—that such decisions are taken sequentially.[1] The firm usually finds it too difficult to make sure that a decision which is taken in order to ensure that a particular aspiration level is reached once again also allows it to continue to reach all its other aspiration levels. To make all such decisions completely consistent would usually be beyond the capabilities of human beings, even if the complexities of large organizations did not play their own part in preventing consistency.

Before leaving this section, we must define sub-optimal decisions. An optimal decision, we have seen, is one which comes as close as possible to achieving a particular objective. (Strictly, an optimal decision will be one which fits in with all the overall objectives of the firm.) A sub-optimal decision is one which provides an optimal solution to a particular problem from the viewpoint of a particular department or manager, but which does not at the same time meet the firm's overall objectives.

There are two main ways in which this can happen. First, the objectives of the individual department may differ from those of the firm. The sales department may seek to maximize the volume of sales, while the firm as a whole is seeking to maximize profit. In operating so as to maximize sales, the sales department is sub-optimizing. Whether it will be allowed to sub-optimize will depend on the way the firm is run. Second, sub-optimization can occur, even though an individual department really is trying to achieve the firm's overall objectives. What may happen is that the department finds that it is too low down in the organization to have the information it needs to be able to optimize. It may then be forced to sub-optimize because it lacks information. For example, the sales department may not have enough information about what effect a change in the sales of particular products will have on the profits of the whole firm. So it may not be able to sell those quantities of products which would enable the whole firm to earn the optimal amount of profit, even though it is attempting to do so.

In our case studies, we did not find any clear examples of sub-

[1] *Op. cit.*, p. 35.

optimal pricing decisions. We did find evidence in one firm (Alpha Ltd) of sub-optimal thinking, though perhaps not of sub-optimal decision taking. There is no reason to believe that the decisions that Alpha Ltd actually took prevented the firm from achieving its overall objectives. Yet the way that pricing and other marketing decisions were discussed in the marketing department suggests that this department was basing its discussions on different objectives from those of the Board. Alpha Ltd itself doubts the correctness of our observations, but we still think we are right. We also feel that these differences of objective must have made it harder for Alpha Ltd to take good pricing decisions, even if they did not actually prevent them being taken.

4.6 TIME PERIODS AND OBJECTIVES

We have seen that the firms we studied distinguished between operational and non-operational objectives. They also distinguished between long-term and short-term objectives. We found it fairly easy to see what the pattern of long-term and short-term objectives was, though it varied more from firm to firm for marketing objectives than for more general objectives. In particular, five firms set marketing objectives for the short-term only, usually for one year. In the other eight firms, which had long-term marketing objectives, the long term usually meant a period of more than a year; usually, it meant five years. Where objectives were identified for the long period, they were set out very tentatively as, for example, in Alpha Ltd.

4.6.1. Long-Term Marketing Objectives

Among the eight firms with long-term marketing objectives, were all four manufacturers of consumer goods. This is not surprising because these firms used sophisticated consumer marketing techniques and the thinking that went with them in highly competitive markets. In no firm were these tentative, long-term objectives of immediate enough concern to be taken seriously into account in pricing decisions. The firm's long-term objectives were concerned with its profitability and, to a smaller extent, its share of the market. The firm's long-term market forecasts played a large part in determining what long-term objectives should be. These long-term objectives were operational objectives for the firm's marketing activities as a whole, because marketing plans were built around them and short-term marketing objectives derived from them. But, even though pricing is part of marketing, long-term objectives usually had no direct influence on pricing decisions in our firms. In each of the decisions we studied, prices were set taking into account relevant factors as they appeared at that particular moment. Five-year forecasts were concerned only with the more remote (in time) of these relevant factors. Firms also felt, as indeed those responsible for national 'plans' in Western economies usually seem to do, that changes in the prices of individual products were unlikely to have much effect on sales of those products over longish periods of time. The implications of this for elasticity of demand are interesting.

We doubt if businessmen really do believe that elasticity of demand for their products is as low as this implies. Changes in relative price levels are important both for businessmen and planners. Changes in absolute price levels occur continuously, because of inflation. The importance of changes in relative levels is recognized, for instance, by the notion of the 'skimming' price used by the Surgical Instrument Company and possibly by Epsilon. However, in some industries productive capacity is the limiting factor rather than price. Even so, a reduction in the relative price charged by an individual manufacturer will often directly increase his sales turnover, always assuming he has spare production capacity available.

Despite what has been said, long-term objectives can sometimes have important consequences for pricing. As time passes, what was once the long-term creeps inexorably nearer, until within the given number of years it has become the short-term. Universal Corporation realized this only too keenly. For each of the years for which it made a long-term demand forecast, Universal Corporation ultimately had to be able to produce the output that consumers demanded. Its plant took a long time to build, so that once a demand forecast had been made for five, six or seven years ahead, Universal Corporation was committed to it; capital expenditure had to be planned as far ahead as that. If demand grew more or less quickly than had been expected—say, because of a change in the general level of economic activity—Universal Corporation would find that it had more or less capacity than was needed to meet actual demand. As a result, it would be faced with a pattern of costs, which, given its need to earn the required rate of return on capital, left it with an undesired pattern of prices for its products. It would be undesired in the sense that it was not the pattern of prices that would have given the required return on capital had demand been correctly forecast.

In most firms, however, long-term objectives had the advantage that they could be changed as they became short-term ones. Alpha Ltd drew up a five-year plan each year, but it had always taken a five-year look ahead as part of its budgeting process. Experience, as well as information, gained between budgets had always been taken into account in budgeting, and this always made it probable that some long-term factors lying behind the budget would change before the next budget was constructed. This flexibility in budgeting was necessary if annual budgets, or short-term plans, were to be based on the most up-to-date information available when they were being drawn up.

The Surgical Instrument Co. made a forward estimate of demand in the fifth year after introducing its new scalpel, even though the firm had no five-year plan as such. For the scalpel, the market forecasts and the objectives for the fifth year after introduction served much the same purpose as did five year plans elsewhere. Fourways Manufacturing was in a similar position. The firm had no comprehensive long-term plan; nor was there a long-term marketing plan for the new product we studied. Instead, objectives for periods more than one year ahead were treated as objectives over the expected life of each new product. Heavy Technology had a rolling, five-year order schedule which was filled in as orders were obtained. The prices currently being tendered reflected the state of this schedule.

4.6.2 Short-Term Objectives

Our firms usually used the phrase 'short term' to describe a period covering the next year or less. In most cases, short-term objectives were specified in annual budgets. Objectives were laid down for a number of different elements: for profit (in absolute money terms, or as a percentage return on sales turnover or capital), for sales volume, for market share, and so on. In other words, overall, long-term plans were used as a basis for laying down specific, measurable objectives which were then included in the firm's detailed short-term operating plans. These short-term plans provided forecasts and targets for departments within the firms. For managers and others concerned with pricing and marketing, the important short-term objectives were either absolute amounts or rates of profit to be earned, or results to be achieved in the product market. By making management control possible, this kind of short-term budgeting was the first step in the feedback process of control.

In the firms we studied, annual budgets were usually divided further into budgets for shorter time periods; monthly and quarterly periods were the most usual. It was thought that unless this was done managers might react too slowly to divergences between actual and budgeted performance. The feeling was that if annual budgets were not split up into budgets for shorter time periods, only rather big divergences from budgeted performance would lead managers to see that immediate remedial action needed to be taken. Control was thought to be easier and cheaper the more quickly a failure to meet the budget was reported to the appropriate manager. The value of these budgeting and feedback arrangements was seen to be that they provided the firm with opportunities to adapt to changes in the environment and that they helped to improve performance within the firm. As the firm's achievements were monitored and compared with its budget, managers were forced to analyse the variances between the two. This helped them to discover the speed and size of changes in significant factors in the environment. The firms' objectives—and the budgets which set them out in detail—could then be modified as necessary.

One firm with quarterly instead of annual budgets was Wessex Timber Industries. There was an interesting situation here, because the firm showed a healthy disregard for the convention of annual budgeting, which is of course linked to the conventional, annual accounting period. It is true that one advantage of drawing up budgets for the full year is that this automatically cancels out the effect of seasonal influences on activity. The fact that Wessex Timber Industries had quarterly budgets may be thought to show that it was keenly aware of the uncertainties of its market, and that it showed a high degree of market orientation. This would be quite wrong. The first step in drawing up the budget was to estimate output for the next quarter; the main factor limiting that output was the supply of labour. The amount of labour which Wessex was able to employ varied over time. Wessex Timber's quarterly budget simply reflected the fact that the amount of output it could produce depended on the size of its labour force, and employment could not be predicted for much more than a quarter at a time.

4.7 CONCLUDING REMARK

In this chapter, we have cleared up a number of general points about objectives. We must now go on to concentrate on pricing objectives.

CHAPTER 5

Pricing Objectives

5.1 INTRODUCTION

In this chapter, we consider the objectives that our firms pursued in setting prices. The most convenient way of doing this turns out to be to consider, first, profit objectives; second, market objectives; and, finally, other objectives.

5.2 HOW PROFIT OBJECTIVES WERE STATED

All the firms we studied had one or more marketing and pricing objectives set in terms of profit. The following were the main ways in which profit objectives were stated.

5.2.1 Money Profits

The first, simplest and most basic measure of profit was as an absolute sum of money. This measure was used by all firms. Having such a measure is a necessary part of the budgeting process, since budgets use the common measure of money to judge all of a firm's activities by a single standard. Calculating profit is a necessary—and legally required—part of the process by which a firm reports on its activities to its shareholders. Equally, it is a vital part of the firm's internal reporting process, though of course it would be unusual for the profit figures used by management to be calculated on exactly the same basis as those given to shareholders in the published accounts. Profit also represents one part of the flow of cash within the company, and between it and the parent company (if any) or the shareholders.

5.2.2. Return on Sales

Our firms always had figures which enabled them to calculate ratios of profit to sales. Absolute levels of both profit and sales turnover were budgeted. However, the return on sales was not a significant profit objective (or even indicator) in all our cases.

The Surgical Instrument Co. did use the rate of profit on sales as one of its criteria for deciding whether to proceed with the development of the new scalpel, but it put more emphasis on return on capital employed. Dee Plastics calculated its gross margin as a percentage of selling price. Other firms using return on sales or turnover in this way included Alpha Ltd and Wensum Engineering. Both Fourways Manufacturing and Heavy Technology made use of a similar concept: return as a margin on costs.

5.2.3 Return on Capital

This measure of profitability was used by all firms. In principle, it is the most useful way of measuring profitability. Yet it is also among the most misleading. This book is not the place for a long discussion of the reasons why this is so, but a brief comment is required.

Rates of return can be defined in several ways, but we must distinguish two. First, there is profit for the period in question, expressed as a percentage of the value of the assets used in earning that profit. Usually, this will be the value at which these assets stand in the balance sheet. We shall describe this rate of return as the rate of return on capital employed.

The second measure of rate of return on capital is used where a new asset is being acquired. More and more firms are calculating the DCF (discounted cash flow) return on such assets. This works out what return the investment is expected to yield over its life—assuming that the predictions of its earnings turn out to be correct. We shall have more to say about DCF returns later. For the moment, our concern is with return on capital employed.

The big problem in calculating the rate of return on capital employed lies in the difficulty of valuing capital assets correctly. Book value (namely, cost less depreciation) will be correct only if there is no inflation, and if the depreciation method used reflects exactly the rate at which the asset actually depreciates. Put this way, we can see that only by a miracle will the book value of an asset equal its actual value in a world where there is both inflation and technical change. Inflation makes the values of both new and existing assets appreciate; technical change makes them depreciate. Depreciation charges are usually best seen as a simple way of ensuring that, when plant has to be replaced, retained profits have been made available to allow for this.

However, it must be emphasized that these profits will not necessarily be available in a liquid form. Effective capital and cash budgeting will be needed for that.

To allow for inflation, more firms will need to do what some firms already do—undertake the regular revaluation of capital assets. This method will still not deal with the other important factor leading to changes in asset values—technical change. If technical improvements reduce the cost of new assets of a particular kind, then the value of existing assets will fall. In the contemporary world where prices rise steadily, though technology improves too, there is merit in using rates of return on the current values of assets to evaluate performance. The reason is that it emphasizes the fact that using book values often overstates rates of return on capital and so makes management's job too easy. This explains why managers frequently resist the revaluation of assets. In addition, revaluation does mean extra work, and careful cost/benefit evaluation is necessary to see how frequently it can economically be undertaken.

It follows, of course, that there are even bigger difficulties in the way of comparison of rates of return on capital employed between firms. Definitions of capital employed vary from firm to firm, as do accounting practices and depreciation conventions. Some firms revalue capital at intervals; others do not. However, useful information can be obtained from comparison of trends from year to year in the return on capital in any given firm, provided that the basis of calculation used remains constant.

Despite all these reservations, we must recognize that achieving a given rate of return on capital is a major objective for most firms. Firms borrow capital with which to trade. For the shareholder (or other lender) who provides that capital, it is the return on each pound invested that matters. Return on capital (measured as accurately as it is profitable to do) is therefore the most significant indicator of the profitability of the firm, even though knowing what rate of return is currently being earned will not necessarily enable the firm to know whether a better one is possible. So long as the firm measures return on capital employed consistently between departments, and uses it for internal comparisons only, there is no serious problem in using it.

It is perhaps worth pointing out that even if the firm is earning a high return on capital employed, as defined above, it may not necessarily be doing the best it can for its shareholders. A major problem in business finance is to ensure that the capital structure of the firm—especially the relationship between fixed-interest borrowing and the issuing of equity capital—is optimal. The ultimate aim of the firm must be to give a high (or maximum) rate of return to equity shareholders. Earning a high (or maximum) return on capital employed is only the first step in this larger process. However, it is an important first step.

In our study, the only firm which tried to calculate the return on capital employed for individual products and product lines was the Surgical Instrument Company. The DCF return on the capital employed in producing the scalpel was therefore one of the main criteria by which the project was evaluated, before the board gave authority for it to be put on the market. In all the other firms we studied, return on capital was one extremely important criterion by which the overall performance of the company was judged, but not the performance of individual products. A specific target rate of return was laid down for the whole firm at some stage in the long-term forecasting or short-term budgeting process. A number of firms judged their performance by looking at their rate of return on capital before tax. Wessex Timber Industries was one of them.

None of our firms appeared to take tax explicitly into account when pricing. Perhaps tax is not very important for pricing decisions so long as the rate of (pre-tax) return required from any product takes account of the level and structure of taxation in a general way and yields a big enough rate of return after tax. It is with investment decisions that the fact that the British system has provided investment and depreciation grants or allowances has made it essential to allow for tax explicitly.

The refusal of the twelve firms, apart from the Surgical Instrument Company, to calculate rates of return on capital for individual products was realistic. Many products were produced jointly with others—with raw materials, labour and plant devoted to making more than one product. For example, Basic Foods processed several foodstuffs from the same raw material on the same machines. Dee Plastics and Wessex Timber Industries produced wide ranges of similar items, of different sizes, on the same plant. In these three firms, no attempt to allocate either current or capital costs to individual products could have given very accurate results. Even for those firms and products where such a calculation would have been less difficult, it was not thought worthwhile.

5.3 PROFIT OBJECTIVES

We now go on to look in detail at the profit objectives pursued in the firms we studied. In the terminology of section 4.5, five of the firms tried to maximize profits. The five were: The Surgical Instrument Company, Dee Plastics, Heavy Technology, Medlock Engineering and Clean Engineering.

5.4 THE MAXIMIZERS

5.4.1 The Surgical Instrument Company Ltd

The Surgical Instrument Company is the odd one out in this list. It was the only one of the five firms which set out to maximize profits that was not virtually compelled to do so either to meet the competitive pressures it faced in a depressed market or in order to reach the level of profit required from it by the parent firm. The Board of the parent firm did not set the Surgical Instrument Company a minimum rate of profit which it was expected to earn on each individual product. However, the parent Board did keep a careful check on the overall return on capital earned by the Surgical Instrument Company. The latter therefore thought it best to take the trouble to work out the rate of return on capital for every product.

The attempt to maximize profits can be split into two distinct stages. In the first, capital was allocated to the production of disposable scalpels only after the Surgical Instrument Company had looked at the known alternative uses for this capital. The only way in which the parent Board could be persuaded to invest funds in a new project was for those concerned with it to show that it would yield a satisfactory rate of return on that investment. The Surgical Instrument Company was seeking a DCF return of at least 12–15 per cent on its investment in any major products, but might accept a lower rate on less important ones. In this case, it was decided that beginning to produce scalpels was the best way of using the funds in question, taking into account all relevant alternatives and the opportunities and constraints for each alternative. The company sought the most profitable use for these assets—it maximized.

In the second stage, the scalpel was priced. In doing this, the marketing manager of the company was under pressure to set whatever price would maximize profit and this was thought likely, for the scalpel, to be a rather high one. He looked at the rate of return both on capital and on turnover. While the company realized that it was easier to reduce a high price than to raise one that had been initially set too low, it had only recently entered the scalpel market and faced a number of competing products. The prices of these products effectively gave the maximum price which could be charged for a new scalpel. If the Surgical Instrument Company had set a price higher than this, it could not reasonably have expected buyers to change from existing products to the new one. Its price was therefore set to maximize return, but taking into account the prices of competing scalpels.

Three of the remaining four firms which tried to maximize profits were operating in very difficult market conditions. They were Heavy Technology, Medlock Engineering and Clean Engineering.

5.4.2 Heavy Technology Ltd

In Heavy Technology, it was the general and sales managers who were responsible for setting pricing objectives fitting in with the company's philosophy. The firm had not defined its profit objectives precisely, though it was generally agreed in the firm that a rate of return of about 15 per cent was required on the funds put into any new investment. The firm was anxious to embody the latest scientific and technological developments in new products, in order to maintain its position as the most technically advanced firm in the industry. It also sought to maintain its market share and to earn sufficient profit to finance an intensive research and development programme. Profitability was thus treated as very important. Without it, research and development would have suffered. As a result, the company had in the past had to satisfy the parent Board that it was earning at least as much as in the previous year, and close to a 15 per cent return on capital employed. New capital was allocated by the Board on the basis of past achievement.

With the market depressed when we studied the firm, things had changed. It would have been unrealistic for the general and sales managers to continue to pursue the objective of earning a 15 per cent return on capital, since Heavy Technology had been forced to reduce its prices in order to obtain business. Holding or increasing its market share, and so maximizing profit (or minimizing loss), were now seen as the most important goals.

The complete set of the objectives which had been pursued by Heavy Technology at one time or another in pricing contracts was as follows:

(a) to earn a profit of about 15 per cent on capital for the company;
(b) to guarantee the company's survival;
(c) to keep its share of the market;
(d) to provide funds for research, development and product innovation; and
(e) to maintain a high level of employment, particularly for staff.

In the difficult market situation, objectives (a), (d) and even (e) had virtually been abandoned, in order to maintain profit and survive. A new profit objective—to minimize losses while increasing market share if possible—had been tacitly adopted. This was effectively profit maximization (loss minimization) but with the hope that it would still be possible to maintain the existing level of employment, especially among staff.

5.4.3 Medlock Engineering Ltd

The competitive position faced by Medlock Engineering was equally difficult. It was very hard in this case to discover operational pricing objectives for the product we studied which were different from the non-operational objectives of the whole firm, and which could give definite guidance to managers. In our study of Medlock we were concerned only with export markets. The (non-operational) objectives there were:

(a) to keep the factories working at a high level of activity;
(b) to provide an acceptable level of contribution to fixed costs and, if possible, profit;
(c) to obtain technical experience that could be of value in the home market in future.

These goals clearly do not represent precise, operational objectives, though they do emphasize the marginal character of export sales in Medlock Engineering. The notion of marginal pricing for such sales was well established.

Medlock Engineering normally set each of its departments to earn a return of 15 per cent on capital employed (at book values). However, it was accepted that it would often be difficult to earn this rate of profit in the export market. While the profit objective was not formally changed on export business, lower rates of return were in fact accepted by the Board. Many export sales were truly marginal, covering variable cost and little more. The objective was to choose the most profitable combination of sales open to the firm. At the time of our study, the emphasis was on using these export sales to minimize losses at a time when the home market was depressed. Given the capacity of the firm, it was hoped to keep employment at current levels, but had it been necessary to choose between lower profit and lower employment, employment would have been allowed to fall. The overriding aim was to minimize losses.

5.4.4 Clean Engineering Ltd

The other case where the market was so depressed that the firm was forced into trying to maximize its profits, was that of Clean Engineering. Here, again, it was not possible to distinguish clearly between operational and non-operational pricing objectives. The company's main pricing objective was to keep its existing (approximately 15 per cent) share of the market for water purification equipment at a time when there was intense competition for business, but when the size of the total market was increasing. Even if it had kept its market share, Clean Engineering would have found it hard to provide the Board with the required rate of profit. The Board ostensibly concentrated its attention on the rate of return on capital employed, requiring Clean Engineering to achieve between 15 per cent and 20 per cent. However, when we studied the firm, it was a matter of attempting to use all plant and equipment at tolerable profit (or loss) levels, knowing that the result would be a return of far less than 15 per cent. Indeed, prices were little above marginal cost. The desire to keep labour, plant and equipment in use was again an important factor, though the desire to maximize profit (minimize losses) was seen as paramount. Fortunately, though trade was bad, it was not quite bad enough to require a cut in employment.

5.4.5 Dee Plastics Ltd

The parent company of Dee Plastics Limited was essentially interested in receiving a given percentage rate of return on the capital that it had invested in the subsidiary. However, the parent company did not attempt to interfere in the running of Dee Plastics. It recognized that only the local management had the expertise needed in manufacturing and marketing venetian blind slats. Within Dee Plastics, the profit objective for each contract was to earn the 'normal' gross margin of about 25 per cent of the selling price, which was thought to be the optimal margin. This was a margin over prime costs, which were defined as raw materials, sundry direct process costs and carriage. The gross margin of about 25 per cent had to cover labour costs, overheads and profit. Higher prices could sometimes be obtained, and the gross margin on some contracts had been as high as 27 per cent.

On the other hand, we have seen that for larger orders Dee Plastics was prepared to accept lower margins. If one customer were to take all the output produced by working two shifts on one production line, the firm would be willing to accept a gross margin for all this business of between 15 per cent and 20 per cent. The lower unit contribution to profit was seen as worth having because a single set of negotiations was needed and a high level of sales guaranteed. Alternatively, if the whole output of a single shift on this one product line had already been sold, it would now have been possible to set a lower profit margin for the output of the second shift. A substantial level of sales would already have been guaranteed, and a substantial proportion of the firm's fixed costs covered, especially because there would have been no significant increase in overhead costs if two shifts were worked instead of one. Nevertheless, Dee was finding it impossible to provide as high a return on capital as the parent firm would have liked. Dee Plastics had little spare capacity, though thought was being given to the desirability of expanding it by putting down another production line in the existing factory, and by building another factory. Because there was this capacity constraint, Dee was a firm trying to maximize profits while accepting that it could not sell more than the output produced by the existing plant when working the two shifts.

5.5 THE SATISFICERS

5.5.1 Alpha Ltd

The eight remaining firms were, quite simply, satisficers. First, there was Alpha Ltd. The operational objectives set for any product group within Alpha Ltd have to be seen in the context of the company's objectives. Alpha Ltd's profit objective was 'to return a satisfactory reward on overall company operations'. This non-operational objective had been made more precise when objectives were set for the product 'Alpha' itself; but some objectives, even for 'Alpha', remained non-operational. For example, the price of 'Alpha' was to be set by taking into account its total profit contribution to the product group and to the company. In this context, 'Alpha' was required to provide a 'satisfactory' margin of profit, after all costs had been met; but the size of a 'satisfactory' margin had not been defined.

On the other hand, 'Alpha' was set the task of providing a specific share of company profits, within the annual budgeting procedure. When the figure for profit in the budget was being set, the objective was a satisfactory, rather than the maximum possible, amount. At product-manager level, the basic strategic aim was to increase both 'Alpha's' market share and the total amount of 'Alpha' sold. There was an explicitly-stated belief that, in the long run, the best guarantee of satisfactory profit would be for the market share held by 'Alpha' to be maintained. However, there was no attempt to quantify this relationship between profit and market share. While it was clearly thought to exist, no one could say exactly what it implied for individual, short-run marketing decisions. These were aimed mainly at achieving short-run market share objectives. The conflicts, actual and potential, which lay behind the attempt to guarantee long-run profit by maintaining short-run market share will be looked at in more detail later.

5.5.2 Gamma Products Ltd

The second satisficer was Gamma. The objectives which Gamma pursued in pricing its battery for shavers were:

(a) to obtain a specified share of the battery market within a year;
(b) to sell x thousand Gamma shavers in the same period;
(c) to distribute Gamma's batteries and shavers through 75 per cent of the total number of electrical shops in the UK (which normally handled Gamma's products) and 75 per cent of barbers' shops (which handled a large proportion of shaver sales, but which had not previously sold Gamma's products).

These objectives were set after the firm had studied forecasts of the markets for batteries and shavers, in terms of both volume and value. The forecasts were made for each year of a five-year period, beginning with the year of Gamma's introduction, and were revised at fairly frequent intervals as experience was gained in the market.

A review of market forecasts undertaken a few months after the introduction of the Gamma shaver, led the firm to reduce its estimates of the total market demand for shaver batteries by about 20 per cent, while its forecast of the total demand for shavers was rather more than doubled. As a result, the sales-volume and market-share objectives for Gamma's batteries were both reduced, whilst those for shavers were both increased very considerably. The Board and the product managers of Gamma had always realized that the initial forecasts might well be wrong. They accepted them as a reasonable basis for planning because so little information was available. The targets based on them were accepted as achievable.

A similar series of estimated figures was prepared for the costs of Gamma batteries and shavers, and for the revenues and profits expected from them. Depending on the assumptions made, a wide range of possible annual profit figures was shown for each of the five years after the forecast was made. Profit was estimated in absolute amounts of money throughout. In the case of shavers, this was because there was no capital investment in shavers by Gamma Products; manufacture was contracted. The profit on turnover from Gamma shavers was small by the firm's normal standards, whatever assumptions were made. But, since the shaver had been developed in order to keep up Gamma's battery sales, the actual rate of profit was regarded as comparatively unimportant so long as sales of batteries, and profits from them, increased.

5.5.3 Wensum Engineering Ltd

Wensum Engineering, too, would have liked to earn more than it was currently earning, in order to satisfy the parent board. In practice, for various reasons, it arrived at a lower profit than it might have done. Wensum Engineering was originally asked by the parent firm to provide a return on capital employed of between 20 per cent and 25 per cent. Wensum explained that 'the broad aim is to obtain a given percentage return on investment rather than a particular market share for each product group'. However, Wensum's managing director felt that past performance, viewed rather cautiously, demonstrated that this rate of return on capital employed could not be reached. He was able to get the target rate of return reduced to a less-ambitious one of 17 per cent. The parent firm had to allow for the fact that Wensum sold a significant proportion of its output to other members of its group on very favourable terms. There was a problem of transfer pricing here. This was to some extent a circular process, because the rates of return Wensum was asked to earn depended in part on the prices at which it was forced to transfer its products to other members of its own group. If the transfer price had been increased, the return on capital employed required of Wensum by its parent board would undoubtedly have been raised too. A great deal of discussion went on about the correctness of these transfer prices, and this is a subject to which we shall return in Chapter 11.

We studied Wensum's annual price review, which was carried out by a committee that did not include the managing director. Its members were the marketing manager, the accountant and the domestic sales manager. The export sales manager's position was ambiguous. Though nominally a member of the committee, he attended only part of the meeting. No specific instructions were given to the members of this committee. They already knew that the minimum goal was a return on turnover of 10 per cent to 12 per cent. It was explained to us that capital would be turned over 1·5 times, giving a return on capital employed of 15 per cent to 18 per cent. The parent firm required 17 per cent. However, in the price review meeting, the minimum return was taken as the required rate of return.

The managing director confirmed that he did not give any specific directive to the review meeting. He said, 'They know what we are trying to get.' As we shall see, things did not work out even as smoothly as this implies. The decisions taken in the meeting did not yield even the minimum rate of return on capital of 17 per cent. This may explain why, after the meeting, the domestic sales manager raised some prices on his own.

5.5.4 Fourways Manufacturing Ltd

Fourways Manufacturing expected each of its products to cover the general overheads which were regarded as being associated with its production, and to make an 'acceptable' contribution to profits as well. In addition to this non-operational objective, there was the operational objective that, for every group of similar products within each product line, there should be a standard percentage rate of recovery, or margin (expressed as gross invoice value less commission, labour cost and material cost). Individual products were expected to provide a margin of this size over an appropriate time period. This was either a year, or the expected life of the product, depending on the particular circumstances. The standard rate of recovery of overheads for each product group was expressed both as an absolute sum of money and as a percentage of costs. From it was calculated a tentative price, which was then adjusted to take market conditions, including the prices of competing products, into account. In the case of the new product whose pricing we studied, the amount expected to be earned over and above commission, labour and material costs, was based on forecasts of several factors. These were the amount to be invested in the product, its launching and development expenses, its manufacturing costs and the expected levels of sales in the first years of its life. The forecasting and profitability exercise was repeated several times during the development of the product.

5.5.5 Basic Foods Ltd

In Basic Foods there was a close link between overall company objectives and the specific objectives for the product studied. This was perhaps because the product accounted for a great deal of Basic Foods' turnover. Overall objectives for the group of which Basic Foods was a member were set when the budget for the following five years was drawn up. (The budget for the first year was worked out in detail, while plans were drawn up for the remaining four years in whatever degree of detail was felt to be appropriate.) The group's overall objectives were set in general terms by the executive board of the parent firm. This general plan provided an outline of intended future developments, which the subsidiaries of the group could use in drawing up their own one-year and five-year plans, tailoring them to meet their own specific objectives.

The objectives of Basic Foods were set by its own Board. They took account of the general, overall objectives laid down by the executive board of the parent, of how far current performance was matching current objectives and of forecasts of those factors which were likely to affect Basic Foods' operations in the future. These objectives for the first year, and for all five years, were presented to the parent's executive board together with Basic Foods' capital budget for the first year. From this document and from discussion on it, detailed objectives were agreed for the first year of the five-year period for each of Basic Foods' products. When we studied Basic Foods, its underlying (non-operational) objective was 'to maintain adequate growth while maintaining profitability so far as this is possible.'

The capital budget outlined Basic Foods' plans for dealing with the main problems it anticipated meeting. It covered all aspects of marketing policy and gave Basic Foods' forecasts of sales volumes, sales value, costs, profit and return on capital employed as well as the internal rate of return expected on its total planned capital expenditure for the period. The capital budget represented a set of intentions based on a limited number of assumptions; from it were developed the annual plans and budgets for all Basic Foods' activities.

The company recognized that with a fluid competitive situation, like the one for the product we studied, the marketing and pricing decisions made by Basic Foods, or by any one of its competitors, were bound to have a substantial impact in the market in which they operated, and not least on market shares. As a result, it was accepted as likely that the budgeted figures for sales, profits etc., would have to be changed. Pricing decisions were made to meet a combination of marketing (i.e. sales volume and market share) and financial (i.e. sales value and profit) objectives, given the overall objective of maintaining growth and profitability.

5.5.6 Epsilon Ltd

Epsilon Ltd seemed to be less concerned with its overall profitability than was Basic Foods, although a target rate of profit on capital employed was set in advance and was aimed at over a period of five years by the whole company. How far any level of profitability either for the whole firm or for an individual product was regarded as satisfactory depended on the current market situation and on the Board's interpretation of the word 'satisfactory'. But what profit had been earned in the past seemed to have a significant influence in determining what was accepted in the present.

To understand the profit objectives for Epsilon, we must look in some detail at the objectives of Epsilon's marketing staff. The operation of launching Epsilon on a national scale was to be carried out in two phases. First, there was to be a limited test-market period, during which Epsilon would be introduced and (it was hoped) successfully established in two different regions. Then the sales coverage for Epsilon was to be extended over the whole country. The two test-market regions were chosen to allow the firm to discover whether consumers in different geographical areas accepted Epsilon's physical attributes and its performance, as well as to test alternative methods of sales promotion. This was to be done before the product could be introduced on a national scale.

Objectives were set for both stages of this operation. Epsilon Limited wished not merely to establish Epsilon in the market, but to establish it as the leading brand in the more expensive part of the market. Specific targets were set for yearly periods up to five years ahead, covering both phases. They were set in terms of profit, sales volume and sales value, market share, the scale of distribution to retail outlets (and hence availability to customers) and the percentage of customers who had tried the product. It was also expected (and indeed intended) that not more than 30 per cent of Epsilon's sales would be at the expense of the company's own similar products. Again, these objectives seem to have been satisficing ones.

5.5.7 Wessex Timber Industries Ltd

Turning now to Wessex Timber Industries, we find that its board had set a pre-tax rate of return on capital employed which was to be achieved from sales of timber. The managers and salesmen of Wessex had to ensure that the budgeted output of timber would be sufficient to provide this level of profitability. However, as labour was the limiting factor for Wessex, its ability to work at high levels of output depended on heavy investment in plant and equipment. Consequently it was important to ensure that, as the scale of the firm's investment increased, it continued to earn an acceptable rate of return on capital employed. Ensuring that increased investment did not reduce the rate of return on capital lay at the heart of Wessex's management problems.

The firm's operational pricing objectives had to take account of two major requirements. Wessex was asked:

(a) to provide the return on capital of $12\frac{1}{2}$ per cent before tax required by the Board;
(b) to work as near to 100 per cent of capacity as possible.

In order to turn these general requirements into precise objectives, the management of Wessex Timber Industries Ltd met quarterly to review past performance and to set budgets for the following quarter. Variances between budgeted and actual performance in the previous quarter were studied to see if they were likely to recur. For example, since the amount of labour that was available for employment was the main factor determining how much of Wessex's capacity could be used, it was particularly important that labour variances should be analysed, and taken into account if necessary, in setting the next quarter's budget.

From these discussions emerged a forecast of output in the next quarter, usually expressed in thousands of feet of processed timber. Since the Board required the 12½ per cent before-tax rate of return on capital, the management had to ensure that selling the budgeted output of timber would achieve this target. The production manager forecast the effects of changes in costs in the coming period. These were incorporated into a build-up of expected costs for the quarter, for each type of timber processed. Cost per foot of timber ready for sale was calculated on the assumption that output targets would be achieved.

To calculate what price had to be charged to ensure that selling the budgeted output would provide the budgeted cost levels was then a simple matter. This price was the salesman's target; his job was to get the best price he could for any sale of timber, but he was given only the freedom of being allowed to charge prices within plus or minus one per cent of those shown in the company's price list. It follows from what has been said that if the salesman really did get the best price he could for any timber sold, then the firm could be regarded as maximizing profits rather than satisficing—given the supply of labour. However, our judgement is that if one considers the way in which the budget was set, the firm was probably satisficing rather than maximizing. We suspect, though we cannot prove, that salesmen might have obtained higher prices if greater pressure for profit had been put on them.

5.5.8 Universal Corporation

The final satisficing firm was Universal Corporation. Its objective, laid down by the parent Board, was to obtain a given return on capital employed over a five-year period. Precise rules were laid down for calculating the rate of return on capital employed, and these regulated all the Corporation's activities. Universal's objectives were defined in this way because of two interdependent factors. First, it had to rely considerably, but not completely, on internal funds to finance investment. It therefore had to earn profit margins big enough to service large amounts of capital expenditure. The second factor was that its plant took a long time to construct. The size of its plants and their complex technology meant that a number of years had to elapse before any newly-planned plant could be put into operation. Because its pricing objectives were framed so as to ensure that it earned the required rate of return on capital, and to some extent because it was traditional, Universal Corporation had set its prices on the basis of unit cost. The definition of this unit cost—and therefore of price—was being changed at the time of our study. The unit cost used had previously been average cost at pre-determined volumes of output. Universal was now beginning to use marginal cost and was relating this to particular ranges of output.

The reasons for adopting a system of marginal cost pricing were complex, and the change was undertaken only after considerable discussion with the parent board and with Universal's distributing agents. The objective in making the change was rather more clear cut. While charging prices related to marginal cost, the corporation aimed to cover its overall expenses in the short run, i.e. in periods of up to a year. Over the longer run (say, one to five years ahead) Universal Corporation wanted to base prices on marginal cost in order to help its distributors to recognise likely future patterns of cost and so of demand. Since it would be easier for them to deduce such patterns from marginal rather than from average costs, marginal cost pricing was intended to enable distributors to make better forecasts of their likely future demands for the products of the Corporation.

5.6 PROFIT OBJECTIVES SUMMARIZED

We may now sum up. All the firms we studied had profit objectives. In every case, the firm had an objective stated in terms of rate of return on capital. The difficulties in measuring capital were usually glossed over and it was usual for the rate of return to be set for the output of the whole firm or department rather than for an individual product. Only some of the firms treated rate of return on turnover as an operational objective in pricing, but all of them set a target profit, in budgets, as an absolute sum of money.

Five of the thirteen firms could be regarded as maximizers, but only one (Surgical Instrument Company) maximized profit as part of a freely-chosen policy. Dee was forced to maximize because the Board of the parent firm was insisting on high (or increased) profits. The other three were seeking to earn as much as they could in markets where trade was depressed. The remaining firms were satisficers.

5.7 MARKET OBJECTIVES

Market objectives provide the firm with criteria by which it can judge its performance in each of its markets. The firms we studied concentrated on three measures: sales volume, sales value and market share. All of them had set specific, measurable market objectives for pricing, using at least one of these criteria.

The terminology used was not the same in every case; for example 'sales volume' was used by Alpha Ltd; 'output' by Wessex Timber Industries. Although, where there are stocks, output need not equal sales volume, in practice the two may come to the same thing. This was obviously true where goods were produced to meet specific orders, as in Wessex Timber and Clean Engineering. Output and sales could differ where goods were produced for stock. They did so in Epsilon Ltd, in Fourways and in Wensum.

5.7.1 Volume of Sales

With the exception of Clean Engineering, all our firms set targets for the volume of sales to be achieved in specific (usually budget) periods. These targets were set in units of output, or in turnover, according to the product. In the case of Clean Engineering, which wanted to keep its 15 per cent share of the growing market for water purification equipment, estimates of market size were available. When sales volume was considered it was therefore as a derivative, rather than as a determinant, of the firm's desired share of a market of the estimated size.

5.7.2 Sales Volume and Capacity

In some cases, targets for sales volume depended upon production capacity. The clearest example of this was in Dee Plastics where, but for the constraint imposed by its limited production capacity, its marketing effort would have been devoted to increasing sales and taking market share from the dominant competitor. A major reason why extra capacity had not been installed was that it was not clear that the extra volume and market share could be obtained at an adequate profit. The case of Wessex Timber was similar, though here it was labour, not plant, that was the limiting factor. In Heavy Technology, the situation was slightly different. The main objective here was to maximize profit (minimize loss) but to hope that this would allow the firm to work near to full capacity in the highly-competitive market situation that the company faced. The benefit that Heavy Technology would obtain from a particular contract was judged by the effect that obtaining it would have on the profit-and-loss position, but with an anxious eye on the proportion of capacity which would be at work. With Medlock Engineering, the situation was broadly similar. Export orders were judged by their 'contribution' to profit and by how far they would fill the gap between demand from British customers and total productive capacity. But the main objective was to maximize profit.

5.7.3 Sales Value

Sales value, or turnover, objectives were normally set in terms of the firm's net receipts, though these were often hard to calculate. For instance, when Epsilon Ltd calculated company revenue, it began from retail prices. Retail prices were notional, because there was no resale price maintenance for 'Epsilon'. The notional unit retail price was multiplied by estimated sales volume, and retail margins, trade discounts, etc. were then deducted. Similar calculations were made by the other consumer good manufacturers, although in the case of Basic Foods sales at below notional retail price were not so numerous as for Alpha Ltd, Gamma Ltd and Epsilon Ltd.

The manufacturers of industrial goods, like The Surgical Instrument Company and Wensum Engineering, used similar concepts when setting their sales-value objectives. They began from ex-works selling prices and allowed for trade discounts. For Heavy Technology calculating turnover meant adding together the values of all individual contracts. A similar position existed in Medlock Engineering and Clean Engineering.

5.7.4 Market Share

Market share objectives were set by most firms, though the importance attached to them varied. They were most important to the consumer-good manufacturers. For Alpha Ltd, whose 'Alpha' was competing with 'Omega' for this particular consumer market, movements in market share were seen as the most significant indicators of success or failure. As a result, market-share objectives had a crucial place in budgeting for 'Alpha'. Market-share objectives were stated as a percentage of the total market both in terms of sales volume and value. Although the remaining consumer goods manufacturers (Basic Foods, Gamma Products and Epsilon Ltd) did not each compete with a single major competitor, they used similar measures of market share to judge market success. In the cases of Gamma Products and Epsilon Ltd, both of which were launching new consumer products, attention was concentrated on the market share which they wanted by the end of the launch period. This would be a major determinant of the product's success or failure.

Most of the industrial goods manufacturers did not regard market-share objectives as so important. However, Heavy Technology, Dee Plastics, Medlock Engineering and Clean Engineering all faced very keen competition. Keeping their positions in their respective markets had become extremely important. So, they had to pay a great deal of attention to market share.

Market share was a less important objective in pricing for the other firms. The Surgical Instrument Company, Wessex Timber Industries and Universal Corporation all had estimates of their current shares of their markets; they all planned on the basis of estimated, future market shares; all of them used these estimates to obtain an idea of how their products were faring on the market. Even so, the projections were far from critical for either marketing or pricing decisions. Medlock Engineering had set no objectives for its share of the world-wide market for its exported product. Although data was available about markets in a number of individual countries, there was no effort to determine what share of these markets the firm should try to obtain or to hold.

5.7.5 Scale of Distribution

The scale on which the consumer goods we studied were distributed was an important criterion of marketing success for their manufacturers. The larger the number of retail outlets selling a product, the greater was the number of potential buyers. Accordingly, consumer goods manufacturers often set objectives for the scale on which they wanted their products to be distributed, in a way that was not always appropriate to the manufacturers of industrial goods.

With Epsilon Ltd and Gamma Products, which were launching new consumer goods, the objective in each case was set as the percentage of all possible retail outlets which were to be selling the product within one year. In test markets, the objective was set for the limited area and for the period of the test market only. Alpha Limited did not treat as an objective the percentage of shops it wanted to stock 'Alpha'. 'Alpha' was an established product, and the number of outlets through which it was available had largely been determined already. While its distribution pattern was measured and reported on, the struggle with 'Omega' was fought by other means.

In addition to its distribution objectives, Epsilon Ltd had set objectives for the trial marketing of 'Epsilon'. The aim was that by the end of the test-market, or introductory period, 'Epsilon' would have been sampled by a given percentage of the available body of consumers. During this trial period, 'Epsilon' was to make use of various forms of sales promotion. It was believed that the scale of such trials was important in determining the rate at which customers would become aware of 'Epsilon'. Once they were aware of it, some of them would be likely to switch their custom from other brands, so increasing 'Epsilon's' chances of achieving its other objectives.

5.8 MARKET OBJECTIVES SUMMARIZED

We must now sum up again. So far as market objectives were concerned, all our firms set sales volume and market share objectives. In a few cases, the market share aimed at was somewhat influenced by the desire to sell enough output to keep employment at current levels.

Market share objectives were of varying importance for our firms. They were more important for consumer goods producers and for the four firms selling in difficult markets. The scale on which the product was available to consumers was an important objective for consumer-good manufacturers.

5.9 OTHER OBJECTIVES

In the check list, we suggested a number of other objectives that might be relevant to particular pricing decisions. Examples suggested were: using capacity to the full (an objective distinguished from that of reaching a given sales volume); setting levels of output or inventory, or reducing variations in them; adjusting to particular aspects of national policy; and attempting to set or alter the public image of the firm.

In our studies, we found two major objectives of this kind. Clearly, our firms were concerned to ensure that their pricing decisions did not result in unacceptable levels of and/or variations in inventory. They were also keen that they should not be unnecessarily criticized either by the Prices and Incomes Board or by the Monopolies Commission. However, the two main 'other objectives' were those of keeping the percentage of capacity employed at a high level and ensuring that the firm kept in the forefront of technological development.

The objective of keeping capacity employed was a significant objective for Heavy Technology, Medlock Engineering and Clean Engineering. We have already discussed its relevance to their sales volume objectives. They put more emphasis on maintaining profit than on maintaining employment, even though the desire to maintain employment could be justified on purely economic grounds. To lay off labour, if depression in the firms' markets was not going to last for very long, would be expensive in terms of redundancy payments, re-training costs and so on. The objective of keeping capacity occupied was more important in the case of Dee, where it was linked to its desire to take market share from its major competitor.

One or two of the firms making technically-advanced products emphasized the need, sometimes, to take orders at low prices in order to gain experience needed to develop advanced products. Heavy Technology and Medlock Engineering were the firms which put most emphasis on this. Heavy Technology, in particular, took export orders for its larger products at low prices because the business gained gave excellent experience in designing and operating products bigger than the UK market would require for some years. This gave them a head-start over domestic competitors who had not done so.

CHAPTER 6

Some Conclusions About Objectives

6.1 THE PLAN OF THE CHAPTER

In this Chapter, we pause to reflect on what we have learned about business objectives. We shall try to draw some conclusions about the way objectives are set, and consider how conflicts between objectives are resolved. A list of the objectives which a writer on these matters—especially an economist—would suggest as the 'classic' business objectives would undoubtedly include the following:

maximizing profit;
maximizing market share;
maximizing sales volume;
attaining technological leadership;
providing employment.

We shall see that all of these objectives figured in our study.

6.2 THE IMPORTANCE OF PROFIT

We begin this chapter by looking at the profit objectives of the firms we studied to see what generalizations we can make about them. Our list of the 'classic' business objectives suggests that profit maximization is an important business aim. However, it appears from our case studies that this traditional idea of economists that firms are above all interested in maximizing profit is defective in several ways. This is not to say that there are no other reasons for attacking the economist's assumption of profit maximization. We do not pretend that ours is anything like a complete list of the possible criticisms of the idea of profit maximization; we can only say that these are the ones we found in our researches.

To ensure that this section is not misinterpreted, it must be stressed at once that we were rather surprised by the emphasis that our firms did put on profit. Over the past twenty or thirty years, it has become fashionable for economists to question their traditional assumptions, and to believe that few firms actually seek maximum profits. The reasons suggested for their failure to do so are that they hesitate to exploit their customers; that they fear that high profits in any line of activity will attract new entrants to it and so eliminate those profits; that high profits will lead to intervention by governments to reduce prices; and so on. Indeed, one had begun to wonder whether supposed philanthropists like doctors (especially American doctors) were the only remaining profit maximizers.

It therefore came as a salutary surprise to discover that five of the thirteen firms studied were anxious to maximize profits. It will be recalled that these firms were: The Surgical Instrument Company, Dee Plastics, Heavy Technology, Medlock Engineering and Clean Engineering. It is true, of course, that Heavy Technology, Medlock Engineering and Clean Engineering would have liked to maintain employment. Nevertheless, in seeking to maximize profits or minimize losses, they would have been prepared to see men laid off rather than abandon this attempt. Dee Plastics was being pressed hard to increase profits, by its parent firm, in a situation where it found it difficult to compete successfully with its much bigger rival.

Of course, there are various ways of increasing profit towards a maximum level, and changing price is are only one of them. Others which a firm seeking to increase its profits should consider would include: cutting overhead costs, eliminating uneconomic customers or products, reducing inventories, reviewing purchasing policy, and so on. Nor should it be forgotten that even if a firm is using pricing policy to increase profit this does not mean that prices have to be put up. If demand for a product is sufficiently responsive to price cutting, profitability may be increased by cutting prices—not by raising them. The willingness to seek increased profits through price *cuts* is one element in the greater flexibility in pricing which we should like to see displayed by more firms, especially in Britain.

It is important to emphasize at once that this proves nothing about the objectives of British firms in general. What we are saying about profit maximization is true for only five of the firms we studied. What is more, there is one very important reason why we should not expect these five firms (or indeed our whole sample) to be typical ones. Six of the firms taking part in this survey (Dee Plastics, Heavy Technology, Medlock Engineering, Clean Engineering, Wensum and Fourways) were firms which were concerned about their overall profitability. They included (somewhat oddly) two of the satisficers—Wensum and Fourways. Indeed, these six firms asked us to look at the products we studied partly because they hoped we might be able to suggest ways of making them more profitable and so increasing overall profit. This being so, it is hardly surprising that a high proportion—five of our thirteen firms—should have sought to maximize profit. This is not to say that no other firms seek to maximize profit. Nor, indeed, can we say whether our satisficers, when pricing other products, sought bigger (or even maximum) profits. Our survey simply does not allow us to know. All we can do is to report the fact that five of the firms we studied were extremely anxious to earn higher profits from all their activities.

Nevertheless, we have already shown that this is not quite the whole story. While these firms were keen to earn high profits, they were also anxious to maintain employment and output. They seemed to hope that a change in price might help to improve profitability in a less painful or disruptive way than would any of the alternative courses of action that they could have followed to increase profits. If necessary, they would have reduced employment—but they hoped it would not be necessary.

So far as profitability is concerned, perhaps the best interpretation is to say that three of the five firms seeking high profits (Heavy Technology, Clean Engineering and Medlock Engineering) were essentially satisficers. Perhaps Dee was too. These firms were reacting in the way satisficers do react when one or more of their aspiration levels fails to be met. Here, the failure was to earn sufficient profit. The reaction was to concentrate on taking decisions to ensure that the firm could once again achieve this one objective (profit) by setting levels of price which, purely from a pricing point of view, were as close to profit maximizing ones as the firm could make them. The aim was to maximize profit, and simultaneously to hope that if pricing policy led to maximum profit it would be possible to avoid significantly changing other aspiration levels—those for production, employment, inventory levels and so on—or indeed the extent to which these aspiration levels were being reached. The attraction of trying to use price alone to improve profitability was that, if the attempt succeeded, all the potentially painful adjustments required in order to do so would have to be made outside, not inside, the firm. Profit could be increased while the constraints represented by the other aspiration levels still held. The firm would increase its profits either at the expense of its competitors, if a cut in price took business from them; or at the expense of its customers, if a rise in price did not cause them to change to other suppliers.

We are therefore convinced that, in at least four of the cases where the firms studied would have liked to maximize profits, they were satisficers, and not maximizers, at heart. In easier conditions, we believe they would have left prices unchanged so long as the aspiration levels for profits were being met.

All this points to a very important conclusion. Pricing is one activity (some marketing and investment decisions may be others) where the main burden of adjustment can be imposed on persons or groups outside the firm. It falls upon expenditure by customers on the firm's products, or upon the market shares, sales receipts and profits of competitors, rather than on the firm's own levels of employment, production, inventories, etc. The reason why our firms behaved as they did seems to be that, when trade is difficult, it is both easier and more attractive to make adjustments at the expense of one's customers and competitors rather than of one's colleagues and employees. We believe that this explains why firms that are satisficers when taking decisions about production, inventories, employment, etc., may become maximizers when they set prices. They are forcing those outside the firm to bear the burden of change.

Even when firms do try to maximize profit through their pricing decisions, however, difficulties arise. What our studies did was to spell out some of the reasons why, as we suggested in Chapter I, profit maximization is a non-operational objective. The main reason is that firms rarely know as much as they would like to know about the relationship between the price of any one of their products and the amount of it which is bought. Because of this, even firms which do want to maximize profits cannot move, all at once, to a position where they earn them—subject, of course, to the constraints mentioned above about maintaining acceptable levels of employment, output, etc. We think that firms often attempt to move towards maximum profit in a series of steps.

The result is this. Unless the firm's market is an extremely stable one, and competitors' actions in that market rare or unimportant, profits are unlikely ever to be maximized, even in a firm that wants to maximize them. The firm will be trying, continually or at discrete intervals, to alter prices so as to move towards maximum profit, perhaps rather slowly. Yet the price for each product which would maximize those profits will also be changing all the time. Perhaps we may use the analogy of the children's game of Hunt the Thimble. Using the loudness of the music as an indicator of how close one is to the thimble, one is always trying to move closer to it, not farther away. The complication here is that, with pricing, the correct analogy is with a situation where the thimble is moving about for most, or all, of the time. In these circumstances, firms are unlikely ever to reach profit-maximizing positions, although they will always be tending towards them. One wonders whether a satisficing philosophy is spilling over here. Perhaps a firm increases its price by less than the profit maximizing amount, partly because it has become accustomed to taking its other business decisions in ways that give less than optimal solutions. At the same time, of course, we must add that business men have had to become accustomed to taking decisions like these with less data than they would ideally like.

What we are saying is, first, that the biggest obstacle to taking pricing decisions so as to maximize profit is that profit maximization would require firms to know too much about the demand relationships for the products of their firms. Either information is unobtainable—like accurate predictions of future changes in the economy—or it can be obtained, but only at a price that would be greater than the value of the information. Second, a subsidiary obstacle is that profit maximization would also imply the need to keep achievement continuously in line with what maximization requires. Third, we are saying that if firms are used to satisficing, then, even if conditions become so difficult that they feel they must try to maximize, they may be timid in doing so. This leads to a fourth difficulty. Even if it knew how to do so, no firm would find it tolerable to be continually and minutely adjusting prices, output, inventories, marketing policy, etc. so as continually to maximize profits within a changing environment. One important reason for this is the sheer administrative inconvenience and cost of changing prices frequently.

To sum up, we have so far seen in this section that five of our firms were anxious to maximize profits. Given the unrepresentative nature of our sample, we cannot say how typical these firms are, but we suspect that four of them were satisficers rather than maximizers at heart.

The remaining firms were nearly all 'straightforward' satisficers, but the case of Wensum Engineering is interesting. Talking to managers in Wensum, it became clear that everyone would have been delighted, in principle, if the firm could have maximized profits, or at any rate have increased them substantially, provided that this could have been done without much disturbing the pattern of employment, output, etc. There would then have been congratulations from the parent firm. Yet Wensum has to be classified here as a satisficer, not a maximizer. As we shall see later, those in Wensum who carried out the annual price review seemed unable to break with satisficing habits of the past. The managing director set Wensum the target of a profit of 10–12 per cent on turnover. Once set, this became, not a minimum to be exceeded if possible, but the profit at which the firm aimed. Indeed, we have already noted that the price review committee found difficulty in bringing itself to increase budgeted profits even by this amount—to the level this 10–12 per cent profit on turnover objective required—partly because it did not allow for the expected rise in wage costs. This seems to us to be an indication of how hard 'satisficing' patterns of behaviour are to break.

6.3 CONFLICTS BETWEEN OBJECTIVES

Perhaps the most important conclusion which emerges from our analysis of pricing objectives is that in every firm these were multiple. While all firms pursued at least one profit objective, they all had some kind of sales volume or market share objective as well. Some firms also had more nebulous objectives, like remaining in the forefront of technological advance.

It is clearly not impossible for a firm to pursue a number of objectives simultaneously, though it is always more difficult than pursuing only one. Ideally, the firm could construct some kind of 'goal index'. It might, for example, decide that it wanted to maximize an index which gave a 50 per cent weight to an increase of one per cent in net profits: a 30 per cent weight to an increase of 1 per cent in market share; and a 20 per cent weight to an increase in employment of 100 men. It could then try to set prices on this basis. Hardly surprisingly, we did not find any firm doing so.

Another way of pursuing more than one objective at a time would be to use a ranking procedure. In practice, it is likely that this would mean deciding which was the most important objective, at any moment or in any set of circumstances, and then giving it absolute priority. Satisficing is simply a variant of this. Several aspiration levels are set. If any one of them fails to be met, priority is given to reaching it again. This is a simple type of ranking. One ranks the objective which is not being met as coming first; the other objectives are then for the time ranked as unimportant.

Of course, the fact that a firm seeks to pursue multiple objectives does not necessarily mean that there will be conflicts between them. If a firm knows that it will earn the maximum possible profit for the following year if it has a 40 per cent share of the market, it can perfectly well pursue the objectives of maximizing profit and holding a 40 per cent market share. However, things are very rarely as certain as this. The fact that a firm is trying to pursue multiple objectives must make it more difficult to specify these objectives precisely than if it has only one. Even when the objectives can be specified, it will be difficult for the firm to ensure that the ones it is pursuing are always mutually consistent. Firms rarely have the knowledge they need in order to pursue mutually-consistent and multiple objectives.

Our studies lead us to think that firms sometimes resolve this problem by treating what appears to be an independent objective as a constraint on another apparently independent objective. For example, we have described five of our firms as profit maximizers. In fact, four of them were also anxious to keep existing capacity and labour fully employed. If they really had treated the employment constraint as absolute, they would have been maximizing profit (or minimizing loss) subject to the over-riding constraint that output was not to fall below the level required to keep men and plant fully employed. One objective would have become a constraint on another. What is more, the constraint (maintaining employment) would have turned out to be a more important objective than what had initially appeared to be the primary objective (maximizing profit).

6.3.1 Conflicts between Objectives—Alpha Ltd

In some other firms, something rather similar seemed to happen. For example, Alpha Ltd was seeking a particular absolute amount of profit, and was also aiming at a particular market share. Any conflict between these objectives was resolved through the budgeting procedures. Alpha aimed to earn a certain absolute amount of profit and to hold at least a certain market share, by the end of five years. If this given market share had turned out to be compatible with the larger money profit, of if the given money profit had turned out to be compatible with a bigger market share, all would obviously be well. However, if either the market share or the money profit proved to be too low, at the desired level of the other objective, the conflict between the two objectives would need to be resolved. This would have been done by changing one (or both) objectives during Alpha Ltd's budgeting process in the way we shall consider later.

We did not observe Alpha Ltd for long enough to see how far the two aims did prove to be compatible, but there was confidence among the firm's managers that there was no conflict between its profit and market-share objectives. This was not based on a knowledge that the particular level of profit and market share were demonstrably compatible. It was expressed in a conviction that maintaining or increasing market share in the short-run was the best guarantee of adequate, even maximum, profit in the long run. We have no way of saying whether this belief was true, because we do not have the data one would need to prove it. Nor did anyone in Alpha Ltd. Yet the fear of conflict between profitability and market share was eliminated. Anyone who feared there was such a conflict convinced himself that it did not exist through the comforting rationalization, propagated by his colleagues, that the two were compatible.

Since there were those in Alpha Ltd who found it hard to see how its two main objectives ever could be incompatible, we should perhaps emphasize that an increase in market share will not always lead to an increase in profit. Beyond some point, an increase in market share will have to be 'bought' so expensively, either by price cuts or by increased expenditure on sales promotion, that it will be accompanied by falling profit. Similarly, for example, a change in inventory control arrangements, intended to minimize costs of holding inventory by reducing stock levels, may have undesired effects elsewhere in the firm. For example, it may lead to shorter production runs and so to higher production costs. The objectives of simultaneously minimizing both inventory and production costs will then conflict.

In fact, Alpha Ltd accepted the objective of achieving, at the end of five years, a certain market share and a given amount of profit. It then used its budgetary machinery to determine what its precise objectives were to be in any particular year. Like other firms, Alpha Ltd was likely to find that some conflicts had to be eliminated during the budgeting process, but the problems raised by these conflicts could then be looked at in precise, numerical terms for specific periods of time. We shall have a little more to say later about the problems of converting broad objectives into precise budgets.

Conflicts occurred in several of our firms between the aims of increasing short-run profits and of building up to the long-run volume of sales which they sought as an assurance of long-run profit. All of them were firms where competition was very keen in the sense that it was oligopolistic and far from impersonal. This kind of conflict was strong in the case of 'Alpha' because the total market for both 'Alpha' and 'Omega' was growing slowly. This slow growth restricted the duopolists largely to fighting each other to keep existing business and gave them little opportunity to attract new custom.

6.3.2 Conflicts between Objectives—Basic Foods Ltd

Basic Foods was another firm which faced a conflict between its objectives for profitability and market share. Basic Foods had decided that it wanted to remain among the two or three firms with the biggest shares of its market. The market was growing, but competition was increasing too, and it had lost its traditional role as market leader. Basic Foods was convinced that it could not afford to hold its own prices at the existing level if the trend of prices for products like its own continued to be downwards. If it did, then an internal memorandum suggested that the result would be 'a rapid and accelerating loss of market share which would soon reach the point where no further growth in volume could be involved'. It is not clear whether this was intended to imply that growth in sales volume was needed in order to maintain Basic Foods' profit or to keep up its level of employment and activity, or both.

Nevertheless, Basic Foods saw that if it tried to keep its existing market share by cutting prices, its profit would fall too far. A middle course was therefore chosen, but was not defined precisely. Basic Foods asked for its increased sales to be made at prices that were not 'totally unprofitable'. It set out to hold back the growth of the small firms in the market, without making quite such big price cuts as they did. It set out to match fully any reductions in the prices charged by the bigger firms. It also aimed to extract 'the maximum profit from the remaining business'.

Like Alpha Ltd, Basic Foods was trying to balance market share objectives against profit objectives. In the way they were stated in the previous paragraph, Basic Foods' objectives were non-operational. For example, it is not clear how much profit it was ready to sacrifice in order to maintain market share. What is clear is that Basic Foods, like Alpha Ltd, believed that too big a loss of short-run market share, even if it protected short-run profit, would lead in the long run to a fall in market share that was too big to be acceptable. Basic Foods did not go on, as Alpha did, to argue that keeping short-run market share was the way of best guaranteeing long-run profit, but the underlying attitude was much the same.

As with Alpha Ltd, Basic Foods translated these vague objectives into specific budgets for profit, sales, etc. for the following year. It was at this stage that the conflict between market-share and profit objectives was resolved. Detailed budgets were worked out which set objectives that were thought to be compatible with each other. As it turned out, the problem of how far to cut prices in order to keep market share was resolved for Basic Foods by the other firms in the market. In particular, one big competitor cut its price and forced Basic Foods to follow. In other words, when finally forced to decide, Basic Foods chose to keep up its market share. It did this, not knowing for certain what the implications for profit would be, except that it was likely to fall. Even if the fall were substantial, Basic Foods felt that it had no choice but to follow its major competitor in cutting prices. This was seen as its only hope for survival.

6.3.3 Conflicts between Objectives—Other Firms

In several of our cases, a conflict between profit and marketing objectives was more potential than actual. For example, the Surgical Instrument Company wanted a good profit, but found that the prices charged by its competitors put a clear upper limit on the price of its scalpel. Similarly, there was thought to be no serious conflict between profit and market objectives in Wensum Engineering, at least during the annual price review. The order budget for the next year had been completed before the price review we studied. When the order budget had been drawn up, no allowance had been made for the effects of price changes that might be made during the price review. It was assumed that any changes would be small, so that they would make no difference to the budgeted figure for sales volume in the next year. We were told that when the price review was completed, budgeted sales figures would be changed only for products whose prices had been altered by more than 5 per cent. Wensum rarely acknowledged an overt link between prices and sales, so that it equally saw no need to acknowledge conflicts between profit and market-share objectives. An increase in profit caused by a price rise of 5 per cent does seem to imply no significant drop in sales. However, we remained suspicious when told by Wensum that sales of *all* its products were quite insensitive to price changes—even within this range of 5 per cent.

At the time of our study, profit was a more important objective for Wensum than sales volume or market share. Wensum seemed to us to be very much a 'satisficer' looking at objectives sequentially. Currently, it was the profit objective that was not being met, so that attention was being concentrated on increasing profits, without much attention being given to what might happen to volume or market share. However, it is only fair to say that Wensum had a fairly large number of competitors, each with a fairly small market share, so that it was not concerned about what happened to market shares in the way that Alpha Ltd and Basic Foods were.

One firm where the process of budgeting really did seem to have carefully eliminated any element of conflict between objectives was Wessex Timber Industries. At their quarterly price-setting meetings, those who set prices in Wessex agreed the results for the previous quarter and compared them with the budget for that quarter. The budgeted output for the next quarter was set in the light of this analysis. The budgeted output, together with the level of costs anticipated in the next quarter, was used to determine the likely—and the budgeted—level of unit costs in that quarter. To obtain its list price, Wessex added to these costs an allowance which would ensure that the firm earned the desired return on capital of 12½ per cent. Everything was consistent with everything else. No conflict was apparent between objectives. Any conflict between objectives and achievement that occurred during those three months could be analysed at the next quarterly pricing meeting and could be taken into account in building the next budget. However, the basic objective was to sell all the output which could be produced, with a labour force that was always smaller than Wessex would have liked, at the best level of prices that could be obtained. Given this shortage of labour, conflicts between objectives did not really exist.

Fourways Manufacturing also had a clearly-expressed set of objectives that would be fully met if the firm achieved its budgeted level of sales at the list prices of its products. As the following figures indicate, with the product we studied, something was radically wrong with the budget.

SALES OF PRODUCT

BUDGET		ACTUAL	
Year 1	*Year 2*	*Year 1*	*Year 2*
96	142	11	38

Fourways' sales forecasting for this product was obviously not good; this could scarcely have been disputed. But, in the short run, Fourways did not go on to alter the price of the product, or the budget, to remove the difference between the actual and budgeted levels of sales. Sales may well have been as low as this because the new model was paying for the deficiencies of its predecessors. An earlier product produced by Fourways Manufacturing had been very unreliable, and had earned the company a bad name. The new product was technically more satisfactory, but there were problems of reliability and performance. Even so, it seems more likely that the new product, which used a revolutionary technique, suffered because buyers thought that its price was very high rather than because of these previous failures. However, the budget remained unrealistic. Conflict here was clearly not within the objectives set, but between these objectives and reality.

6.4 PROBLEMS OF RECONCILING CONFLICTS BETWEEN OBJECTIVES

Two major aspects of conflicts between objectives remain to be discussed. First, we need to see how successfully detailed figures worked out during budgeting removed conflicts between broad objectives. This seemed to be done most successfully in firms like Alpha Ltd, Basic Foods, Wessex Timber and the Surgical Instrument Company. The vagueness of what were effectively non-operational objectives for the whole firm enabled everyone within the firm to accept them with little hesitation. The process of budgeting forced choices, especially between market share and profitability. So far as we can tell, the firm was setting aspiration levels rather than trying to maximize. So long as all the aspiration levels continued to be met, there was no difficulty. If one aspiration level failed to be met, a great deal of effort was devoted to ensuring that this particular objective was reached again. We have seen that price cutting by its rival forced Basic Foods to cut its own prices in order to maintain its market share, and that this was done even though it was by no means certain that profit would continue to be satisfactory at the lower price. We think that, faced with a similar choice, Alpha Ltd would have set out to hold or maintain its market share as the best guarantee of long-run profit, even though this might have reduced short-run profit below the aspiration level. Market share was, or seemed to be, the main objective.

Our studies show that, if it is in a really difficult position, a firm is likely to concentrate on meeting the threatened aspiration level, almost irrespective of the effects on the others. In less-difficult situations it seems that, at the very least, the figures in budgets are made consistent. The number of objectives seriously pursued by our firms was limited, certainly in any given period of time. The pursuit of only one objective was often felt to be enough of a problem for the firm to face at any given moment; difficulties arose when two were being simultaneously pursued. On at least some occasions, when these difficulties became too great, one objective was abandoned in favour of the other(s).

While the firm's budgetary procedures turn disputes over broad objectives into more limited arguments over the objectives of particular departments or products, the problem of setting detailed objectives through budgets is nevertheless a very complicated one. Indeed, once it resolves itself into a matter of which figures are to go into detailed budgets, conflict over objectives raises the second issue that we must discuss. This is that individual departments have their own objectives and will press to be allowed to pursue them. While this brings the possibility of sub-optimization, it may also make things easier rather than more difficult. Instead of strategic debates at Board level about, say, precisely how much profit is to be sacrificed for precisely how much extra sales volume or market share, one has disagreements between departmental managers over what is to happen. These are likely to be treated in a more routine way than would be possible at Board level, without the honour of any top manager becoming too much involved.

The result is that the issues that arise when basic objectives are being converted into budgets and targets are very detailed and technical. A lot of the acrimony which accompanies disputes over broad objectives at Board level is lost in a mass of detail. Conflicting interests and pressures seem less important. It also seems that the process of budgeting will often convert maximizing procedures into satisficing ones. Once enshrined in a budget, a profit or market share figure is likely to become a floor one should not fall below rather than a minimum figure which is to be exceeded by as much as possible.

6.5 CONCLUSIONS

It is clear from this chapter that, on objectives, our survey has reached very similar conclusions to those of Simon, Cyert and March. Our firms rarely pursued a single objective. Objectives were almost always multiple. Because of this, there were often conflicts, if not contradictions, between objectives. Where these conflicts and contradictions became too difficult to deal with, our firms took one of two ways out. Either they concentrated on two objectives, or even one, at the expense of the others; or they pushed the resolution of conflict down into the detailed budgeting procedure. This often led in the end to the same result, with firms emphasizing one objective—if only for a time—to the exclusion of others. What is more important, once this kind of conflict was resolved through the budgeting process it became very difficult for us to see exactly how it was being dealt with, even though it also became more of a routine matter. We did not have the time or the resources needed to follow through the whole budgetary procedure in detail.

One should therefore not be surprised in pricing if conflicts between objectives occur, given the complexity of modern business, the number of people taking decisions and the intricacy of information and control systems. Conflicts between objectives are bound to arise. It may be hard to define, let alone reach, just that mixture of values for the firm's objectives which gives the best, the optimum, result for the whole organization. Firms must also accept that many decisions will be taken which are best from the point of view only of a particular part of the firm; they must accept that a good deal of sub-optimization is inevitable. Yet, while carrying out our research, we found that businessmen were often trying to conceal conflicts between different objectives, as though feeling that they should be ashamed of them.

A number of recommendations flow from our findings. First, since firms may well be forced to sub-optimize, pricing decisions may have to be taken with a limited number of objectives in view. Pricing decisions may well mean sub-optimization. Not all the firm's objectives will be seen as relevant to a particular pricing decision. This is partly because to look at all of them would make the decision too complicated; it is partly because pricing decisions are often not being taken at the top of the firm. It is therefore important for those who take pricing decisions to be quite clear which objectives the firm sees as relevant to each pricing decision and how these objectives are to be related, or ranked. Perhaps its easier with pricing decisions than with any other decisions for the firm to take optimal decisions. The effects of optimization are borne by those outside rather than inside the firm.

Second, pricing objectives should be clearly stated. Where it is sensible to do so, they should be stated in numerical or other precise terms. This makes both the pricing decisions, and the later control of operations and analysis of results, much easier. However, it is important not to over-emphasize numerical objectives. Firms must not concentrate too much on numbers. It is easy to do this. Numbers are the things one knows; qualitative, but nevertheless important elements in the problem, are therefore often given too little weight.

Third, contradictions between objectives which cannot be eliminated should be recognized and accepted. Some conflict between objecttives is inevitable. There is no need for businessmen to be ashamed of these conflicts. They should bring them out into the open, acknowledge them and look carefully at their implications.

Fourth, it is not enough for top management alone to understand what the firm's objectives are and what is the relative importance of each of them. Continuing efforts should be made to ensure that all those at lower levels in the firm are fully informed about those objectives of the firm which are relevant to them in their own decisions.

To sum up—it is usually impossible or impracticable for the firm to devise a comprehensive set of objectives that is completely consistent. In pricing, the important thing is for those taking pricing decisions to isolate the objectives that are relevant to each individual decision. At the very least, they must understand how objectives are to be ranked in taking each decision and then give priority to the most important. At best, they should decide on a mutually-consistent set of objectives for each decision.

CHAPTER 7

External Information for Pricing Decisions

7.1 THE INFORMATION NEEDED

In this chapter, we explain what information about conditions in their external environment was available to price setters in the firms we studied. We begin, however, by looking briefly at the external information which should be available if price setters are to determine optimal prices for the products they sell. We are here describing an extreme and unusual situation, where a vast amount of information is available. It is not even clear that it would be an ideal situation, since price setters would inevitably face serious problems in making good use of what would in most cases be an enormous amount of information. It might prove difficult to reach any decision at all; there would be too many possible choices and too much information about them.

This statement implies that one can have too much information for effective decision taking as well as too little. This will often be the case when a number of interrelated variables have to be taken into account in making a particular decision. Even if the precise nature of the relationships between the variables in question is known, the human brain is incapable of handling more than one or two quite simple relationships of the kind met with in most pricing problems. With computers, things are different. They can handle large amounts of complex information with ease. Where computers are used, information must simply meet three requirements. It must be necessary to the solution of the problem; it must not duplicate or contradict other information; and the relationships between relevant variables must be known.

What we are saying is that the ideal amount of information is only as much as the decision taker needs in order to take good decisions. To provide more would be unnecessary. But this is merely a special case of a much more important proposition. It is never worth spending more on collecting information for solving business problems than the information will be worth when it has been collected.

So far, we have been implying that information is freely available. In the real world, the problem of how much information it is economic to collect is the important one. To say this is simply to emphasize that the collection of information is itself an economic activity.

The statement that one should never spend more in collecting information than the information is worth, does, of course, oversimplify what is often known as the problem of optimal search—of how much time and money it is worth spending on obtaining extra information to solve a particular problem. It is very hard indeed to know in advance what the value of any information will be and, therefore, how much can profitably be spent on collecting it. Nevertheless, this is the problem which efficient information collection requires businesses to solve. One wonders how many of them solve it.

Three things emerge from this discussion which need emphasizing. First, it is by no means certain that the correct solution of a pricing problem will require anyone to use all the information which appears to be relevant to its solution. In Chapter 11, we shall suggest that sensitivity analysis can help to show which information is more and which less essential to any decision. Second, even if a given piece of information is relevant to a particular problem, it may be too expensive to collect. The third point is a corollary of the two previous ones. Assuming that an item of information is both necessary and available, firms should ensure that it is used in decision making. Problems of communication sometimes prevent the most efficient use by decision makers of relevant information that is available elsewhere in the firm.

At the beginning of this Chapter, we consider the kinds of information about the external environment that are likely to be relevant to pricing decisions, while emphasizing that not every type of information mentioned will be relevant to any particular pricing decision. We are concerned with the whole range of potentially-relevant pricing information.

7.2 MARKETS

This chapter looks at information about conditions outside the firm—about the environment in which the firm operates. It is the job of market research to provide some or all of this information. Looked at from within a business, such information has three parts. First, there is the market (demand); second, the firm's own industry or other industries whose products do, or may, compete with it (supply); third, there is the Government. The Government may be a purchaser (part of the market) or it may be important because, through tax or other measures, it influences the whole or part of the firm's market. Our main topic here is the market for the firm's products, taking into account competitors and Government activities. The market for any product, like motor-cars or clothing, is large and varied. To analyse it for pricing purposes, it is usually necessary to divide it into a number of smaller segments. Although the precise division made will depend on the particular firm and product, most firms will find it necessary to identify the total market available to them and their competitors for each of their products.

The total market for one firm may be smaller than the complete market for all similar types of product or service with the same general name. For example, an individual firm in the car industry is unlikely to sell every possible type of car. The total market which is relevant, even when an automobile firm is pricing its whole range of cars, will therefore be limited. At any moment, it will mean the market for cars of the kinds which compete significantly with the products of the given firm, in those countries where it sells.

Turning to the case studies, we find that although Universal Corporation was the only supplier of its particular product, and therefore a 'monopolist' for that product, the market to be considered for pricing purposes was much broader than this single product. Universal Corporation had to take into account the prices and the performance of all the products which could do the same task as its own. On the other hand, 'Alpha' was a product with a clearly defined use, competing against 'Omega', marketed by its rival. Although there may have been some slight competition with other products which could be used instead of either, the market was effectively a duopolistic one.

In pricing, the total market often has to be defined very narrowly, as the market for an individual item or class of goods; or it has to be split into geographical areas, each of which is separated from the rest of the market by tariff barriers, by distance or by some marked regional feature; or there may have to be a division within one of these geographical areas.

There has often been uncertainty among economists over how this concept of the 'market' is related to that of the 'industry', a term which is often used in every-day discussion. An industry is a group of firms using similar production processes and/or similar types of labour to supply similar customers. Clearly, an industry defined in this way will rarely be selling a single product or group of products. Even the steel or the wool-textile industries will be selling a number of distinct, though perhaps related, products coming from a number of firms each of which gives those products somewhat different characteristics. With more complex manufactured goods, the various products of the industry will be even more clearly differentiated, for example, by using different brand names.

It has been argued by Professor Joan Robinson, we think decisively, that the best procedure is to use a double classification. Where one is concerned with issues like pricing, competition, monopoly, etc. one must consider them in terms of markets. The concept of an industry can then be reserved for discussion of 'questions concerning labour, profits, technical progress, localisation and so forth'.[1] Because we accept Professor Robinson's argument, we shall confine our attention in this chapter to the concept of the market. However, readers may find it useful to bear our distinction between the market and the industry in mind while reading the remainder of the book.

When a firm delineates its market, it will be concerned not only with the products competing in that market, but also with its geographical area, especially where the firm sells in a number of separate export markets, as well as in the home market. The Surgical Instrument Company, Wensum Engineering, Fourways Engineering and Medlock Engineering are all firms which served several geographically-separate markets.

In trying to decide what is the size of the total market, the firm will often (perhaps always) be well advised to ask the question: The total market for what? For example, Wessex Timber Industries was in a situation where its total market was not as clearly defined as it appeared to be. Wessex was a considerable operator in the timber trade, but the market for timber was both large and fragmented into many different parts. That fragmentation does not directly concern us, except to note that it complicated the task of gathering information about the total market. The basic difficulties faced by Wessex Timber were these. First, how did one define the total market—was it for timber alone, or for timber and timber substitutes? At what

[1] Joan Robinson, 'The Industry and the Market', *Economic Journal*, Vol. LXVI (1956), pp. 360–1.

point should one begin—or cease—to consider timber substitutes? Second, by looking forward in time, what was likely to happen to the demand for timber—and for its substitutes—in the future? How far ahead should Wessex look? What new uses for timber, and what new substitutes for timber, could be foreseen? And could Wessex Timber hope to move easily into the production of these substitutes as they developed? If not, could it find ways of doing so, for example by a merger with a firm producing timber substitutes? Or could timber itself become a substitute for the products in question?

An important concept is therefore that of a 'need market' where one considers all the ways of meeting a given need. One has to go even further. Other products might become substitutes for timber—for example, plastic materials. However, we have seen that timber might itself be able to move into 'need markets' where it has not previously been used, if its products were changed in some ways. This is a classic policy dilemma. Should the firm follow the existing market, and if necessary alter the range of products it is offering to compete with substitutes coming in from other industries? Or should it stick to its existing products, and seek opportunities to move into new 'need markets' previously supplied by others?

These are the factors to be considered in the defining of the firm's total market. They are therefore the factors which the firm should first consider in developing a marketing policy. All firms need to consider this basic problem before setting their market strategies. This is not to say that every single pricing decision must be preceded by a review of the firm's whole marketing strategy. But marketing strategies do not remain correct for ever. The firm must discover quickly if its current strategy has ceased to be appropriate. This will be possible only if it is continually obtaining the necessary information from its review and feed-back processes.

Because it is essential for firms to recognize what markets they are in, we began in constructing the check list by examining the need for information about the total market. Firms must go on to ask what are the various sub-markets which make up this total market for the product which is being priced. As we have seen, the geographical spread of its markets may well be important. In particular, it is important to know how far its markets are international and whether the division between the domestic and overseas parts of them is a relevant one. Are there other significant factors which distinguish particular parts of the total market from each other?

While the current size and structure of the total market is important, whether measured in terms of money, units of output sold or in some other way, its growth prospects are even more important. What is its prospective growth rate? In deciding this, the firm may have to take technological developments into account if these mean new models or new substitute for the products in question, and especially if they will take sales away from the existing product. If the best way of looking at the total market is to see it as split up into various sub-markets, it will also be important to know how the different sectors of the total market will interact as growth and technological change occur. Finally, it will be very important to know which are the main firms producing in this market now and which will be in the future. It is the number of firms selling in it which determine whether the market is an oligopolistic one, as was the case with most of the firms we studied, or whether some other type of competitive situation exists.

Having determined the characteristics, size and rate of growth of the total market, it will then be necessary for the firm to obtain the information it needs if it is to understand the competitive situation in each sub-market for its products. The price in each sub-market must be decided in the light of competitive conditions within that sub-market.

Looking first at products, the firm will want to know which are the firms and products against which it is competing. It can then attempt to judge the relative merits of its own and competitors' products—a judgement which is of great importance when placed alongside the answers to the questions: What do the buyers require of our product? Why do, or should, they buy our product rather than the competing ones? Similarly, of course, it is often a good idea to put the same questions about competitors' products. This sort of competitive product evaluation, which can be taken to considerable lengths, is an important factor in determining what the price of the product should be.

The firm will then wish to move on to more detailed study of trends in the market. Having earlier established the size and growth rate of the total market, the firm will wish to compare these with the volume of its own sales and the rate at which these are growing. At the same time, it will be looking at its competitors' sales and at the rate at which they are growing. This will enable the firm to calculate the market share of all firms in the relevant market and to find out how market shares have been changing over recent months or years. Clearly, market shares will be of differing importance in different situations, but we found in our studies that consumer good firms put special emphasis on them. Alpha and Basic Foods were two firms where market-share information was given very great weight in pricing and marketing decisions generally. As was explained above, all this had to be done in the light of probable technological changes. Among industrial goods firms, Medlock, Clean and Heavy Technology put particular emphasis on maintaining market shares of not less than 15 per cent of their particular markets.

In making its predictions about market growth and market shares, the firm will be interested in how its own financial situation and those of its competitors are likely to develop. It will therefore want to look at the implications of these financial situations for its own and its competitors' marketing and investment plans. The firm will find it useful, in predicting the way market shares will alter, if it knows what kind of financial situation has accompanied the market shares of at least its main competitors. Again, only if it can make reasonable predictions of its own investment plans and those of its competitors, will a firm be able to forecast at all accurately the rate at which the outputs of the firms in a given market will grow in the foreseeable future.

Perhaps most important of all in the marketing field, the firm will need to have some idea of how its competitors will react to changes in its own marketing policy. Our main interest in this book is in pricing. In pricing under oligopoly, the most important thing is to know how competitors will react to a change in the price of one's own product. Since our own study has been mainly concerned with oligopolistic markets, it is hardly surprising that this turned out to be an important issue. It has long been accepted, both in economic theory and by businessmen, that it is in oligopolistic situations that one's own price changes are most likely to lead to immediate and substantial price changes by one's competitors. One need only recall the way in which detergent producers in the UK reacted to each others' price changes during the 1950s to see how true this is. In our studies, Basic Foods was forced to react abruptly, and in a way in which it would not have freely chosen, to a major change in price by one of its rivals. All oligopolistic firms need to be sure how they will react to price changes by competitors, as well as how they think that competitors will react to their own price changes.

It is clearly important, in oligopolistic situations of this kind, to know whether there is a price leader in the market, and if so which firm it is. Among the firms we studied, Dee Plastics had become accustomed to following the lead of its very big competitor. For many years, Basic Foods had itself been the price leader in its market, though this was no longer so when we carried out our study. If there is a price leader in a particular market, it will be necessary to decide whether, in a particular situation, the price leader must be allowed to make the first move in changing price, or whether on this occasion one's own firm can move independently. However, what may appear to be price leadership can sometimes be rather different. A firm may simply be attempting to 'match' competitors' pricing, where there is no price leader at all, and the first firm to alter prices on each occasion is different.

Since we are concerned with pricing, it is obvious that having information about the prices at which one's competitors' products are being sold is very important. One difficulty, which became clear in our study of Wensum Engineering, is that in some industries, while there may be a standard product with a known price, a number of optional extras will also be available which can be bought to add to the capacity or versatility of this product. The problem is that, in these circumstances, it is not always clear exactly what price customers are paying for particular characteristics of the products of competitors. This will be especially true if, as with the products of Wensum and its competitors, allowances and discounts are given to customers. Indeed, the problem may be worse even than this. For example, Wensum Engineering had great difficulty in deciding precisely which characteristics of its own products consumers rated most highly, though it was beginning to try to obtain a greater understanding of this.

A further piece of information whose importance has been emphasized (perhaps over-emphasized) by economists is that of the relationship between the various possible prices at which any good might be sold and the amount that consumers would buy at each of those prices. Economists describe this relationship by a function like:

$$q = f(p).$$

where q denotes the quantity of the product sold at price p. We are here concerned with the total demand for a class of commodity, like butter, tea, wheat, etc. The relationship in the equation can be shown on a diagram by a 'demand curve' (which will be a straight line in some cases), like the one in Figure 7.1.

Here, price is shown on the vertical axis. The quantity of the good which would be bought at each price by all consumers taken together is shown along the horizontal axis. The curve shown takes the shape usually assumed by economists—with less of the good demanded (bought) at a higher price than at a lower one. The main reason for the downward slope is that the curve is drawn on the assumption that the prices of all other goods remain unchanged as the price of this one falls. It can then be assumed that as this product becomes cheaper it will be substituted, to some extent, for all other goods, which are now

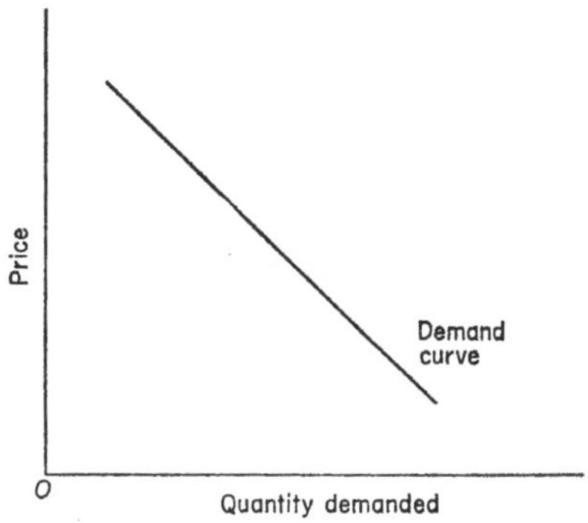

FIGURE 7.1

relatively dearer. The demand curve relates to the broad market for products—aggregating the demand for all firms in the market. However, the curve showing the relationship between price and quantity demanded for a particular firm's version of the general product will be different.

An individual firm (or farm) in these circumstances will be able to sell very large quantities of the product at the ruling price. Indeed, this ruling price will be determined by the general balance between supply and demand in the total market, and will be beyond the influence of the individual firm. The firm will be too small, relatively to the total market and all products will be identical, or nearly so. The curve showing the price-quantity relationship for the product of an *individual* firm will be like that shown in Figure 7.2. It is known as an average revenue curve to distinguish it from the demand curve relating to the total market. Here, the price is determined by the balance between supply and demand in the total market, and it is *OP*. At this price, this individual firm (and indeed any other individual firm) can sell as much as it is able. Even if it sells all that it can produce, its own output is too small relatively to the total supply for its own actions to be able to influence price. This analysis is legitimate provided there are enough competing firms and products in any market for a reduction in the price of the product we are considering have only minor effects on the sales of all other products. With oligopoly, and therefore few firms, this is not a realistic assumption. Indeed, among our firms, even Wessex (with a good deal of competition) seemed to behave as though it was oligopolistic.

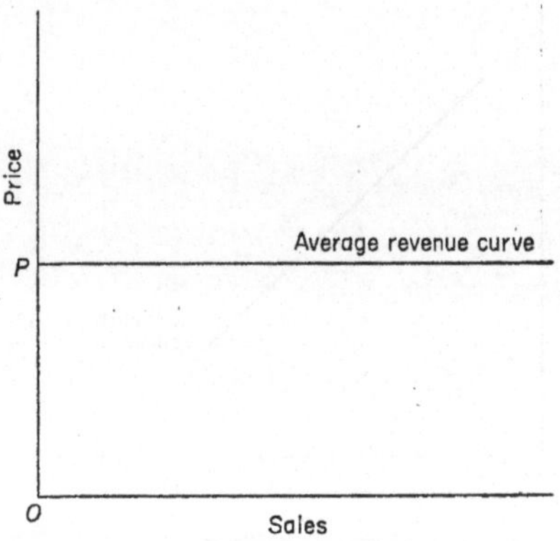

FIGURE 7.2

We can also draw an average revenue curve for a monopolistic product. It will be realized by this that we mean a product for which there is no close substitute. Then, the average revenue curve will be similar to the demand curve shown in Figure 7.1. For the monopolistic product, there are no close substitutes any more than there are close substitutes for a good like tea or wheat, as shown in Figure 7.1.

This discussion raises two problems. First, in those situations—namely, 'competition' and monopoly—where a demand curve or an average revenue curve is a realistic concept, it is extremely difficult to discover its shape and position. This is one of the biggest problems in pricing. Second, in those cases where there is oligopoly—the majority of cases in our study—it may not be possible to use an average revenue curve at all.

While the problem is difficult, we can say this. First, it is almost always possible to derive a total demand curve of some sort for *all* the products together of *all* the oligopolists operating in the given market. Second, it is frequently *not* possible to draw an average revenue curve for the individual oligopolist. This will be so, especially, where a cut in the price of one oligopolist leads to such a big fall in the sales of the other oligopolists that they have to reduce their own prices in retaliation. This will alter the shape and position of the whole average revenue curve for the individual price cutter. Something more complicated than a simple curve is then needed.

However, we can go further. First, where the price change is comparatively small, it may not have a significant effect on competitors' sales. Second, the oligopolists may differentiate their products successfully, by, for example, branding or small changes in specification or presentation. Then, even a comparatively large price cut may not lead to price cuts by competitors. The British car industry is perhaps a good example of this. In these circumstances, demand curves can be, and indeed have been, constructed for the products of oligopolists, though their use appears to be unusual.

We shall have to look later at the role of mathematical models in analysing pricing problems in oligopoly. However, it is perhaps worth mentioning one ingenious attempt to continue to use something like a traditional demand curve. This is the 'kinked' average revenue curve, one example of which is shown in Figure 7.3.

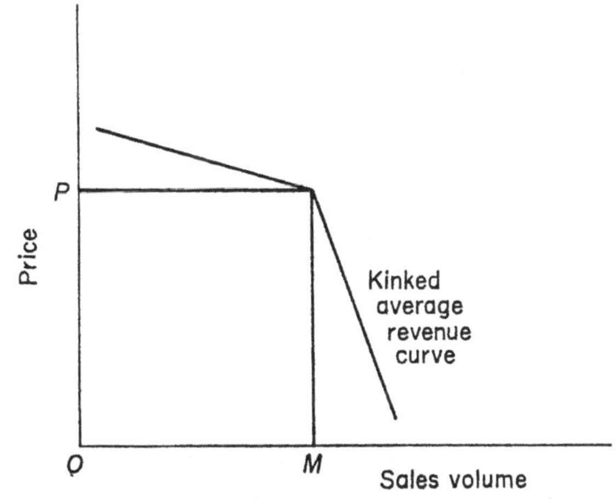

FIGURE 7.3

Here, it is assumed that all the oligopolists begin by charging the price *OP*. At this price, our firm, shown in Figure 7.3, is selling *OM*. We now suppose that the firm is considering whether to alter its price. If it raises its price, the assumption on which Figure 7.3 is drawn is that all the other firms will leave their prices at *OP*. Our firm, therefore, will suffer a sharp fall in the sales if it raises its prices; the upper part of the average revenue curve is quite flat. On the other hand, if our firm cuts its price, then it is assumed that all the other oligopolists will match the price cut exactly. They will then, again, all be charging the same price, but now a price lower than *OP*. Because it is assumed that price cuts will be met, the kinked average revenue curve for our firm will slope steeply downwards below a price of *OP*. It should be obvious that the reason why an average revenue curve can be used, even though there is oligopoly, is that the assumptions are restrictive. Either all firms are charging the same price (of *OP* or less); or all firms except our firm, depicted in Figure 7.3, are charging the same price. These are simple enough conditions for a demand curve to be drawn, in principle if not in practice.

It should also be clear that the curve in Figure 7.3 is most appropriate where the demand for all products is depressed. It is in such circumstances that one's competitors are most likely to match price cuts and to refuse to follow price increases. These were the trading conditions most frequently met with in the 1930s, when the 'kinked' average revenue curve was first used.

The implication of this curve was that prices would tend to be stable or 'sticky'. Once established at the 'kink' (*OP* in Figure 7.3) they would tend to stay there. If one firm increased its prices, the others would refuse to follow because the market was depressed; once the first firm reduced them, the others would all follow. In both cases, profits would most likely be reduced, so that the price change would not pay. Economists have argued a good deal over how far prices really are 'sticky' in depressed markets. There is still disagreement on this, and our study does not throw any more light on this particular issue.

While it is possible to use a kinked average revenue curve in other situations than that of a depressed market, it is clear that it can deal only with very simple situations. Only some kind of mathematical model can handle the complex relationships that usually exist in oligopoly pricing. What is more, such a model would have to allow for the view which any given firm took of the way in which its competitors would react to changes in its own pricing or marketing policy.

Where a demand (or average revenue) curve can be drawn, economists find it useful to be able to measure the responsiveness of demand on that curve to changes in price. The measure most often used is that of 'elasticity of demand'. This is given by the formula:

$$\text{Elasticity of demand} = \frac{\text{percentage change in amount demanded}}{\text{percentage change in price}}.$$

This formula gives what is known as 'point' elasticity of demand—elasticity of demand at a point on the demand curve. Strictly, it should be used to calculate elasticity of demand for infinitesimal changes in price only. Measures are available for calculating 'arc' elasticity of demand over a large price range. Readers who wish to know more about elasticity should consult a text book of economics.[1]

Our industrial goods firms were less interested in elasticity of demand than the consumer good firms were.

Having done what it can to establish the nature of the relationship between price and quantity demanded for the product it is pricing, the firm should go on to look in more detail at pricing practices and structures in its particular market. For example, it needs to be certain about any discounts and rebates which are given in the particular market, as well as about associated charges like those for packing, delivery, etc. As we shall see in our study of Clean Engineering, discounts can be the means by which price competition takes place. Similarly, more favourable credit arrangements can be used as the equivalent of price cuts. So can aggregated rebates, related to quantities bought over a period. The firm needs to know about these and all the other elements, like advertising and sales promotion practices and expenditures, which make up the detailed structure of the market.

Finally, there is Government policy. One needs to know what influence the government has on the market, whether by its actions as a customer or through its general economic policy. The whole range of fiscal and monetary policy has to be considered here. Tax cuts and easy money will increase the demand for most products; tax increases and tight money have the opposite effect. In recent years, anti-monopoly legislation and institutions like the Prices and Incomes

[1] See, for example, D. C. Hague, *Managerial Economics*, London, Longmans (1969), pp. 52–9.

Board have been of growing importance in the UK. The former has made collusion in price-fixing illegal for many products. The latter has brought another variable—the need to convince expert economists and others that there is a case for increasing prices—into the firm's calculations. Firms which specialize in products which are required by the Government tend to suffer from the antique notions which the Civil Service has about the way price and cost should be related. Perhaps they put up with these notions too readily, because of the importance of the Government as a customer.

In looking at the influence of Government policy, the important thing is to understand which activities of the Government are relevant to the firm and how they will affect the firm's market. If possible, however, one should go beyond understanding the nature of changes in economic policy or government purchasing that will be of importance to the firm and attempt to forecast their effects on its markets.

Having looked at the kinds of information relevant to pricing decisions, we now go on to see what information our firms actually had.

7.3 FIRMS WITH ADEQUATE MARKET INFORMATION

Eight firms, Alpha Ltd, Basic Foods, The Surgical Instrument Company, Heavy Technology, Epsilon, Wessex Timber, Clean Engineering, and Universal Corporation had what they considered to be reasonable information about their current markets. We look at them in turn.

7.3.1 Heavy Technology Ltd

Heavy Technology relied very much on its salesmen for obtaining up-to-date information about the kind of equipment its customers required, and about any special preferences of individual customers which might affect the company's chances of being successful in obtaining business for which it tendered. Salesmen were able to obtain such information because of their personal contacts with the staff of customer firms. Indeed, they were expected to provide the Head Office with regular reports on business in their areas. Heavy Technology felt that its salesmen were a very useful source of information about customer demand and, on occasion, about the activities of competitors. For example, a customer would often tell one of Heavy

Technology's salesmen how the price it had quoted compared with that of a competitor. This happened particularly when Heavy Technology had recently failed to obtain a contract because it had quoted a price that was rather too high. The salesmen of Heavy Technology visited all customers' offices regularly and so were able to pass this kind of information on to the sales manager during regular meetings they each had with him. These meetings with an individual salesman were held more frequently when a contract was being quoted for in his sales area. He was then expected to provide as much information as he could about the intentions of the customer.

At the same time, Heavy Technology did have a market research department. This department provided the managers responsible for pricing with information about the activities both of customers and of competitors. Customers' ordering methods and trading strategies were carefully studied by the section. Particular emphasis was put on acquiring information about the state of the order books of the company's chief competitors. This was felt to be useful in Heavy Technology's depressed market. If it were known that a rival company already had enough business to keep it working at or near capacity, then Heavy Technology knew that it was less likely to make a real effort to obtain more business. Hence, Heavy Technology could afford to quote fairly high prices when tendering. This information allowed some degree of market forecasting, but was more concerned with what had happened in the past. Information on the future was obtained from market research plus what salesmen reported. However, one here has the paradox that when business was extremely difficult to obtain, this aspect of market research increased in importance; at the same time, one knew that it was likely to be harder than in more prosperous times to know just how much spare capacity competitors had.

7.3.2 Wessex Timber Industries Ltd

Wessex Timber Industries was in a very different position. The firms in its industry were selling products that were much more homogenous than in Heavy Technology. The timber industry had a number of trade associations which provided a good deal of information about various aspects of the business. Some of these associations were sponsored by the Government, but others were operated by the industry. Between them, they gave information about the amounts of various kinds of timber that were being imported, about domestic output of various timber products, and about the consumption of the industry's products by the trades which used them. It was also possible to obtain more detailed market (not competitor) information from these associations, if an individual firm wished to ask for it.

While this kind of information was clearly valuable for long-term planning, and indeed for various kinds of decision-taking within the company, information of more direct use in pricing was often difficult to obtain. Wessex could discover what prices were being charged by its competitors for any type of product only by its own efforts. Prices for some standard timber products were quoted in various trade journals. However, they gave only a range of prices at which these products were being sold after basic processing. If it wished to obtain more detailed information about prices, Wessex had to rely heavily on its salesmen. They were able to discover what prices competitors had been quoting to customers; they could often acquire information about prices in the course of casual conversations with other people in the timber trade. Because it was selling a homogenous product, Wessex Timber Industries felt that the market information it had was adequate.

7.3.3 Clean Engineering Ltd

Clean Engineering was in a slightly different position, but again felt that it had a great deal of market information. Nearly all of its customers were public authorities, who provided large amounts of data about their activities and plans in their annual reports, in answers to questions in the House of Commons or in evidence to the Select Committee on Nationalized Industries. Such information assisted Clean Engineering in the long-term planning of sales and production. However, while this information was available about the long-term plans which local authorities had for buying water purification equipment, it was often difficult to discover at what precise date work on a particular scheme would start. Much of the more detailed information needed in order to discover the dates at which tenders for equipment would be issued by given local authorities therefore had to be obtained by the firm's sales representatives. They were expected to report anything of interest to the Head Office after they had visited local authorities in their area. As has been implied, the vital pieces of information were usually the delivery date which the authority would be expecting manufacturers to meet and the dates on which tenders for large items of equipment would have to be put in. These were the facts that Clean Engineering really needed to know. Clean Engineering had a good deal of reliable information about its current market position and also a market which was very sensitive to change in the level of economic activity as a whole, which could also be predicted. It would make good market forecasts and these were regularly reviewed, every three months.

7.3.4 Universal Corporation

In Universal Corporation the main problem was to obtain information about the demand for its products far enough ahead. Because plant took a long time to build, demand forecasts were required for up to ten years ahead. This provided the basis for decisions about how much plant should be built, how much money would have to be borrowed and what interest and dividend payments this implied. Apart from these long-term projections, forecasts of demand for the product in the next year were made annually by Universal Corporation, as well as by its parent firm and its distributors. The forecasts were then discussed by all three parties, and an agreed output forecast for the next year arrived at and issued by the parent firm. After further discussion with the distributors, the parent firm broke down this total demand forecast into expected demands from each of the various distributors. It then gave these forecasts to Universal Corporation's commercial department. This detailed breakdown of forecast market demand was passed to Universal's production department, which used it as the main determinant of the production budget. The detailed forecasts were also used by the commercial department in its computer simulation model, which used information about the sales and costs of each distributor.

The computer model of Universal's production and distribution system enabled the commercial department to forecast what production would be required for individual plants during the next year. The model also allowed the commercial department to calculate optimum production schedules and production costs for these plants, given the forecast demand. The figures produced by the model tended to be idealized. For, although the solution which the computer simulation model provided was optimal, given the constraints which were built into it, it was possible to introduce only a limited number of constraints. In the real world, there were far more. Nevertheless, Universal Corporation claimed that the forecasts which its model had produced had turned out to be much more consistent than any obtained by other means. The model was also the only device which Universal Corporation had that would quickly show the effect on production costs of changes in the size and composition of demand.

7.3.5 The Surgical Instrument Company Ltd

The Surgical Instrument Company had its own market research section, comprising ten people at the time of our study. The section was responsible for preparing market statistics—like estimates of the market for any product—and forecasts and surveys on any country or product in which the company was interested. As far as we know there was no form of exchange of information between various countries in the surgical instrument market in the UK or with other countries. There were several organizations where manfacturers, and sometimes people from hospitals met, but we do not know what was done at those meetings. At the time of our study, there was no information on the change in size of the market for the scalpel produced by the Surgical Instrument Company since its introduction. However, we think that this market research department was a good one.

7.3.6 Alpha Ltd

So far, we have considered only the market information which was available to producers of industrial goods. Three out of the four consumer goods manufacturers were among the eight firms which had reasonable statistical information on market size. All these had taken a good deal of trouble to set up their own facilities for providing this information every month or quarter, or to buy it where they did not find that possible. Alpha Ltd, for example, provided detailed and fairly accurate information about various aspects of the external environment for both product and product group managers. They received the information quarterly. It covered such things as the total size of the market; 'Alpha's' market share; the market shares of competitors; the number of shops selling 'Alpha' and/or competitors' products; and the amount of competitive activity in the form of, for example, test marketing and price cutting. Every two years, surveys were made by Alpha Ltd. to discover, for example: the social and other characteristics of the members of the public who bought 'Alpha'; general trends in the national consumption of products of the same type as 'Alpha'; and the reasons why consumers did or did not buy 'Alpha' or the competing products.

7.3.7 Basic Foods Ltd

Basic Foods was well supplied with market information. The firm had data about the size of the market in earlier years and therefore about its recent rate of growth. This was provided monthly through an industry information agreement operated by the trade association. The agreement gave information only about the total size of the market, but Basic Foods could easily calculate its own market share during any month by comparing its own sales figures with these reported figures for total sales. Similar calculations, using estimated sales figures for competitors, gave estimates of their market shares. Forecasts of future total market size, rate of growth and the market share were also calculated, both for Basic Foods and for its competitors, by the marketing economics staff.

7.3.8 Epsilon Ltd

In Epsilon Ltd, both quantitative and qualitative information about the market and about competitors was available from a number of sources, especially from market research studies both by specialist market research agencies and by the staff of Epsilon Ltd itself. Epsilon Ltd also carried out test marketing. Each such exercise involved a full-scale marketing effort by the product group's sales and technical staffs for the product tested. But it was an effort limited both geographically and in time.

The quantitative market data collected by Epsilon Ltd was for market size and growth; for the sales volume, sales value and market shares of individual brands (both those of Epsilon Ltd and of its competitors); and for the scale of test marketing and promotional campaigns by the various producers of products like 'Epsilon' during the preceding period. These figures were not thought to be particularly accurate, although Epsilon Ltd had accurate information about its own activities from its sales department. Estimates of future market size, market shares, etc. were provided by Epsilon Ltd's market research and marketing staff for all its products. In the market for 'Epsilon' itself, it was thought that an indication of likely future trends could be obtained by studying experience in the USA and in other overseas markets.

One general point needs to be made. We have already mentioned that both Wessex Timber Industries and Basic Foods received substantial amounts of information regularly from their trade associations, although in the case of Basic Foods this was only for the size of its total market. Four of the thirteen firms we studied were producing highly technical industrial products and in their markets some statistical information could be obtained from Government departments. However, we found that there was a good deal of reluctance to approach Government departments in order to obtain extra information where published Government statistics were not adequate. For example, firms would sometimes have liked to have information which was published by Government departments classified in different ways, or analysed in more detail. These firms were reluctant to believe that Government departments would, as they sometimes will, provide more information than is published, or analyse published information in different ways.

We have now seen, in some detail, how the eight firms with reasonably adequate market data collected it. We go on to look at firms with less-adequate market information.

7.4 FIRMS WITH LESS-ADEQUATE MARKET INFORMATION

The information that the remaining five firms, Dee, Medlock, Wensum and Fourways, had about current or past market size was less adequate.

7.4.1 Dee Plastics Ltd

Dee Plastics Ltd was operating in a market where the overall rate of growth had been 7½ per cent per annum over the previous few years. There were a number of sub-sections in this market, and each had its own rate of growth. For some, growth was greater than 15 per cent per annum. One problem was how to forecast the future growth rates for these markets. Forecasts had been made, but there was little consensus about the likely rate of growth for individual sub-sectors. So, for one section, estimates for rates of growth varied from a 40 per cent growth in the next twelve months to a 70 per cent one. Part of the reason for this, as will be seen later, was that Dee Plastics had no market research department. The task of discovering what the rate of growth was likely to be was undertaken by the commercial manager. Because it was not his full-time job, the latter could not afford the time needed for analytical work, other than to discover the views of colleagues and customers.

However, there did appear to be agreement that over the next ten years there would be an annual increase in sales, in value terms, for the total market for plastic slats, of at least 5½ per cent per annum. There was a feeling in Dee Plastics that there was a large potential export market, particular in Europe. At the time when we made our study, Dee's big competitor, which had subsidiaries in Europe, dominated export sales of plastic slats. As far as we could discover, information on the potential size of the European market was limited to forecasts of one or two potential customers' demands. There did not seem to be any detailed predictions of growth in the European market as a whole. So, while Dee Plastics did have a certain amount of market information, it was by no means one of the best-placed of our firms in this respect.

7.4.2 Gamma Products Ltd

We have seen that Gamma Ltd was selling a battery for electric razors. It had launched this some two or three years earlier, and had hoped to obtain about half the battery market. Although this market was small, it was thought to be valuable (with an estimated total turnover of about £1m). In the event, Gamma's battery turnover had risen to only £200,000. There were two reasons for this. First, the battery market had turned out to be smaller than had been anticipated. Second, firms making rechargeable batteries had captured a larger proportion of the smaller market than had been expected.

Besides over-estimating the existing size of the total market for batteries, Gamma had launched its battery at a time when it was predicting rapid growth in the demand for battery-operated razors. This rapid growth did not occur and the rate of growth in the demand for razor batteries reflected this. At the time of our study, Gamma's sales of razor batteries were growing at only 2 per cent per annum. Nevertheless, the product manager responsible for battery sales pointed out that if American trends were followed in the UK, the percentage of men owning battery operated razors in ten years' time could be as high as 40 per cent compared with the current percentage of 3 per cent. This prediction was based on several assumptions, the most important of which was that the price of battery razors would fall relatively to the prices of other consumer goods and increase their relative attractiveness to the customer.

7.4.3 Medlock Engineering Ltd

Medlock Engineering was in some difficulty over obtaining adequate market information when we studied it. It will be remembered that we were studying the pricing activities of Medlock Engineering in overseas countries. The chief source of market information was overseas agents, who usually lived in the country in which they represented Medlock Engineering. The agents were usually shared with other UK companies operating in their country—either firms in quite different industries, or associates or subsidiaries of Medlock Engineering. It was often found difficult to persuade these agents to collect the right sort of market information, not least because they had little training in market research techniques. However, once these difficulties could be overcome, by training and other means, Medlock Engineering felt that its agents were able to provide invaluable information about prospects in individual countries.

As one way of overcoming its difficulties, Medlock Engineering had instituted studies of market conditions in a few countries which seemed to offer particularly attractive export opportunities. These studies were carried out by the market research department under the supervision of the sales manager. Using all the sources of information open to it, the market research department was able to provide a complete picture of the market which that country would provide for Medlock's product. The study provided an assessment of the extent to which local manufacturers in the country studied were developing their own capacity for making products like Medlock's. It considered the probable pattern of demand for the product, and forecast the rate of growth of the market. There was an assessment of the underlying economic situation; an assessment of the political situation, where this seemed likely to affect exports to the country in question; and information about the country's preferences about which firms it should give business to. Medlock could then avoid expending too much effort in countries which would not buy British goods.

Finally, there was an assessment of the price at which Medlock Engineering could hope to sell its product in the country in question. A good deal of information on prices could usually be obtained by looking at the actual prices obtained for previous work, but if no contracts had previously been obtained and it was impossible to discover the prices obtained by competitors, Medlock Engineering had to make its own assessment of the situation. This problem arose acutely in the products we studied in Medlock, because they were all sold in the export market. If they were larger than in the past, or if they were of a new kind, there was little information about past experience. Once it had an idea of the price levels at which business could be obtained, Medlock Engineering could calculate whether or not it would be commercially profitable to increase its selling effort in the particular country.

Although we have classified Medlock Engineering as a firm with inadequate market information, it can be seen that a good deal of effort was being given, at the time of our study, to improving the supply of information about the external situation. Medlock could now almost certainly be classified as a firm with good market information.

7.4.4 Wensum Engineering Ltd and Fourways Engineering Ltd

Wensum had difficulty in obtaining enough market information both for home and export markets. This was true for Wensum's output as a whole, but Wensum had found it very hard to split its total market into separate markets for individual products or product groups. A major difficulty in studying the UK market was the way in which Government statistics were published. Wensum's products were almost always aggregated with other, different products. Like other firms, Wensum was reluctant to try to get the Government department in question to give it more detailed figures. Fourways was in a very similar position to Wensum. Its product was much the same, and it found market information equally difficult to obtain.

One thing that worried a number of the firms we studied, was the difficulty they found in discovering how their markets were divided between different types of customer and between different geographical areas. This complaint was made particularly strongly by Wensum and Fourways. In the light of this, we were struck by the fact that some of the firms we studied, including Wensum and Fourways, did not get as much information as they could have done from their own sales records. These records were usually detailed enough to provide a good deal of information about the characteristics of customers and about the geographical distribution of sales. We were rather surprised that these firms, which complained so much about the lack of market information, did not make full use of the information they already had.

7.5 MARKET INFORMATION IN OUR FIRMS: A SUMMING UP

To sum up, eight of our thirteen firms had adequate market information. Those which had not found deficiencies in statistics, or difficulties in obtaining information from salesmen. However, some of these firms could have made better use of statistics which they did have. Since decisions always have to be taken for the future, it is clearly important to try to go beyond information about the existing market to forecast what will happen in future. Three of the firms we studied, Universal, Gamma and Medlock had made explicit and detailed forecasts for the future, though Gamma's forecasts turned out to be less accurate than those of any other firm. Other firms made fairly simple forecasts, and only Wensum and Fourways did not normally make forecasts at all, except for the figures that went into the budget for the next year.

One important qualification needs to be added about all of this, and it is not easy to know how to make it. All the managers we studied were making continual mental, and even written, notes about the marketing activities of their own firms or their competitors. It is far from easy to allow for this in research findings, since to do so adequately one would need to get inside the minds of those concerned. However, we feel we should call attention to this important fact.

7.6 MARKET RESEARCH DEPARTMENTS

Apart from Wensum Ltd and Universal Corporation, all the firms we studied had their own market research departments. However, three of these were virtually out of action at the time of our study. No one in Dee Plastics had been employed full time on market research for about two years. The only market research officer had left and had not been replaced. Instead, the commercial manager had carried out what market research there was. With his other work taking most of his time, the commercial manager was simply unable to spend enough on the analytical aspects of market research. He admitted to us that most of the time he did give to market research was concentrated on those aspects which interested him, rather than on taking the more detached view of the market researcher. Consequently, he had relied very heavily on his contacts with men from other firms in the trade in obtaining the information he needed about the market. The danger of doing this was obviously that collecting information in this way gave him a considerable range of figures for forecasts of future growth rates in the market. Yet, because he had not made the forecasts himself, he could not be sure of the assumptions underlying any of the forecasts or of the precise forecasting methods used.

While we were making our study, the firm appointed a new market research officer. Although he was appointed to provide Dee Plastics with market information about a number of other products, he quickly provided the firm with significantly more information about the market for plastic slats than it had previously had. It is interesting that the market research officer got a good deal of information about the market from the Board of Trade, and that he also acquired some market information because of his good contacts with one of Dee's competitors. Some of those who provided him with this information from the competing firm were quite senior employees.

Wensum and Fourways both had similar problems. Neither company had a full-time market research department. The job of market research had therefore come to be shared by a few individuals, none of whom had specific responsibilities for market research assigned to him. As a result, market information was not always available to those who needed it for pricing. There was also a certain amount of rivalry between at least two of those in Wensum who were responsible for collecting market information, and this had led to difficulties.

In Alpha Ltd and Epsilon Ltd, outside specialists were employed to collect market information to supplement that provided by their own market research departments. We have seen that Heavy Technology and Medlock Engineering obtained market information from contacts that its salesmen had with customers as well as from trade associations. It also had a small market research department of its own.

We think it would be an interesting hypothesis, though our information does not allow us to test it on an adequate scale, to suggest that firms with good market research departments are also those which make most use of market research specialists from outside. We also suspect that the reverse is true; that firms without their own market research department are also reluctant to use outside market research. Certainly, several of the firms we studied complained that they found it too expensive to employ outside consultants at all, though they tended to be small firms making industrial goods.

Only one of the firms we studied gave us detailed information to substantiate this claim. This was Wensum Engineering, where we were able to look a little more deeply into the question. The commercial manager, who had recently been appointed, was surprised that the company's market research effort over the preceding five years had been so unsuccessful in providing the facts about its markets. His view was that the cost of providing what, in his previous job, he had regarded as a normal amount of information about the market for any product was surprisingly high. He saw this as one of the costs of product variety, and it is certainly true that Wensum Engineering sold a very wide range of products. As we were ending our study of the firm, the commercial manager was beginning to try to increase the amount of market information he had, but there had so far been no reduction in the large range of products sold.

7.7 MARKET SHARES

Having described what information our firms had, and the arrangements they made to collect it, we now look in detail at a number of aspects of market information, beginning with market shares. Using the information described above, all the firms did what they could to calculate their own shares of their various markets for given time periods. They compared the outputs of their own products with total sales in the market. In Basic Foods, where detailed information about market size was provided each month through the industry information agreement, we have seen that the company could calculate its market share easily and accurately. The market share of each of the firm's competitors was estimated by the company's marketing economics staff, who compared their own estimates of competitors' sales with the size of the total market. Basic Foods believed that its estimates of market shares were very accurate. Alpha Ltd and Epsilon Ltd also believed that they made accurate calculations of market shares, making use of their own information and of some obtained from outside market research firms. Gamma's figures for market share were less good, because information about the market itself was so bad.

Obviously, it is only where one of a particular firm's pricing objectives relates to market share that this figure is of direct relevance in pricing. Eight of our thirteen firms did have market share objectives, so that this was an important figure for them to know. However, these eight firms included all four consumer manufacturers. Only four of the nine industrial-good firms we studied were calculating a figure for market share because this was a pricing objective. All firms which calculated market shares believed that they could make good estimates of the market shares of their competitors.

7.8 BUYERS' ATTITUDES TO PRODUCTS

Three of the consumer goods manufacturers, Alpha, Gamma and Epsilon, believed that their products sold because they provided their consumers with a persuasive combination of characteristics. Among these they put advertising impact, performance, appearance, price, and sales promotion methods. They used specialized market research techniques to judge the importance of such characteristics.

The industrial goods manufacturers did not use these specialized techniques to learn about buyers' attitudes. However, they did meet their buyers socially, at trade functions, demonstrations, etc. They therefore had first-hand knowledge of their buyers, although they did not collect this information formally as the consumer goods firms did. However, it did accumulate. What we find difficult is to determine just how much information of this kind was useful. Dee Plastics relied on reports by its executives, particularly its commercial manager, although we have seen that this was partly because the firm had no market research department when we studied it. Other firms depended heavily on reports by salesmen and agents who were in direct contact with customers but who had not usually been trained in the techniques of market research.

Wessex Timber, for example, employed a number of salesmen who between them sold the entire output of the firm. The salesmen had to negotiate the size and price of individual orders with customers. Every salesman spent a long period being trained in every aspect of timber production and knew the uses for each of Wessex's products. Wessex asked its salesmen to predict customers' future requirements, in order to build up a detailed knowledge of each customer's business. Wessex regarded this as very important. It felt that when trade was difficult, and a major customer was pressing for a lower price, the salesmen would know enough about the customer's business to be able to decide what product characteristics were important to him and so whether it was possible to lower the price of timber for him.

This rather special kind of market information was kept in his head by the salesman, but he was also in close touch with the executive in Wessex who set list prices. It is important to remember that a significant percentage of Wessex's output went to other firms in the group. Wessex therefore knew these buyers personally, in addition to being well informed about buyers in firms outside the group.

7.9 PRICES

For the products they were competing against, all the firms we studied knew the broad levels of price for individual products and classes of products. In several firms there was a problem because the price actually charged for a unit of product could differ considerably from the basic (perhaps list) price. There were two reasons for this. First, details of competitors' arrangements for giving discounts were not always known. Dee Plastics, for example, had found it very difficult to obtain a copy of its major competitor's price list, although it ultimately found a way of doing so. Even having the price list did not help very much, since Dee could only guess what discounts its competitor was offering to particular customers. Information about discounts could be obtained by asking customers what prices they were actually paying, but one then invited them to bluff. No customer was likely to tell Dee exactly what discounts it was being given by its major competitor, if by exaggerating the size of the discount he could get a bigger one from Dee itself.

The other problem was that firms deliberately engaged in what we have already followed economists in calling product differentiation. The firm would attempt to make its own product just a little different from (and if possible more attractive than) its rivals' products. This sometimes made it rather difficult to know exactly what it was that a customer was (or thought he was) getting from the competitor's product. For example, Wensum Engineering found that all its competitors offered a basic model of each product at a known price. But they also offered optional extras, and Wensum Engineering was rarely able to discover exactly what the price of any optional extra was. Even when it did, with a wide range of varieties of each product, it was by no means easy to be sure what it was that the customer felt he was getting for his money.

Yet, where there was product differentiation, optimal pricing clearly required each firm to do precisely this—to judge what combination of price and product characteristics was being offered by each competitor. A number of firms, including Alpha and Wensum, went to a good deal of trouble to analyse the design and the material content of the competitors' products. They then tried to decide what differences there were between these products and their own.

In several firms producing industrial goods, managers visited competitors' plants in order to study similarities and differences between products and processes and so to improve the design and manufacture of their own products. Managers who made such visits could provide a good deal of the information that was required for analysing the price and product specifications of competitors' products. However, only Alpha, Basic Foods and Epsilon, all of them producing consumer goods, carried out this sort of analysis in detail. None of our firms had enough information to be confident that it really understood the price/product specification relationships for competitors' products. As with Wensum, the main reason was that given differences in specification could rarely be associated with specific differences in price.

7.10 PRICE-VOLUME RELATIONSHIPS

All the firms we studied believed that they knew something about the relationship between the general level of prices for all individual products of a particular type, and the total volume of sales for all those products in the whole market. In other words, they felt they knew something about elasticity of demand. However, underlying this belief seemed to be the feeling that the total demand for each product depended much less on price than on some more basic factor, perhaps an element in the environment like population growth. Within unstated, but fairly broad limits, firms felt that total demand was unresponsive to changes in price. We were not given any empirical data to justify this assumption, but our firms insisted that this was how they felt. It did not, however, lead them collectively to raise prices.

7.10.1 Elasticity of Demand

Unfortunately, as we have seen, the information which price fixers really needed about elasticity of demand was not for the whole market but for individual products and brands. All our firms agreed that this information would have been valuable if they could have obtained it, since it would have shown them how the amount of each product sold would have altered as its price changed. Some firms had made efforts to identify this relationship for their own products.

Basic Foods was one of the firms with no very precise information about elasticity of demand. The general view in Basic Foods was that total demand for all of its products taken together was inelastic, and that this was shown by past experience in the trade. However, it was also believed that the demand for some individual products sold by Basic Foods' was very elastic, provided only that the price of one of these products changed, while the price of all competing brands remained unaltered. Economists use the slightly narrower concept of cross-elasticity of demand, where the price of one product is changed but the price of the competing product remains unaltered. Basic Foods thought that cross-elasticity was high for any one of their products and each of a number of different products made by competitors. However, Basic Foods believed that unless there was a difference in retail prices of about 5 per cent between any two products, cross-elasticity would be very low. Because of this, and because retail prices were not maintained, there was quite significant price cutting on Basic Foods' products in most shops at the time of our study. This happened even though retail prices were recommended by all manufacturers. We shall see that Wensum also seemed to believe that a 5 per cent change was required before there was any significant effect on the demand of any of its products. It felt that changes of less than 5 per cent in prices did not significantly affect sales. However, we have too little information to judge whether this was correct or not.

In Basic Foods, price cutting was most frequently engaged in for those products which had the smallest market shares. But it was not limited to them. Several of these products had recommended retail prices below those recommended for the products with big market shares. The general view in the trade was that cross-elasticity of demand was high enough, and most shops' prices stable enough, for an energetic retailer, with a suitably situated shop, to more than double his sales if he charged retail prices 10 per cent below the recommended ones. It was not believed that such big price cuts were often made. However, these examples give an idea of the benefits which sellers of these products with small markets could get from price cutting where the producers of the products with big market shares did not respond by cutting the recommended prices for their own products. One safe generalization about oligopoly seems to be that once one of these products with a small market share reaches a share somewhere between 5 per cent and 10 per cent, the big firms in the market will take notice of it. This certainly happened in the market served by Basic Foods.

One of the few firms which had carefully studied elasticity of demand for its products was Epsilon Ltd. An experiment had been made during the nine months before 'Epsilon' was sold on a significant scale. During the whole of that period, 'Epsilon' was sold in a number of carefully chosen shops at prices varying from 2s 6d to 3s 10d. The aim was to find the most profitable price for 'Epsilon' by selling it at different prices in a number of shops, each chosen because it had characteristics similar to those of the total market.

TABLE 7.1

Price per Unit (P)	2s 6d		3s 2d		3s 10d
Change in Price: (ΔP)		27%		22%	
Unit Sales (Q)	100		61		46
Change in Sales: (ΔQ)		39%		25%	
Elasticity of Demand $\left(\frac{\Delta Q}{Q} \div \frac{\Delta P}{P}\right)$		1·4		1·1	
Unit Profit	100		182		275
Total Profit	100		109		125

An estimate of elasticity of demand was obtained from the price/quantity information so acquired. For 'Epsilon', both the quantity demanded and the elasticity of demand was found to be higher at comparatively low prices. Demand in absolute terms was smaller and elasticity of demand lower at higher prices. Profit, per unit and in total, was greater at higher prices. The results of this experiment are summarized in Table 7.1 which gives index numbers for both sales and profit.

Because this was a limited experiment, one cannot deduce that the elasticity of demand for the whole market was the same as for this part of it. However, Epsilon used the information to conclude that elasticity of demand was low enough for there to be no justification for selling 'Epsilon' at a price of less than 3s 10d.

As the case study shows, Fourways Engineering had also tried to estimate elasticity of demand for one of its products. The company's agents had been asked to fill in a questionnaire showing what they would expect sales for the product to be at various prices ranging, by steps of £50, from £250 to £450. They were asked to distinguish between home and export sales. Elasticity of demand was not itself calculated but the figures show that, if they were correct, total receipts from the product would have been greatest at the lowest price of £250. Given the pattern of costs, it was thought that profit would be greatest at a price of £350. Unfortunately, it turned out later that the estimates for material and labour costs were wrong. The conclusions of the whole exercise were therefore ignored.

7.11 PROBABILITIES OF OBTAINING BUSINESS

It will be remembered that Heavy Technology was a firm which had to tender for its business. The right tender price had to take account of the percentage of capacity which would be employed at the time when Heavy Technology was actually making the product in question. At the time of our study, Heavy Technology was paying a good deal of attention to the possibility of discovering what the relationship was between the price at which a tender was put in and the probability of obtaining the contract in question. This is not quite the concept of elasticity of demand.

Elasticity of demand is concerned with a definite (though often undiscoverable) relationship between the price charged for a product and the quantity which would be sold at that price. Heavy Technology was concerned with probabilities rather than certainties. It wanted to know how likely it was that particular business would be obtained at a particular price, at a particular time, given the reactions which could be expected from competitors. The sales manager of Heavy Technology played an important role in calculating these probabilities. He was in close touch with his opposite numbers in the main competing firms, and therefore in a good position to be able to judge what each major competitor was likely to do when tendering for a particular contract. It was vital for Heavy Technology, in its difficult market, that the probabilities the sales manager assigned should be accurate. The information he used in doing so was mainly historical. He depended heavily on prices, so far as they were known, at which Heavy Technology and other manufacturers had taken business in the past. At the time of our study, more sophisticated methods were being introduced in the hope of getting a better idea of the probability that Heavy Technology would take given business at a particular price.

7.12 OTHER ELEMENTS IN THE MARKETING MIX

Our studies showed that firms always found it difficult to distinguish between the effect of a change in price on the volume of sales and the effects of changes in other variables, like product design, advertising or sales promotion expenditure. Changes in product design seemed to be particularly important in stimulating sales for Dee, Gamma, Wensum, Fourways, Basic Foods, Epsilon and Medlock. Advertising and sales promotion were also important for Alpha, Gamma and Epsilon, that is to say, for three of the four consumer goods firms. Where there was no price difference between competing products, as happened with 'Alpha' and its competitor 'Omega', the influence of these other marketing variables was obviously very important.

Apart from the experiment carried out by Epsilon Ltd, none of our firms had any information about price-volume relationships that was based on continuing observations over a period of time. Nor did they have information about price-volume relationships over a significant range of prices and sales volumes. Nor, again, could our firms effectively eliminate the effects of non-price elements like advertising on the volume of sales, though Alpha had figures going back fifteen years for price, volume, market size and market shares. Alpha had also constructed a simple mathematical model for its market, relating advertising expenditure to sales.

7.13. INFORMATION ABOUT COMPETITORS

Much of the information which our firms had about their competitors has already been mentioned in our discussion of market information. However, besides having information about competing products and prices, price setters required other information about competing firms. The information they had is discussed below.

7.13.1 Competitors' Marketing Practices

We have explained that the details of competitors' discount arrangements were not always available, and that this made pricing rather difficult in some cases. The absence of information about discounts made it hard for firms to draw useful conclusions about how important discount policies were for their competitors. For example, Dee Plastics was in a trade where discounts were extremely significant. These could be divided into exclusivity discounts, paid to any customer who took all his plastic slats from one company, and quantity discounts which were given according to the annual purchases of slats made from one particular firm. Dee Plastics was in difficulties because it rarely knew exactly what discounts its competitors were offering, though it did know that the exclusivity discount offered by its major competitor made it hard for Dee to take new business. Because of its shortage of capacity, Dee Plastics was often unable to supply all the plastic slats that were required by a prospective customer. Yet, if that customer gave Dee Plastics any business, he lost the whole of his exclusivity discount from his existing supplier. Exclusivity discounts clearly helped large suppliers, with spare production capacity available, to keep business despite keen competition from smaller producers whose capacity was not fully occupied.

Clean Engineering also found that discounts were important. At the time of our study, a good deal of time was being spent by the firm in trying to build up a correct understanding of the discounts being offered by major competitors. Otherwise, Clean feared that a good, even superior, product could fail to take a contract because more favourable discount terms were being offered by the competitor.

Our firms did not have much difficulty in obtaining information about other aspects of competitors' marketing arrangements, such as transport, distribution, advertising or other sales promotion activities. This was partly because all the firms competing in a particular market used similar marketing and promotional methods, and partly because such information was not difficult to obtain from salesmen, customers, newspapers, trade journals, etc.

7.13.2 Competitors' Plans

Information about competitors' plans for marketing individual products, for developing new products and for expanding their plant was not easily obtained by our firms. In two consumer good firms (Alpha Ltd and Epsilon Ltd) it was possible to deduce something about what competing products were being developed and what the marketing plans for them were, by looking at the design and specification of competitors' new or modified products when these were being test marketed. However, it was not always possible to learn enough about such new or modified products as early as they would have liked.

Information about competitors' plans for expanding plant and other facilities was also difficult to obtain in good time. What was done was to keep a watch on the newspapers for any announcements of investment plans. Basic Foods and Heavy Technology found that they could obtain a good deal of useful information in this way. Basic Foods, for example, obtained some information, often qualitative rather than quantitative, from newspapers, public announcements and personal contacts. Our firms usually tried to use their knowledge and experience to predict competitors' marketing plans and investment activities. For example, they would assume that known technological developments would be applied. Basic Foods saw such knowledge as very important in its oligopolistic market, and part of its marketing economics department was continually engaged on analysing the activities of competitors. Even so, Basic Foods would have liked more information than it had, though it thought that it could not obtain this without engaging in industrial espionage, which it was unwilling to do.

7.13.3 The Financial Position of Competitors

Details of competitors' production and selling costs were rarely available. Firms therefore tended to assume that competitors' costs were much the same as their own and judged the profitability of competitors' activities on this basis. Basic Foods, for example, made this assumption, except where it knew that competitors' costs were different from their own. Allowance was therefore made for this. Similarly, Alpha Ltd and Epsilon Ltd allowed for known differences in competitors' product designs, production methods and advertising arrangements. What surprised us was that in some of our firms, especially Clean Engineering, the assumption that competitors' costs were in line with their own continued to be made even after it became clear that they were lower.

We found that only four of our firms analysed the overall financial situations of their competitors. These four used published information to obtain an impression of the comparative efficiency of competitors' manufacturing methods, the profitability of individual products and the effect which each competitor's current financial position was likely to have on its pricing policy. Given the distinctly unrevealing character of the financial accounts of most British firms, it was rarely possible to obtain satisfactory information about competitors' financial positions, but it was felt that some information was better than none. One wonders if it is in any way significant that among the firms which did study the financial accounts of competitors' were two which continually over-estimated competitors' production costs.

7.13.4 Competitors' Reactions

Eleven of our firms devoted a good deal of time to studying the reactions of competitors to changes in the market situation. The remaining two, selling in markets where there were large numbers of competing firms, studied general changes in their markets, and especially changes in the general price level. Individual firms did not play a large enough role for their reactions to be important. In the eleven firms where there was oligopoly or duopoly, attempts were made to predict the reactions of competitors to price or advertising changes, but few firms used sophisticated mathematical techniques in doing so. This was partly because of unfamiliarity with and/or scepticism over the value of such techniques, but partly because of the lack of data. Such assessments were usually based on an indefinable managerial 'feel' for the competitive situation, though in one or two cases mathematical techniques, using probability, were beginning to be introduced. We have seen that Heavy Technology, for example, was trying to find out whether it could assign a probability to being awarded a given contract, at given prices. It seems likely that, in the situation faced by Heavy Technology, this method could be very helpful to price fixers. Alpha Ltd and Basic Foods were both in situations where it was important to predict competitors' reactions; Alpha Ltd was using mathematical models, though Basic Foods was not.

7.14 GOVERNMENT POLICY

All our firms were to some extent affected by Government policy. Some had to take the likely reactions of institutions like the Prices and Incomes Board into account. All had to consider the effects that changes in the general economic climate would have on their businesses. Relevant information was collected as and when necessary, and made available to price setters. However, information about the general economy was much less important to our firms than information about the market.

7.15 DYNAMIC FACTORS

One thing which greatly surprised us about the market information our firms had was their neglect of dynamic factors. In particular, we found no mention of the product cycle. It is now generally recognized that there is a product cycle for most (if not all) products with rapidly-increasing sales at the start of a product's life followed later by a decline, though sometimes a slow one. The product cycle is obviously most important for products with relatively short lives, because the firm must then be continually ready to bring in new products as existing ones decline. Product life-cycles were probably least important for those firms which made fairly standardized, intermediate parts, like Wessex Timber, Dee Plastics and Universal Corporation, or a fairly standard consumer goods, like Basic Foods. For the remaining firms, product cycles were of varying importance—though rarely mentioned in our studies.

Wensum is perhaps a good example of a firm which had paid too little attention to the product cycle. It will be remembered that one of Wensum's main problems was that it was not earning as high a rate of return on capital as its parent firm wished. We are convinced that a major reason for this was that pricing in Wensum did not take account of the product cycles.

Wensum was a successful innovator, so that when a product was first introduced, it often had no direct competitor. As was suggested in Chapter 1, Wensum was a monopolist for a number of products during the period before its competitors began to make them. Once this happened, the competitor often had a cost advantage over Wensum, which seems to have been better at innovation than at routine production. This accentuated the product cycle. When first introduced, Wensum was assured of good sales because it often had the only product of the particular type; once competitors moved in, it lost ground rapidly.

We believe that Wensum should have taken advantage of this. Perhaps because engineers were important in Wensum, it had taken the view that it would not 'soak' its customers in the early stages of a product's life. Later, with its relatively high production costs, Wensum had no alternative but to cut prices as competitors moved in—

often to very unprofitable levels. The result was that Wensum did not make as much profit as it could have done when innovation gave it a monopoly. Yet it was quite unable to make much profit when other firms entered the market. In addition to its failure to take advantage of the product cycle in the early stages of the product's life (even at the cost of reducing initial sales) Wensum seemed to have been reluctant to drop products when they were in the later part of their lives. It seems to be an excellent example of a firm which needs to make its profits in the early years of each product's life, and to be prepared to drop the product quickly, once it becomes 'old'. A side benefit of this policy would have been that it would eliminate some of Wensum's market research problems. As we have already seen, these arose because its very wide product range made market research very expensive.

So far, we have looked only at the dynamic aspects of the demand for a product, and especially at the need to check on the way each product is moving through its life-cycle. However, dynamic factors come in on the cost side too, though we must not dwell on them here since they relate to cost and not demand. Just as firms should pay more attention than ours did to the cycle of demand for a product, so they should equally pay attention to the dynamics of cost. Increasing emphasis is rightly being put today on the role of experience in reducing the costs of a product over time. The concept of the 'learning curve' is now widely understood, yet too few firms link their pricing policy to it. As the aggregate output of a product increases, there is a tendency for costs to fall, because experience in making the product has accumulated. It is true that the benefits to cost from experience in making products are often masked, as they have been during the 1960s, by high rates of inflation. However, there is a great deal of empirical evidence to suggest that the costs of making any product fall over time, as experience in manufacturing it is gained.[1]

The way in which costs fall with experience should not be separated from the firm's strategy over market shares. If there are two firms in a market where experience has important effects on costs, the firm with the bigger market share will obviously have more accumulated experience. It is therefore likely to have lower costs, and so the ability to reduce prices, and perhaps to drive the other firm from the

[1] See, for example, *Perspectives on Experience*, The Boston Consulting Group, Boston, Mass., *USA*, pp. 69–85.

market. This relationship between market share and cost is an important one to watch. Yet, in common with other dynamic elements in pricing, it was one that our firms neglected. All too often, they were pursuing a pricing policy designed for a static world in a manifestly dynamic one.

7.16 CONCLUSIONS

The main conclusions from this chapter are these. First, firms rarely have all the information about markets and competitors that they would like. Some information is not available; some is uncertain. Some requires the price setter to make guesses about, for example, which moves competitors are going to make. Some information will be obtainable, but will be too expensive. Even so, this is a field where improvements are possible, though price setters must always weigh the costs of getting more information against the benefits of having it. The benefits of having information can frequently be increased by analysing it more thoroughly. As we have seen, some of our firms failed to make use of the information they already had.

Firms should therefore consider the following:

(a) whether they could improve the quality of their information, if necessary by using more sources;
(b) whether to develop and use better methods of forecasting;
(c) whether they are making optimal use of the information they already have.

Potential sources of good market information that merit investigation are specialist market researchers, trade associations and information agreements. The potential costs and benefits of using the firm's own market research facilities should be compared with the costs and benefits of employing outside specialists, if only for some parts of market research. This is because outside specialists will often have developed techniques and sources of information not available to the firm itself. There seems to be little reason why specialist market research techniques should be applied only in the consumer-good field. Manufacturers of industrial goods may find that some of these techniques can provide them with valuable information about their customers.

Trade associations often supply information that is not relevant to the individual markets and requirements of individual firms. But since a trade association is (or should be) the servant of the companies forming it, it may be able to produce the information they want. In two cases (Basic Foods and Wessex) trade associations gathered information on market size and supplied it to their members. We can see no reason, in principle, why trade associations should not provide market research facilities for all their members, or make projections of future market size and developments for them. Information on sales, production, stocks, capital investment (or virtually any other aspect of an industry's activities) could be gathered by trade associations and circulated to their members. This could be done in such a way that information cannot be attributed to individual firms, as is already done by some organizations operating in this field. Or information could be circulated directly between member firms under an industry-wide information agreement. Trade associations could be invaluable in the administration of such agreements, as they already are in some industries.

Information agreements are satisfactorily operated in a number of industries. So long as they are restricted to exchanges of information, and cannot be operated to have the effect of price agreements, there is no reason for them to contravene British Restricted Practices legislation. Wider use of information agreements could provide much new information on the market and on competitors. But firms will also need a more enlightened attitude towards the disclosure of information. In British business, an illogical fear of giving information to competitors currently seems to carry more weight than an understanding of the benefits to be obtained from obtaining good information about competitors. Our study shows that some work had been done on forecasting, but that the forecasting methods used were often rather simple ones. Better forecasting would mean, among other things, the application of mathematical, statistical and computer techniques to business-information problems. The construction of mathematical models and the use of computer simulation can provide managers with important aids to forecasting. These techniques allow managers and their staff to spend more time on analysis relative to calculation, with the advantage that problems, and alternative solutions to them, can be analysed more systematically and rigorously. Perhaps, most important, sensitivity analysis (discussed more fully in Chapter 11) could then be used to discover which market information would be most worthwhile, if it could be obtained. As the real costs of computer installations continue to decrease, these techniques will become increasingly worthwhile to firms prepared to use them.

At present, however, firms may find that the amount and quality of information available, and the relatively limited forecasting skills currently available to them, make it difficult to move far in this direction. At present, the results of sophisticated forecasting techniques may not be good enough to justify spending much money in this direction. However, it is important that a watch should be kept on developments here since it is likely that the cost/benefit position of forecasting techniques will improve very greatly in the next decade.

Improvements in looking at pricing problems in a more dynamic way are, however, already necessary and possible. As we have seen, there was too little emphasis in our firms on the influence that the product cycle should have on pricing policy. There was also too little understanding of the way that experience affected costs. Firms failed to see the consequent need to set market shares for products with appropriate emphasis on the cost-reducing effects of experience in manufacturing a product.

CHAPTER 8

Internal Information Required for Pricing Decisions

8.1 THE ACCOUNTANT'S ROLE

In the previous chapter we discussed the difficulties that our firms faced in obtaining adequate and relevant information about the external environment which they could use in pricing decisions. This chapter looks in a similar way at information about the position within the firm. What information was made available to those taking pricing decisions in the firms we studied and what were its deficiencies?

Inevitably, the internal information system of any firm has been concentrated around its accounting section, although computers are beginning to change this. Much of the information about the internal operations of the firm is quantitative. Until the recent improvements in the quantity and quality of management education available in the UK, the majority of those who were qualified to produce and interpret financial information about the commercial activities of the firm were accountants. Even now the influence of those who have been formally educated in management is very small. The number of those with master's degrees in business is minute. The resulting concentration of power in the accountant's hands has given rise to many problems for price setters, especially because accounting systems were originally designed to provide historical information for management and shareholders. The provision of management accounting data for managers taking decisions, instead of financial accounting data for shareholders and others, is comparatively new. For example, the Institute of Cost and Works Accountants was incorporated only in 1919.

All the firms we studied could call on the services of two distinct types of accountant. The financial, or stewardship, accountant was concerned with presenting financial figures telling management and outside observers what had happened to the firm in financial terms and giving a general picture of its financial position. These accountants were rarely involved in management decision making, except where taxation was involved—especially the tax aspects of capital-investment decisions. The second type of accountant, the management accountant, was concerned with the day-to-day running of the firm, and especially with providing data regularly, in a standard form, for control purposes. This information allowed firms to take control decisions—keeping the firm's performance in line with its budgets. Some of the information provided to managers for control purposes could also be used for less-routine decisions. For example, information provided, either in control accounts or on an *ad hoc* basis, helped decisions to be made on stock levels, material purchases, advertising outlays and on pricing. If extra information was sought for pricing, it usually came from the management accountants.

8.2 PROBLEMS IN IDENTIFYING COSTS

We begin this chapter by looking at cost information. It was from management accountants that most of the firms we studied obtained their cost information. Heavy Technology was something of an exception, because it used technologists to draw up its cost estimates, although accountants did provide the basic data about cost and revenue. Universal Corporation was also unusual, because its cost data were prepared by the production department. In Wensum, too, cost figures were based on estimates from the production department. In other words, while financial information about marketing, administrative and similar costs came from accountants in all firms, production cost information sometimes came from engineers.

What a unit of production 'costs', or, indeed what anything 'costs' and how this 'cost' should be measured, has probably been the subject of more discussion and dispute than anything else in the literature of accounting or economics. For example, one of the burning questions in most restaurants is what is the 'cost' of a meal. The correct answer is that the identifiable costs of a meal are an amount of money for food, another amount for fuel and a further amount for identifiable labour. The rest of the 'cost' of the meal will be an unknown proportion of the amount spent on keeping the restaurant open, clean, heated and lit; of wages of supervisory staff; and so on. The fact is that no one knows exactly what a meal 'costs'. One knows only the identifiable costs. Yet, if a business schoolteacher said this to the proprietor of a restaurant who was working out his price list, he would be regarded as either unhelpful or frivolous. Like most of us, the proprietor of the restaurant feels that there must be a 'correct' or 'right' price for everything. If this is so, then there must be 'a' or 'the' 'correct' cost for everything as well. Otherwise we should have nothing to base the 'right' price on. As we shall see, the problem of how far 'the' cost of any product should be identified, and how one should relate the price of the product to that cost was a major problem in the firms we studied.

In industry, as with our hypothetical restaurant, difficult problems are encountered in calculating cost. The firm's accounting system has evolved from the fundamental methods of double entry book-keeping, and has a history very much longer than that of any of the firms participating in our study. In some of the firms we studied, the management accounting system had failed to develop sufficiently from its financial accounting origins to meet the needs of those who set prices, especially where up-to-date managerial decision techniques or ideas were used. Even where firms had intricate systems for calculating costs, arithmetic manipulation often seemed to play a bigger role than rigorous, logical thought.

8.2.1 Average Cost

Those who calculated costs were concerned, as we have suggested they would be, with the deceptively simple question: How much does this product 'cost' to produce? Even where a firm is manufacturing a single product, this is not an easy question to answer. If one aggregates all the expenditure of the firm and divides it by the number of units of product produced, one obtains cost per unit of output produced in a given period of time—what economists call average cost. Although this is only one way of stating cost, there are major difficulties in its calculation, like that of how to allocate to the product the cost of the capital assets which make its production possible, and which will be used up over a number of years. Even when these have been resolved, other problems remain. Most important, prices frequently have to be set in a series of short-run situations; they cannot always be set to maintain a given relationship with costs over a long period of time. For costs will be changing. What is needed is therefore an understanding of what cost per unit of production is expected to be at likely levels of output and in given periods of time. Relevant costs are future costs in a dynamic changing world. Inflation tends to raise costs over time; 'learning' tends to reduce them.

It follows that a manager faced with a pricing decision will not have sufficient cost information if he accepts the costs which the historical costing system shows were incurred in the past in producing at the actual level of output. What he needs is data specifically related to, and probably specially processed for, a particular decision. He needs to know: Will cost vary with output? How will it be affected by future changes in labour or material costs? How will it alter if new capacity is installed? Will 'learning' reduce costs over time?

8.2.2 Marginal Cost

Above all, the decision taker (whether the price setter or someone else) will need to look at marginal costs. The words 'marginal cost' appear to be highly emotive to many businessmen. We should therefore perhaps emphasize, at the earliest possible moment, that neither we, nor anyone else in his senses, advocates actually charging marginal cost, except when a firm is in quite desperate trouble. The aim is not to charge marginal cost but to relate price to marginal cost. As we shall see, the whole essence of the marginal analysis we shall advocate is that one asks this question: What is the optimal margin, over and above marginal cost, for us to charge on this occasion?

The economist's definition of marginal cost is that it is the addition to total cost incurred if a small extra amount of output (usually one unit) is produced. (Mathematically, it is the derivative of the total cost function.) Calculating marginal cost enables the manager to see how much will be added to his total costs if a few extra units of output are sold, whether as the result of price cuts or for some other reason. He is concerned with what we may call 'incremental marginal cost'. He is concerned with the alteration in total costs if there is a small change in the output of an existing product. Of course, it will not always be easy to work out the change in total costs if output increases by a fairly large amount. If marginal cost is constant, or nearly so, one can easily work out the effect on total cost of a largish increase in output. One simply multiplies (unit) marginal cost by the number of extra units of output to be produced. However, it may be necessary to calculate marginal cost more carefully in order to work out the addition to total cost when output is substantially increased, either in an existing plant or by building a new one. In these cases, one is concerned with what may be called 'quantum-jump marginal cost'.

Those whose job it is to estimate costs must develop an expertise in calculating marginal cost. As we shall constantly emphasize, it is relevant costs which price setters need to know, and relevant costs will usually be marginal costs.

The reason is easy to see. The manager needs to take a decision only in a situation where that decision will alter at least one variable —perhaps profit, turnover or cost. If no variable alters as a result of his decision, there is no meaningful decision at all. (Strictly, there is a 'no change' decision.) He therefore needs to know what will be the effect of possible changes in relevant variables. When the variable in question is cost, he needs to know marginal cost (correctly identified): he needs to know how total costs will alter as output changes.

Where a firm sells a number of products, or product lines, it is even more difficult to answer the question: How much does this product cost? It may be that raw-material and direct-labour costs can be apportioned fairly easily between products and this will simplify the problem. Even if this were the case, however, the problems we discussed for a single-product firm would all arise again. And, in practice, there will always be some inaccuracy in the allocation of some costs between products.

In particular, there are indirect expenses, or overheads. An indirect expense is one that cannot be directly allocated to any product. For example, it may be the cost of electricity used to drive machines making several products, or it may be the managing director's salary. What the businessman usually does in these circumstances is to use what looks like a fair basis of allocation, hoping (because he can never know) that it will be reasonably close to the 'correct' allocation. Power costs may be allocated in proportion to the number of machines engaged in the production of each product; rent in proportion to the floor area taken up with the manufacture and storage of each product; or the costs of service departments in proportion to the outputs of the departments using those services. Whatever is done, it is unlikely that indirect costs will be allocated accurately. As a firm's production becomes more complex or more diversified, it becomes increasingly difficult to arrive at 'a' cost figure that gives 'the' cost of a unit of product. The need for subjective judgement and the complex structure of the modern firm makes this impossible. Cost becomes, within limits, what we make it. However, relevant costs are still what managers need to know, and relevant costs are almost always marginal costs of one kind or another.

It is perhaps worth pointing out that investment analysis based on DCF techniques also uses marginal analysis. One calculates what extra revenues can be earned *only* if the asset is bought; one calculates what costs will be incurred if the asset is acquired, but *not* incurred if it is *not* acquired. The correct analysis of all business decisions is the same. It is always a marginal analysis. This is why it is so important for price fixers to use a marginal approach, separating fixed and variable costs.

8.3 THE COST FIGURES USED IN THE FIRMS WE STUDIED

We shall now outline the way in which the firms we studied calculated the costs they used in their pricing decisions. There was some similarity in the methods which our firms used to arrive at cost data, but we shall see that this did not involve anything like the universal calculation of marginal cost.

Each firm had tried to project its historical costs far enough into the future to act as a basis for decision making. Forecasts of future changes in cost were therefore usually considered, though not always adequately. In most cases, this still left the firms with only a very broad understanding of a complex interrelated cost structure. The data used in taking pricing decisions came from the existing cost information system and in some cases we felt that this is not really suitable for providing data for the decisions in which it was used. In particular, it often failed to distinguish clearly and carefully between fixed and variable costs; it did not make it easy for price setters to calculate marginal cost in order to make a given decision.

We have seen that each firm had some system of annual budgeting, and that most firms extended this to cover a five-year period, bringing the figures up to date each year. Each departmental head took part in the process of drawing up these budgets and was given details of what was expected of him over the budgeting period. However, price setters played an insignificant part in this budgeting activity, except where the level of prices was expected to be important in determining whether the budgeted profit was reached. In order to obtain useful information for pricing purposes, detailed and difficult numerical analyses had to be carried out, based on accurate forecasting, clearly-stated objectives and good, subjective assessments of the situation. All the firms tackled this problem in their different ways. However, it is fair to say that most of the price setters we studied were slow to demand truly relevant information from the accounting system to help them in their pricing decisions. They relied too much on data that had come to them simply because it formed part of the routine flow of accounting information.

8.4 COSTS OF ESTABLISHED PRODUCTS

The pricing decisions we studied were of various kinds. We shall therefore look first at the way in which cost information was collected in each of these different types of pricing situation. We studied four firms which were concerned with the pricing of established products, two of them consumer products and two industrial goods.

8.4.1 Alpha Ltd

We begin with the consumer-good firm, Alpha Ltd. The core of Alpha Ltd's information system was a monthly report by the accounting department. This was primarily intended as a document circulated to managers to allow them to keep adequate control over the firm's activities. From this report, the price setters could obtain information about costs of raw materials, packaging and manufacturing as well as about distribution and selling costs. The monthly report also gave details of head office expenditure on research and development, specialist services and other activities not carried out by the divisions concerned with production or selling. The amount of 'Alpha's' 'contribution' to the firm's total indirect (but not necessarily fixed) expenses was also shown, together with figures for the number of units of 'Alpha' sold, its money turnover, its stock levels and its production schedules. The management of Alpha Ltd, regarded the information on costs as some of the most accurate it had for pricing decisions. Alpha Ltd was one of the few firms which had prepared, in some detail, a breakdown of the cost structure of the products of other firms competing in its market.

In Alpha Ltd, the costs that were given most weight in pricing were (a) manufacturing costs and (b) delivery costs. Manufacturing costs were subdivided into (1) the cost of raw materials; and (2) the cost of packaging. Delivery costs covered all the direct costs incurred between the time when the packed product left the factory and the moment of its delivery into the hands of the retailer. Direct costs were split into their fixed and variable elements, to help management decision taking. Indirect expenses, in the case of Alpha Ltd, accounted for approximately 15 per cent of the company's turnover, and included all the usual items which cannot be allocated separately in Alpha Ltd, and charged against profit, not being seen by the company as 'normal' indirect costs. Costs incurred in such activities as test marketing were also treated differently from the other indirect expenses and were allocated in a way that was peculiar to the needs of the firm.

8.4.2 Basic Foods Ltd

The other firm pricing established consumer goods was Basic Foods Ltd. Basic Foods was engaged in mass production, using a process which enabled it to produce several products simultaneously from common raw materials. The company had decided that the only satisfactory way to allocate costs was to use a carefully thought-out method of attributing costs to the products being manufactured. Indirect expenses were allocated to individual products on the basis of an estimate of the extent to which each product contributed to the total indirect expenses of the company.

The situation facing Basic Foods Ltd was more complex than in most firms. Because there were joint products, its production costs were 'joint costs'. It was impossible to separate even the direct costs of producing any unit of one product from those of producing any unit of any other product being manufactured in the factory. Yet the whole point about identifying 'direct' costs, as normally defined, is that they are costs which can be directly attributed to individual products. With joint products this cannot be done. These problems led Basic Foods to allocate direct costs, as well as indirect costs, by rule-of-thumb methods, though it must be said that the methods worked to the satisfaction of the firm's management. Cost estimates prepared by these methods were used in pricing decisions. The emphasis was on changes in cost—on marginal cost. The firm asked: What extra costs will arise if the pricing decision is taken and the expected changes in sales volume occur? Basic Foods was one of the few firms in our study which not only calculated marginal costs explicitly, but also set out in detail how its costs would change if it took each of the various alternative courses of action which were being considered. Even so, computers were not used in doing this and the complexity of Basic Foods' cost calculations was probably great enough to warrant using them.

8.4.3 Wessex Timber Industries Ltd

We turn now to the industrial goods producers. One was Wessex Timber Industries, a mass-producer with fairly standard product. We have seen that the supply of labour determined how big an output Wessex could produce. Labour was also the second most important cost, after the raw material—imported timber. Labour was a stable cost, however, while the price of timber fluctuated. To help its salesmen, who were given the discretion to alter list prices by 1 per cent, a target price was provided by the cost department. This target price was calculated on the assumption that the production budget for the following period would be achieved—a budget for feet of timber leaving the factory. Given this production budget, it was relatively easy to calculate the amount, and so the cost, of raw material on a replacement cost basis. It was also easy to calculate the cost of the labour which would be needed to produce this output. Indirect expenses were allocated by long-established rules of thumb. This gave Wessex a cost per foot of timber, to which was added expected distribution and packaging costs. The resulting figure was a total cost per foot of timber. It was from this that the target price was set, which the salesman used when negotiating the actual price with the customer. He took into account the quantity of timber being ordered. In calculating the target price, the cost department added to total cost per foot of timber an amount sufficient to provide a return of 12½ per cent before tax on the capital employed. This gave the target selling price for the salesman. Wessex Timber provided a good example of cost-plus pricing, although even here we have already seen that market forces were reflected to some extent in the final price agreed by the salesman with his customer. The salesman could use his own discretion in fixing a price within plus or minus 1 per cent of the target figure.

8.4.4 Wensum Engineering Ltd

In Wensum Engineering, we studied the annual price review of a firm making quite complex industrial goods. A good deal of cost information was provided for the review meeting by the accountant and his staff, using information produced by the production department. A working paper from them gave the decision makers cost information which was subdivided in the firm's usual way—into material, labour and works overhead costs. The total of these three elements was known as the *works cost*.[1] In producing these figures, the accountant used information provided by the works manager. Wensum then proceeded to list, for each product, three different figures for what was called the *calculated selling price*. To reach the first figure the firm would multiply works cost by 2·2. The justification given for this was if the factory worked at 'normal' capacity, and a price equal to works cost multiplied by 2·2 was charged for each product, all overhead costs would be recovered, and the desired amount of profit earned. The second figure was a calculated selling price arrived at by taking works cost and adding 20 per cent of material costs and 212 per cent of the total of labour costs and factory overheads. The third figure was reached by taking works cost price and then adding 65 per cent of the material and labour costs included in it. A final column on the working paper provided for the price review meeting gave the existing list price of each product, so that this could be compared with the calculated price.

The reason for providing three different calculated prices was that it was felt that the three elements in works cost (materials, labour and factory overheads) probably needed treating in different ways with different products. We find it hard to see what logic there was in any of these formulae—except that they gave three sets of prices; and that any one set, if charged over the whole range of products, would have given the firm its desired rate of profit. However, the price charged for many products was different from all three 'formula' prices. It was therefore virtually impossible for those engaged on the price review to work out what set of alterations would be required in the whole range of the firm's prices in order to obtain the desired overall level of profit. To have done so would not only have required information about the extent to which sales of the various products would alter if their prices were changed (i.e. elasticity of demand). It would also have required a knowledge of marginal cost—something that the way Wensum presented cost data did not give. Moreover, the complexity of the necessary calculations means that they would have required at least a desk calculating machine for use by the members of the price review meeting. What the accountant's information did do was to provide the starting point for pricing discussions and to suggest

[1] In fact, Wensum used the extraordinary but quite commonly-used term *works cost price*. The fact that such a contradictory term (for it is a cost, not a price) is used, shows how much confusion there is between price and cost, as we noted in Chapter 2.

possible courses of action to the meeting. It did not in itself enforce any prices on the meeting though, as we shall see, the 'formula' price often seemed to be treated as something to move away from rather than to charge.

Up to about two weeks before the price review meeting, there had been no discussion about possible changes in wages. Then the accountant was told by the works manager that there was likely to be an increase in wage costs of about 4 per cent. As we shall see, these increases were not allowed for in the cost figures used in the review meeting. Partly because of this, the price review meeting made very heavy weather indeed of taking changes in labour costs into account.

The study of Wensum throws light on the way in which research like ours can alter the behaviour of the firms being studied. A subordinate of the domestic sales manager, having been told that we were to study the price review, produced his own list of calculated prices, but using only one of the formulae—that of works cost multiplied by 2·2. Because out-of-date cost figures were used, this produced a list of calculated prices which was different in many instances from those provided in the accountant's working paper. The result was that there was some confusion in the review meeting where the two lists had to be reconciled. Neither party had consulted the other in preparing the two lists, even though the domestic sales manager thought that the accountant would be providing such a list and that it might well be based on more up-to-date information than he had. However well-intentioned they are, it seems that researchers in the social sciences can cause changes in behaviour simply by carrying out research at all. Not, of course, that Heisenberg's atoms were different.

8.5 COSTS OF NEW PRODUCTS

We must now look at the cost figures provided when new products were priced. First, we look at two industrial products.

8.5.1 Surgical Instrument Company Ltd

Because its scalpel was a new product, the Surgical Instrument Company had to work out its costs from experience gained in trial runs rather than from historical cost data from the accounting system. Once the sales department had estimated likely prices for the new scalpel and likely levels of sales at these prices, the production accountants provided a cost sheet setting out in some detail the actual costs which had been incurred in manufacturing trial quantities of sample scalpels. These cost figures were used to work out the costs of making the quantities of scalpels shown in the sales estimates.

The Surgical Instrument Company went on to work out a minimum price for the price setter. If price were below this, it would not be profitable for the firm to sell the scalpel. To calculate this minimum price, the various departmental heads held a meeting with the accountant. They produced a profitability statement which began from a series of sales and price estimates, deducted the relevant expected costs, and showed the gross margins expected at each price. The various indirect expenses were then subtracted from the gross margin to give a figure for net profit at each price. Net profit was then divided between home and export business. Finally, calculations were made of the DCF rate of return on capital that would be earned if each of the various possible prices were charged and the assumed volume of sales were to be achieved at each price.

This very detailed statement of estimated costs was then given to the price setter. It showed him the lowest level of price which would produce a satisfactory DCF return on investment in the scalpel.

8.5.2 Fourways Manufacturing Ltd

Fourways Manufacturing was also concerned with the original pricing of a product which had not yet been marketed. The price, when set, was to be announced to customers in the company's price list. The pricing meeting was given details of design and construction methods for the few development models so far produced. These details were also given to the cost estimator whose job it was to work out likely production costs before the meeting. His estimates set out labour and raw material costs, indirect expenses and sub-contracting costs. Initially, this gave a total cost of some £270 per unit, a figure later reduced to £210 after a reduction in estimated sub-contracting expenses. The company had become accustomed to link price to cost by multiplying cost by a given percentage. If achieved for every individual product, this would give the firm its target profit. It was much the same kind of calculation as we have already seen being used in the case of Wensum. Multiplying the cost figure by the traditional Fourways' percentage, suggested a price of £260 per unit. However, a large amount of indirect cost had been incurred in producing the product, including the cost of designing the original product, tooling up, manufacturing development models and carrying out market research and initial sales promotion. When all these costs were included in the cost of each unit it was hoped to sell, a target price of £410 was reached. This was far above the price of similar products already on the market, which was about £350. A year later, by which time a further £6,000 had been added to the initial investment in the product, the prices of competitive products had risen to about £390.

8.5.3 Epsilon Ltd

We now turn to two customer good firms. Epsilon Ltd was a firm introducing a mass-produced consumer product, with emphasis in pricing on market factors and on the attitude of consumers to the product, rather than on a cost formula. The first pieces of information to reach the price setter were estimates of what costs would be at several possible levels of output. These cost figures showed the effects of possible changes in raw material prices and of possible alterations that it was thought might be needed in the product specification to match changes in the specifications of products made by competitors. Estimates of revenue and profit for each alternative output level were also provided for the managers setting prices.

8.5.4 Gamma Products Ltd

Gamma was in a slightly different position. It was always intended to sub-contract the manufacture of Gamma's battery-operated razors. Quotations were therefore obtained from possible manufacturers and these showed Gamma that it could market its razor at a price similar to those of razors already on the market. Gamma took the lowest cost tendered by a sub-contractor and added distribution and selling costs, including retailers' margins and discounts. These costs provided the basis for the pricing decision, in much the same way as they did for the Surgical Instrument Company. They gave a figure to which margins could be added, and which could then be judged in the light of prices for competing shavers. Initially, a 50 per cent margin was added to manufacturers' costs. This brought the price of Gamma shavers into line with those of battery-operated razors already on the market. Our case study showed us that Gamma miscalculated the size of the total market and also wrongly predicted the way in which its product was likely to be received. These errors far outweighed the influence on the final result of any possible mistakes in making cost calculations.

8.5.5 Dee Plastics Ltd

Dee Plastics was in a slightly different situation. Dee was involved in pricing its existing product, but in doing so for a new customer. It therefore had an advantage over the firms pricing new products, because it possessed historical cost information which it could use when quoting prices for the new customer. Dee's product was reasonably standardized and was produced in large quantities so that the allocation of costs was fairly simple. Dee Plastics aimed at maintaining and, if possible, increasing the gross margin it earned over cost. Cost here was measured per 1,000 venetian blind slats produced. The price setter was given the prime cost of 1,000 slats. This did not include labour costs, so that materials represented by far the largest proportion of prime cost. Indirect expenses were allocated on a formula worked out by the accountant. Out of every £1,000 worth of indirect expenses, approximately £500 was regarded as attributable to the factory; a further £350 was classified as outside the control of the factory, and covered such items as electricity, rates and depreciation. The remaining £150 was allocated in the form of head office expenditures and works administration costs. This £150 included the cost of interest on mortgages and debentures.

With venetian blind slats, direct material costs accounted for about 75 per cent of the price to the consumer. Attempts were continually being made to reduce this material cost in order to raise profits. While the price setter was given detailed forecasts of the cost of producing 1,000 slats, he was more interested, when deciding on the quotation, in what prices competitors would be offering to the same customer for the order. He rarely offered a price below 'full' cost, but he was not tied to any given gross margin when deciding on his price. The margin varied with the nature and keenness of competition and with the size of the order. The cost information provided a basis for the pricing decision, but gave no ready-made formula for setting prices.

8.6 FIRMS CALCULATING MARGINAL COSTS

We now turn to four firms which cannot be easily classified, except that, for one reason or another, they had to take marginal cost into account when pricing.

8.6.1 Heavy Technology Ltd

The first was Heavy Technology. Because this firm was manufacturing extremely complicated and expensive capital equipment, a product would often have to be made to a design which had not yet been tested. Most pricing decisions were therefore based on historical cost data but with skill needed in applying it to the new product. Heavy Technology relied very heavily on the technical ability of its estimators. Everyone in the estimating section was a trained engineer or technologist, often with earlier experience in the design department. It is hard to say exactly how these estimators compared in their expertise with cost accountants, but the role they performed was much the same. A cost estimate was presented to management, which contained the best available prediction of costs, based on what technical knowledge and experience there was within the firm. These estimates had been accurate enough for acceptable pricing decisions in the past, and more recently had helped greatly in pricing in extremely competitive situations.

The direct costs of production incurred in producing any unit of output were estimated by drawing on the firm's past experience in making similar or identical products, with appropriate allowances for changes in design or for alterations in materials used. With an untried design, the firm normally relied on its estimators to make whatever contingency allowances they felt were needed. Indirect expenses were then allocated to the product, using a formula based on detailed analysis of the available historical cost data. For much of its business, Heavy Technology was engaged in competitive tendering. This meant that indirect expenses had to be allocated to products in a way which took account of the amount of work that was expected to be passing through the factory when the product whose cost was being estimated would actually be manufactured. It was therefore necessary to predict the level of activity in the factory months, even years, in advance. This was the most difficult problem facing the firm's estimators as they sought to allocate indirect expenses. If the level of activity was underestimated, so that too big an allowance was made for indirect expenses in the tender, this could well result in the order being lost. There was then a danger that this would increase the problem of obtaining future business. If indirect costs were to be recovered, they would have to be recovered from a smaller volume of remaining tenders, and there would be a temptation to raise tender prices too far to allow for this.

The firm's accountants had little or nothing to do with drawing up cost estimates for management, though they did supply data about the current revenue and profit position, as well as information about the whole historical cost pattern. They played this supporting role because a large amount of technical knowledge was required to understand the precise characteristics of each product being manufactured. Without this knowledge, it would have been difficult to estimate correctly. Where a product with a new design was being manufactured, cost was believed to be the most important determinant of price, and an appropriate mark-up was added to the total cost figure to provide a price for the tender. With established products, market factors were the biggest influences on the manager setting prices. However, it must constantly be remembered that Heavy Technology was operating in an extremely depressed market. In some decisions which we observed there was little point in thinking of setting a price above the one at which the most recent contract for the type of product concerned had been accepted. The price which the successful firm had tendered for the most recent contract formed the basis for the pricing decision.

Cost data was therefore needed to show the manager the price at which he would begin to lose money by accepting the contract. In other words, it became essential to calculate marginal cost. Heavy Technology had put a great deal of effort into separating fixed from variable costs. It had become expert at deciding which costs were, and which were not, to be treated as marginal for an individual contract.

8.6.2 Medlock Engineering Ltd

Medlock Engineering was another firm where cost estimates were used as a basis for pricing. This time, the market in which the firm was competing was an international one. Historical cost information was used to provide a basis for allocating relevant costs to each unit of production. Business was again obtained by competitive tender. Occasionally very large products were ordered by a foreign buyer. When this happened, the firm had to spend considerable amounts on research and development, in order to produce design specifications acceptable to the customer. As the tenders had to be put in several months before actual manufacture could begin if the contract were won, indirect expenses had to be allocated in the light of past experience in much the same way as was done by Heavy Technology.

The main problem was how to obtain an accurate estimate of how much capacity would already be occupied when the products covered by a particular contract came to be manufactured. Medlock Engineering saw that there was no point in allocating indirect costs to a product in inverse proportion to the percentage of its capacity that was expected to be in use at the time of manufacture. There was no point in charging huge indirect expenses to a contract, simply because little other work was expected to be going through the factory when it was obtained. This would only ensure that the firm was priced right out of the market for that contract, so reducing further its chances of covering its indirect costs. Instead, Medlock Engineering had also learned to think marginally.

In Medlock Engineering, cost estimates were prepared by the costing section of the accounting department, where all employees had been especially trained for the work, and understood the technical aspects of products well enough to provide good estimates. This section presented a cost estimate to the manager making each pricing decision, and included in it a minimum cost below which he should not consider setting his tender quotation. As with Heavy Technology, it was this minimum price which showed the manager what were his marginal costs. Unless these were covered, there would be a negative contribution towares the fixed costs of the firm. For Medlock, marginal cost comprised labour cost, raw material cost, and an amount to cover the indirect expenses which would be incurred if the particular tender were successful. These indirect expenses were allocated on the basis of the estimator's experience and of careful analysis of historical data.

8.6.3 Clean Engineering Ltd

The remaining firm selling in difficult trading conditions was Clean Engineering Ltd. It was engaged in the manufacture of a technically-advanced product, using batch production to meet customers' specifications. Because of very strong competition in the industry, prices had been pushed downward steadily for a number of years. Profitability and cost were therefore as closely linked as in any firm we studied. Cost information for pricing decisions was provided by the cost department and by the firm's estimators. The design for each piece of water purification plant was passed to the estimators. Using records prepared by the cost accountants, as well as their own data, they estimated the cost of producing the order.

The figures for labour and material content were easily calculated. The estimators also allocated overhead costs to the product. The method used was to take the accounting records and see how indirect costs for units of the product being considered had behaved on any recent occasions when it had been made. The path which the unit would take through the factory was plotted, to see where, and in what proportion, indirect expenses would be incurred. A formula was then used which allowed each element of indirect expense to be attributed to the product in proportion to the man-hours spent on making that product or in proportion to its material content. The formula was then used by the estimators to provide a cost estimate for the product, as well as details of its labour and material content. The final estimate was passed to the manager who set the price to be charged to the customer.

The firm would have been happy to use some form of cost-plus pricing method, adding to cost a desired amount of profit in order to obtain the rate of return on capital required by the Board. Since the market and the competitive situation made this impossible, the cost estimate showed the manager in charge of setting prices how much he could cut them and yet still make some contribution to fixed expense. Once again, this marginal cost estimate treated labour cost as a variable cost. However, difficult market conditions had sometimes forced prices to a level where any further fall would almost certainly have caused some salaries to be treated as a fixed cost, at least in the short-run.

The reason was this. Clean Engineering decided what would be the optimal level of activity for the period immediately ahead, by discovering which level of activity would give maximum possible profit. Because trade was depressed, this maximum profit was below what Clean Engineering really wanted to earn—about 15 per cent on capital employed. However, Clean Engineering found that, in its industry, changes in the number of staff employed could not be made quickly. Some labour costs were fixed, at least for the period immediately ahead, for which the decision on what would be the optimum level of activity had already been taken.

8.6.4 Universal Corporation

Finally, we turn to Universal Corporation. This was a mass-producer of a standardized product, made with expensive and very advanced equipment. The firm set its prices so as both to cover its costs and to earn the rate of return on capital employed required by the Board. Fixed costs were calculated by the finance department. Together with variable costs, they were used in a computer model of the firm's production and distribution systems to forecast total costs at various likely levels of output. What the firm did was interesting, because it was moving towards using marginal cost per unit of output as the basis for the prices to be charged to its customers. The firm was trying to set an overall level of price which enabled it to earn the desired rate of return on capital; but to base each price (and therefore relative prices) on marginal, not average, cost. This is something we shall look at in more detail later.

Universal Corporation began from its output forecasts. These were made for several years into the future, but what matters here is the forecast for the next year. Universal Corporation also worked out demand patterns, based on past experience, showing how demand was likely to be spread over shorter periods within that year. This could be done quite accurately because Universal Corporation had found that short-term demand patterns changed only slowly from year to year.

With this information, Universal Corporation could do two things. First, it could use the total demand forecasts to work out in advance how big demand was likely to be at any time during the year. Second, it could therefore predict which of its machines would be in use at any time during the year and what its costs were likely to be at those times. Universal Corporation tried to arrange that demand was always met by its most efficient equipment. This was possible because Universal's commercial department had up-to-date information about the running costs of each of its machines and about when new machines would become available or when existing ones would be under repair.

From information about the operating costs of each of its machines, and from the predicted pattern of output, the commercial department worked out expected costs for the next year. In doing this, Universal Corporation carefully separated fixed and variable costs. All this data was then fed into the computer model, which gave Universal a prediction of total costs. It also predicted the marginal costs which would be incurred in producing a little extra output during peak periods, normal periods, and slack periods. We shall see later that these three different marginal costs were important in enabling Universal Corporation to charge its customers prices closely linked to the costs of supplying them during each of these three types of period.

It must be added that while, in this section, we have dealt with four firms that are best classified as calculating marginal costs, Basic Foods tried to do this as well. However, the fact that it was producing 'joint products' made the calculation of marginal cost very difficult. In addition, it did 'allocate' indirect costs to its products.

8.7 RELEVANT COSTS

The previous section shows that there was no shortage of cost information in our firms. The essential question is therefore whether the cost figures provided really were relevant to pricing decisions. The cost figure most often given to management was, at best, a simple extrapolation of data from the historical accounting system. At worst, it was a detailed record of what happened in the previous accounting period. Analysis of the data was often left to the manager. In either situation, the firm was sticking to the concepts and time periods of the formal accounting system. These are rarely the ones which would be chosen by a manager interested only in good decision making.

We must therefore look at the information we have about our firms to discover, first, who produced the cost information and, second, how relevant it was.

The basic cost data came from accountants in all but two of our firms—Universal Corporation and Heavy Technology. There, it came from engineers or others who had learned to prepare cost data. In every firm, the accountants were also producing figures for the financial and control accounting system or systems, using conventional time periods and methods of cost allocation.

In Alpha Ltd and Epsilon Ltd, accountants were attached to product groups, and provided accounting data for marketing departments. In Basic Foods, a specialist management information section worked alongside the accounting department. Among the industrial goods manufacturers, with two exceptions noted above (Heavy Technology and Universal Corporation), accounting information needed for pricing purposes was supplied by factory or works accountants. They used either ordinary management accounting routines or worked with specialist technical estimating teams.

What kind of cost information was provided? Historical cost data, or estimates derived from this data, was the basis for the greater proportion of the pricing decisions we studied. We shall not argue that such information should be ignored in pricing decisions. This would obviously be foolhardy. Data on past levels of production and sales, on the commercial success of the product so far, and on costs, are the only hard facts available to the manager setting prices. One can hardly be surprised if pricing frequently begins from cost figures, when these are often the only figures there are. The fact that pricing *begins* from cost figures certainly does not mean that it will be necessarily cost-plus pricing. It need not and should not be. What we would question is the weight given to historical cost data. In Wensum Engineering, for example, the annual price review would have taken place much more smoothly if the expected increase in wage costs and planned cuts in overheads had been explicitly shown in its cost estimates.

None the less, in practice, the fact that pricing begins from cost figures frequently means that it *is* cost-plus pricing. There are simple psychological reasons for this. The firm argues this way. Cost is what we have data about, and market information is what we frequently lack. Therefore we tend: (a) to begin with what we have; (b) concentrate on what we have; (c) to ignore what we do not have.

The essential point can be put as follows:

(i) in logic, the market should be considered first, since it determines what one can sell and the price at which one can sell it;
(ii) in fact, cost is usually considered first, since cost data are available;
(iii) yet it does not matter which is considered first, provided *only* that both the market and cost are given the correct weights, and provided that one understands just how much additional information about each it is economically worth acquiring.

There is another problem too. Not only do costs of inputs like raw materials, labour, etc., change over time. For any firm, the average (and marginal) cost of producing one unit of output is rarely exactly the same from one period to the next, even if costs of inputs are constant. If the volume of output increases between two periods, then cost per unit may rise or fall. It may rise if less efficient plant has to be brought into use; it may fall if resources can be used more effectively when levels of production rise, with more output coming from the same inputs. And, underlying all this, are the longer-term effects of 'learning' in reducing costs. Historical cost figures must be adjusted to take account of these factors when predictions of costs are being made.

However, it is not simply a matter of providing the right cost data, which means having good estimates of future costs. The data must be analysed in the right way. A pricing decision is at least as complex and difficult as any manager has to make. The fact that so many variables, alternatives and assumptions have to be studied, weighed and assessed makes it hard to ensure that the price taker has sufficient cost information and that this is presented to him in the most useful and relevant form. In our firms, only Universal Corporation, with its computer model for analysing cost information, was doing this fully. Basic Foods came close to it. While providing more adequate cost information than most other firms, however, it may have been hampered because it did not use a computer. It found that a good deal of effort was needed to calculate what costs would be in enough possible situations and to do it very quickly. Alpha Ltd's cost information was also good, though cost calculations were required less frequently and less quickly than in Basic Foods.

What we are saying is that, in setting his prices, the manager must work out what amounts of his product he expects to sell at different prices, and what effects selling these expected quantities of product will have on cost, profit and market share. To do this, future levels of cost, price, sales volume, market share and profit have to be linked. Very little of the necessary information will be obtained easily. When it has been obtained, it will often require difficult analysis, covering too many variables for the unaided human brain to do the calculations quickly.

None of this is original. Most managers realize the deficiencies of their information systems. Yet they appear slow to improve them. One reason may be that they confuse the quantity of information with its quality. Perhaps more important is the tension and conflict which inevitably seems to build up between accountants and the managers to whom accounting information is provided. Indeed, in one of our firms accountants refused to give detailed cost information to price setters, because they could not see its relevance. This tension arises partly because managers often feel at a disadvantage when faced with the expertise and the jargon of specialist accountants. In part, it comes from the accountant's unhappiness that, although he has much of the information and expertise needed for pricing and other decisions, he has to leave these decisions to managers who often do not seem to respect his specialist knowledge, or his ability.

Whether or not there are such problems, it always helps if certain steps are always followed in obtaining and analysing cost data. We shall look at these now. How deep and sophisticated the analysis needs to be will depend on the particular pricing decision being made. Perhaps the most important thing, though this sounds too obvious to need saying, is to make sure that all the relevant information that is available is used, and that information that will not be used, whether relevant or not, is not collected. We found several instances in our case studies where information that had been laboriously collected was left lying in filing cabinets when decisions to which it could have contributed were being taken. In two cases, the information was ignored because of rivalry between those concerned with its collection. In two other cases, managers seemed to feel that they could demonstrate their prowess by showing that they kept much or all of the information that was needed 'in their heads'.

8.8 COST INFORMATION NEEDED IN PRICING

The basic principle which should be followed in designing an information system to provide cost data for pricing decisions can be stated easily enough. Relevant information, and relevant information alone, should be provided. This is much more easily said than done. One problem is knowing whether some pieces of relevant information will cost more to collect than they will be worth. Another is that the information which is relevant to pricing decisions may be changing more rapidly than is the firm's information system. The problem then is how fast the accounting system should be allowed to change to catch up. If it changes too quickly, there will be confusion. If it changes too slowly, information that is no longer needed will go on being collected.

8.8.1 What Should the Information System Provide?

The first step is for the manager to ask himself a simple question: What do I need to know about costs for this decision? Inevitably, other questions flow from this one. What costs are going to be incurred, or altered, by the decision? What is the time period over which these costs need to be known? Which cost information would it be most useful to have reported regularly so that prices can be set, reviewed, and altered in the light of changes in internal and external conditions? What routine needs to be established for providing easy access to such information? And what routine can ensure that the information system itself is always kept up to date?

Let us first recall what cost information our firms did possess. Our studies show that, with consumer products like 'Alpha', the emphasis was on regular reporting of information which was needed to allow the firm to control its costs. The overall level of prices charged by Alpha Ltd was stable, though there was a good deal of variation in the actual prices paid by individual customers, with resale price maintenance no longer operating. Regular reports on the way changes in output had altered costs and profits were what management needed. This information was produced more frequently in consumer good firms like Alpha Ltd, than in firms making industrial products, though we are not sure that it was always communicated to price setters. Certainly, the consumer good manufacturers were more aware of the problems and the importance of marketing than most of the other firms. This sharpened their enthusiasm for obtaining regular reports about the factors that were likely to affect prices, sales volumes, market shares, costs, and so profits.

With industrial goods, like those made by Wensum or Wessex Timber, there was still a lively interest in cost and profit but less frequent reports on them. Wessex Timber, like Alpha Ltd sold products which were reported on in bulk. In Wessex, regular reports were useful to managers in setting prices because cost per unit of production was related to volume, even though the accountants worked in terms of average, not marginal, cost. The industrial products of firms like Heavy Technology and Clean Engineering were large and expensive, and managers were given detailed cost and output figures. While the cost/volume relationship was important to them, too, this was mainly at the estimating stage.

In answering the question: 'What cost information do I need for this decision?' the manager is almost certain to turn to his accountants for at least part of the answer. Whether or not the accountants know what information really is needed, the manager will find it useful to make up his own mind about the information he requires. Left to himself, the accountant may well rely too heavily on the information he can easily obtain from the existing accounting system.

Whatever the product, its costs will need to be divided up in some detail. It is important to be quite clear what is included in each subdivision before using such cost figures for decision taking. For example, the 'cost' of raw materials is apparently unambiguous, particularly for pricing. Yet one can quickly see that it is not. One needs to know, for example, whether materials are consistent in quality, whether material costs include the costs of loss or wastage in storage or transportation, whether they allow for discounts, and so on. Similarly, there are problems in how materials are valued when taken out of inventory. Is L.I.F.O., F.I.F.O., average cost, standard cost, or some other figure used? And what indirect expenses, if any, are included in the 'cost' of materials? The price setter must know.

Another major cost element will be direct labour—labour used in turning materials into output. Usually, direct labour can be treated as a variable cost, but we have seen that this is not always correct. It is possible that a firm may be operating in such difficult conditions that it is forced to decide exactly which of its employees it will be determined to go on employing even if this means increasing the size of its losses. The wages or salaries of those employees who are to be kept, at particular levels of loss, then become part of fixed, not variable, cost. The calculation of how much labour cost is to be treated as fixed and how much variable has to be explicitly made.

For pricing decisions, the important questions are usually: How much more (or less) labour will we have to employ, and at what wage, if we take this decision? How efficient will it be? So, what will be the cost of the output it produces? Labour costs need to be known over relevant ranges of output. If labour *is* a variable cost, one needs to be able to calculate the change in total cost resulting from changes in the level of employment that are caused by changes in the volume of output resulting from pricing decisions.

Another major cost element will usually be the all-embracing one of indirect, or overhead, cost. This will cover everything that is not a direct cost of production, or of producing ancillary services. Indirect costs are therefore very hard (often impossible) to attribute accurately to individual products, or even groups of products. Indirect costs will include the cost of such things as light, heat, supervisory staff, stores, office staff, and so on. They will also include rent, rates, and insurance, as well as depreciation, which is a very special kind of cost. Depreciation is simply a way of setting off against profits, over several years, expenditure on capital assets that has already been incurred.

Part of depreciation can be attributed to the use of the asset in question; part can be related only to the passage of time, though this split is rarely made in practice.

Indirect cost is often the most difficult cost to understand. Yet, annoyingly, it is also often the most important cost for rational decision making. Assumptions have to be made about the characteristics and behaviour of indirect costs, and the ones that *are* made often turn out to be unwarranted on closer inspection. Indirect costs are more misunderstood by managers and accountants than any other type of cost. All our firms had problems in dealing with them. In each firm, a large proportion of indirect cost had to be 'allocated' by some rule of thumb. When there was simultaneous production of many products, the difficulties in doing this were compounded.

Price setters must therefore be certain what has been included in indirect cost, and what assumptions have been made in allocating indirect cost to products. These assumptions will affect the apparent 'profitability' of each product. Indeed, we shall go on to argue that it is dangerous to think at all of the 'profit' from an individual product, because the correct allocation of indirect costs is usually impossible.

It may seem that what has just been said about accountants is unfair. This is certainly not the intention. Someone in the firm has to decide how indirect costs should be allocated. It may even be necessary to allocate them to individual products, and this will usually be done by the accountant. Two things *are* being said. First, a manager taking a pricing decision should be quite clear what the accountant has done, and this does not always happen. If a manager has accepted the wrong data as a basis for his decisions, or if he has not understood information which would have been perfectly adequate had he done so, the manager must take the blame. It is no one else's responsibility. Second, even if costs have to be allocated to individual products (or product groups) in order to calculate profit for control or other purposes, it does not follow that this need be done for pricing decisions.

Methods for allocating indirect expenses to products are numerous, but they often mean adding a given percentage to one or other element of direct cost, frequently direct labour or materials. There is little to recommend this method of allocation except that it is simple to operate and understand. Like all rules and methods, it has its faults. For example, in Clean Engineering the 'cost' of metalwork could vary considerably, depending on which division of the firm undertook it. Different rates were being used in allocating indirect cost to such work in different divisions.

While there are many other methods of allocating indirect costs to production, and while each has its merits and defects, some firms decided against using any form of allocation at all. Alpha Ltd was one. It took the view that as there was no uniquely correct basis for allocating indirect expenses to individual products, it would not allocate them at all, but would work in terms of each product's 'contribution margin'.

Let us look at this problem more closely. If the firm is to prosper, then the prices of all its products taken together must be set at a level which allows the firm to cover all its indirect costs. However, it is a managerial, not an accounting task, to work out how much each product is to contribute towards covering indirect costs. It is not essential for prices to be set on the basis of the same information as is used in the firm's financial, or control, accounts. What is necessary is that the prices charged, in the aggregate and for all products, should cover the firm's total costs and leave an acceptable amount for profit. The accountant's fear seems to be that unless every pound's worth of cost is explicitly allocated to an individual product, some costs will be left uncovered. In our study, this fear was most acute in Wensum Engineering, where there was a big gap between works cost and price. Overall, the former was only some 35 per cent of the latter —even though works cost itself included some overheads. This explains why Wensum put so much emphasis on working out cost formulae which, if only they could have been applied exactly in pricing every product, would have ensured that all costs were covered and the desired profit earned. Wensum genuinely feared that, since it was hard to allocate 65 per cent of total costs accurately, some of these costs would be 'forgotten'. It saw the use of its cost formulae as a way of ensuring that all costs were covered.

Clearly, it is vital for an efficient method to be used to ensure that all costs are covered and a profit earned. But this does not mean that the price of every individual product must cover the costs allocated to it by the firm's accountants and go on to earn exactly the same margin of 'profit'. Indeed, because no one knows exactly what it 'costs' to produce any individual product, one cannot legitimately speak of the 'profit' or 'loss 'on an individual product at all. The best approach is more difficult than simply to suppose that the accountants' arithmetic can be taken literally; once learned, it is much more rewarding. The best approach is a marginal one.

One must remember that if firms make wrong assumptions about the way competitors have allocated indirect costs, they will get mistaken ideas about competitors' cost structures and efficiency. This can lead to bad pricing. It is not easy for one firm to assess another's cost structure unless it knows what assumptions the latter's management is making about the allocation of indirect costs, and these usually make up a sizeable proportion of total cost. Wessex Timber faced this problem in an extreme form. Small, often family concerns which cut, shaped and cured timber for small, local markets had long been in direct competition with Wessex, a national company. Wessex had not found it easy to under-cut these competitors, despite its size, modern machinery and skill. Indeed, the reverse had been true. The smaller firms took a different view of which costs should be charged against the production of finished timber. They were not trying to cover the cost of replacing their ageing drills, saws and other machinery. If they were family firms, perhaps once the family died, or lost interest, the firm would be wound up. Wages in all firms were very similar, as were the costs of material used; yet the fact that the small firms did not cover their indirect costs made it hard for the bigger ones to match their prices. The lower prices of the smaller firms did not reflect their efficiency—only their willingness to leave some overhead costs uncovered.

Clean Engineering had often been faced with a similar problem in tendering for water purification contracts. On the whole, over recent years the problem had not been as acute for Wessex Timber, but there had been short periods when it had been even more acute. Clean Engineering might find its price undercut on a particular contract because, though they had similar direct costs, its competitors had used different bases for allocating indirect expenses to that contract. Other firms studied faced the same problem. Medlock Engineering was one of them. Particularly in Medlock Engineering's international market, the cost allocation methods used by competitors were often something of a mystery. Medlock wondered how the price differences met at the time of our study could be accounted for when all firms were bidding for contracts with identical specifications.

All this emphasizes the fact that the nature and complexity of cost structures varied from firm to firm depending, in part at least, on the way particular costs were treated. Unless he fully understands the way cost is linked to the variables that can be changed by pricing decisions, it is impossible for the manager to be quite sure what changes in costs his pricing decision will cause.

8.8.2 Fixed and Variable Costs

In looking at the way costs are divided up, we have so far emphasized the distinction between direct and indirect costs. For pricing purposes the more important distinction is between fixed and variable costs. The manager needs to know which costs are fixed and which variable for any particular pricing decision. Fixed costs are those that do not vary significantly as a result of any particular decision. For pricing decisions, the criterion is usually whether costs are fixed or variable in relation to changes in output. Fixed costs are irrelevant for a given pricing decision, unless that decision is expected to change output so much that even fixed costs have to be increased or reduced. Then, of course, they cease to be fixed and become variable. The convention is therefore that the phrase 'fixed costs' means fixed in relation to the volume of output. Even if output falls to zero, the same amount of fixed cost will be incurred, at least in the short run; this is what makes fixed costs so important to the price setter. In the long run, the firm's total receipts must be big enough to cover all its fixed costs, but there is no way of saying how much fixed cost 'should' be covered by any individual product.

Variable costs are those costs which change in total as output alters though, of course, variable costs per unit of output will often be constant as output changes. Businessmen often assume that variable costs alter in direct proportion with output; doing this certainly often leads to good business decisions. Variable costs usually include the wages of shop-floor workers, as well as material and power costs. However, we have seen that if the firm is not prepared to let employment fall below a certain level, even some labour costs have to be treated as fixed. Some distribution costs vary in proportion to the volume of output going through the distribution network though, in our studies, distribution costs were important mainly for the consumer goods manufacturers.

Obviously, not all costs fall neatly into one of these two categories. Costs may be 'semi-variable'. Two quite different kinds of semi-variable cost can be identified. Foremen's wages are an example of one kind. As output rises from zero to some level, one foreman is able to deal with it; once that level is exceeded, the job becomes too big for him and a second foreman has to be taken on. There will then be a discontinuous jump in costs at this level of output. Indeed, there will probably be further jumps at other, bigger outputs as more foremen are needed.

Another kind of semi-variable cost is exemplified by depreciation. One part of depreciation is the cost of obsolescence. This is a fixed cost because its size depends on how far the passage of time makes the asset less efficient because it is older, not on how much output it produces. However, depreciation contains a second element; what economists call 'user cost'. This alters in proportion to the amount of output being made with the capital asset. It is the cost of using the asset, rather than leaving it idle.

Semi-variable costs are often very difficult to measure. It is not always easy to know, with the one kind, how big the steps are; or, with the other, how big a percentage of semi-variable cost is fixed and how much variable.

The manager must be sure exactly what happens to cost as he changes the decision variables under his control. In pricing, it is important to know how cost changes with output. So, having identified the various costs associated with a particular product, and having quantified them, the manager must go on to separate out fixed, variable and stepped costs. He can then relate costs to output for the product and work out a cost function for it. Indeed, in appropriate cases, he can go on to construct a more complex model which takes into account all the relevant costs for a given product, as Universal Corporation did.

To show the kind of cost function we are discussing, we give a simple diagram relating the cost of a product to its output in Figure 8.1. This shows a simple cost function—what economists call the total cost curve, or function—for the product in question. Strictly speaking, the curve is likely to hold only for a relatively short period of time, during which all the costs entering into it are unchanged. The total cost curve here is *CL*. It shows that fixed costs of *OC* are incurred whatever the level of output, and that, in addition, increasing total amounts of variable cost are incurred if more of the product is made. The fact that *CL* is a straight line shows that variable cost per unit of output is constant. In Figure 8.1 total variable cost is *LM* at an output of *ON*. Variable cost per unit of output, or average variable cost, is *LM*/*ON*.

A truly accurate representation of the firm's total cost curve might well show that it really was a curve and/or that there were 'steps' at some points. Indeed, the total cost curve may well become vertical at its right-hand end, if output cannot be increased beyond some level, in the short run, whatever the firm does. If the firm goes on to expand its capacity, it will then incur a bigger total amount of fixed cost and there will probably be a new slope (or slopes) for the total cost curve as well. Variable cost will still be constant over a given range of output if the curve is a straight line, but the slope of the line may be different over different (in this case higher) ranges of output. The physical efficiency of the new plant may be different from that of the old, and/or money costs may have risen because of inflation.

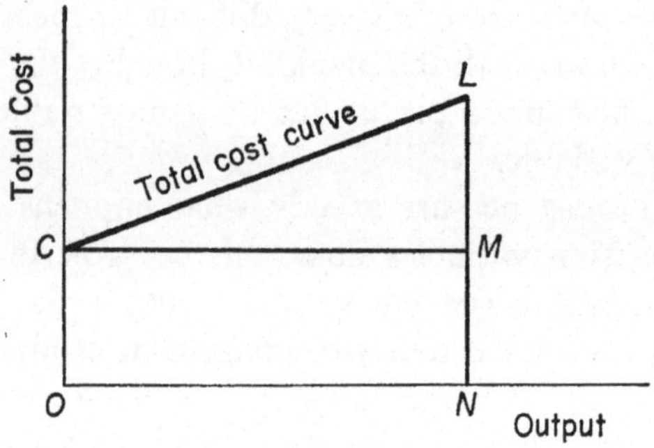

FIGURE 8.1

Such a situation is shown in Figure 8.2. Here, the firm shown in Figure 8.1 increases the size of its plant by adding a second unit, keeping the first one in operation. Its total cost curve now has a vertical section *AR*, at an output of *ON*. *AR* represents the fixed costs incurred in order to be able to produce in the second plant. The curve then traces out the line *PARD*. *RD* is less steep than *PA* (*CL*), showing that variable cost per unit of output is lower beyond *ON* than it was up to *ON*. *PA*, of course, is the same line as *CL* in Figure 8.1. However, since extra fixed costs of *AR* have been incurred in order to raise output, average cost (including fixed cost) will be bigger for outputs just above *ON* than for outputs just below it. The slope of *OA*(*AN*/*ON*) shows average cost per unit of output at an output of *ON*. The slope of *OT* shows the (higher) unit cost (*TM*/*OM*) at an output of *OM*. By the time output has risen to *OS*, average cost per unit is lower (*ES*/*OS*) than at *ON*. Though extra fixed costs of *AR* have been incurred to raise output beyond *ON*, lower variable costs per unit mean that total cost per unit is lower at an output of *OS* than for one of *ON*. It should be noted that Figure 8.2 assumes that the old plant is fully occupied (producing *ON* units) before the new one is brought into operation. It also implies that, if output falls, the new plant will be closed as soon as output falls to *ON*. However, especially if the new plant has lower variable costs than the old one, it may be the *new* plant which is given preference over the old one in sharing output between them. The total cost curve shown in Figure 8.2 would then have to be re-drawn, to show the true situation.

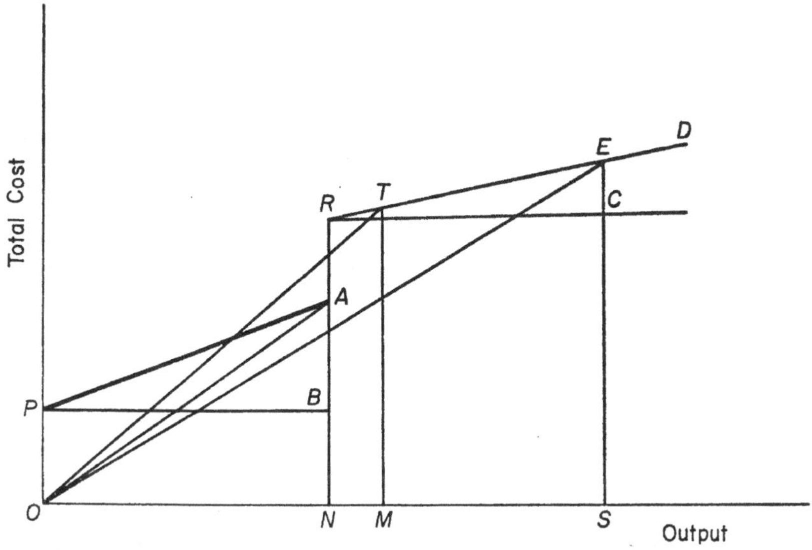

FIGURE 8.2

The kind of model which a firm will need to use if it wants to understand the relationship between relevant cost variables will be more complex even than this. The essential thing is that the manager should use a model that gives him an adequate understanding of the relationships between the cost and other variables relevant to his decision and which really does represent how plant will be used. How complex the 'model' will need to be will depend on the particular decision and on the manager. Managers in several of our firms would have found their decisions easier if they had possessed 'models' of this kind.

8.8.3 Changing the Information System

We have now looked at two of the three main steps which have to be taken if the manager is to obtain relevant cost data. We have considered what kinds of cost are relevant to pricing decisions, and we have seen how costs can be expected to alter when those decisions change one variable—the size of the firm's output. We went on to explain that other relevant relationships must be identified if good pricing decisions are to be made. The third step is therefore for the manager to be quite sure what cost data he needs from his firm's information system in order to specify relevant relationships precisely and which of this data he needs *ad hoc* and which on a continuing basis. Where necessary, the manager can then have the information system changed so that his needs are met.

Most managers will be working in firms with well-established information systems, centred on the accounting department. It is not always easy to change the information system and it is important that any changes that are made are both necessary and profitable. Our study has shown that managers often allow the way in which the information system has become accustomed to presenting costs to influence their decision making. This should not happen.

8.9 MARGINAL COST

In our discussion of cost information needed for pricing decisions, we have emphasized the necessity to distinguish between fixed and variable costs. However, this may not be sufficient. It may be necessary to use the economist's rather more sophisticated concept of marginal cost. There is no doubt that marginal cost information can be of great use in pricing decisions though, in a moment, we shall look at some of the problems one of our firms faced in trying to introduce marginal costing. We shall find that, in this case, using marginal cost did not prove easy.

We are concerned with pricing. If the firm is considering altering its price, it needs to know how sales will alter if price is changed and how big the consequent change in costs will be. It can then compare the change in total cost with the expected change in total receipts. Often, the basic piece of information needed is therefore what additional cost will be incurred in producing and selling one extra unit of output—that is, what we have already defined as 'incremental marginal cost' on page 139. It is often a useful concept as it stands.

Firms like Clean Engineering and Universal Corporation used it. However, in firms mass-producing consumer goods, a number of units of output may have to be considered instead of just one. Thus, Dee Plastics looked at the marginal cost of producing an extra 1,000 blind slats, and Basic Foods worked in terms of thousands of units of output rather than one. What incremental unit of output is the relevant one therefore depends on the industry and the firm.

One point must be cleared up at once. So far, we have written as though variable cost per unit of output is constant—as for example it was in Figure 8.1. Under this simplifying assumption, marginal cost is also constant, and indeed equal to variable cost per unit.

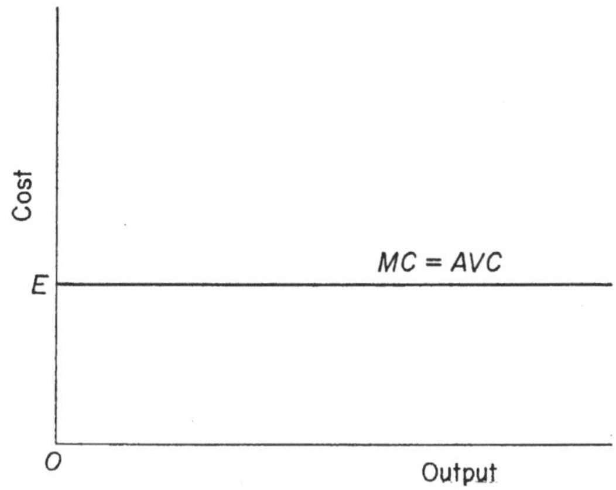

FIGURE 8.3a

This is why it has so far been possible for us to talk mainly of variable and fixed cost. On these assumptions, if one works with variable cost per unit, one is automatically working with marginal cost. Figure 8.3a shows variable cost per unit—or average variable cost, as the economist calls it—in a situation where variable cost per unit is constant. The average variable cost curve in Figure 8.3a can therefore be taken to show the behaviour of variable cost in Figure 8.1. The slope (*CL*) of the total cost curve in Figure 8.1 is represented by the height (*OE*) of the average variable cost curve in Figure 8.3a. Marginal cost (*MC*), in Figure 8.3a, is *OE* and is equal to average variable cost (*AVC*). Each extra unit of output costs the same amount to produce as each previous unit did. Variable cost is constant; it is also equal to marginal cost at every level of output.

In Figure 8.3b, however, the average variable cost curve (*AVC*) really is a curve. Variable cost per unit falls as output increases up to a given level (here *OM*) and then rises as output exceeds it. In these circumstances, not only is the marginal cost curve (*MC*) a curve; it is a *different* curve from the average variable cost curve—as Figure 8.3b shows. This is why it is so much easier to estimate marginal cost where the average variable cost curve really *is* a straight line; or where a straight line gives a good approximation to the true curve. Marginal and average variable cost are then equal.

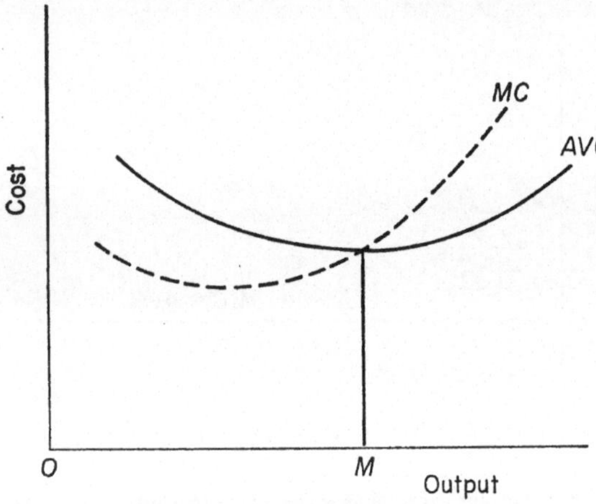

FIGURE 8.3b

Marginal cost is a vital concept for managers, because marginal costs are relevant costs. They are the costs which have to be included in the models managers should use in analysing pricing information. In Medlock Engineering, where selling in the export market earned very little profit, marginal cost computations told the sales manager what was the lowest price he could quote for a particular tender, and yet cover variable costs. With average costing, it would have been difficult, even impossible, for the manager to decide which were fixed and which variable costs. If trade is very depressed, it is essential to know just how low a price one can charge; otherwise one may miss worthwhile business. At the same time, working out what will be the addition to total cost if the business is taken gives one a figure below which it would be dangerous to go, because one would then not be recouping even all variable costs by taking the contract. Marginal cost therefore provides the key to pricing decisions in difficult trading conditions. It enables the manager to work out, before he decides what price to charge, what the implications will be if he cuts price to rock bottom.

Marginal pricing has been much less widely used than it should have been and both economists and accounts are to blame for this. Economists have been too blind to the difficulties businessmen meet in trying to calculate marginal cost, and to the danger of going bankrupt if the price they charge is too close to marginal cost (or even below it). Accountants do not seem to have tried hard enough to understand the logic that economists use in defining and applying marginal cost.

The concept of marginal cost is simple enough, and offers great benefits to managers in pricing and other decisions; but it is still widely ignored and even more widely misunderstood. One manager said that his firm did not use marginal cost because its products were too big! Wessex Timber, with some justification, argued that its methods of average costing gave as good data for pricing decisions as marginal costing would; or, at least, that any further information would not be worth as much as it would cost to collect it. For Wessex, because it was mass-producing timber with only a few separate operations carried out on the raw material, the marginal cost of producing, say, 100 cubic feet of finished timber was normally very close to the average variable cost of producing it.

Other managers did not see how marginal cost data could help them in pricing. Indeed, of the five firms which used marginal costing for pricing, three had been forced to do so by difficult trading conditions; otherwise, some variant of average cost would probably still have been used. Only Universal Corporation and Basic Foods were continually making use of marginal cost figures. Both firms found marginal costing an ideal tool and their managements were interested in new economic ideas like this. Wensum Engineering, which needed to use marginal costing if it was to increase profitability as it wished, had tried to introduce it but had failed to do so successfully.

Clean Engineering had begun to use marginal costing in preparing tender quotations for local authority business. It had wanted to pursue a more vigorous pricing policy in a market where its market share was continually being eroded by its competitors. Average costing did not allow its sales manager to pursue a sufficiently aggressive pricing policy. Without marginal costing, he would have been forced to work out his own split between fixed and variable costs in order to get the information he needed for setting prices. Once it became necessary to have marginal cost information, the firm's accounting system was reorganized to provide it.

8.10 'CONTRIBUTION'

As we have explained, the attraction of marginal costing is that it enables one to get a clearer picture of relevant costs, and so shows the likely behaviour of these costs in given circumstances. It also allows one to use a very important concept—'contribution'. If we split the firm's costs into fixed and variable costs, then to make a profit the firm must cover both variable and fixed costs and have something left over. We have argued that while it will be possible to identify the variable costs incurred in producing different amounts of a given product, it will often not be possible to do the same with fixed costs. It follows that the most one can legitimately say about the profitability of any individual product is that it has covered the variable costs incurred in its production and contributed a certain amount towards covering fixed cost and, hopefully, profit. This is why 'contribution' is a key concept if marginal costing is used. One needs to know what 'contribution' each product is making, over and above its variable cost, towards meeting the firm's total fixed cost and enabling it to earn a profit. How easy it is to define 'contribution' will depend on the cost and revenue functions facing the firm. Perhaps it is worth adding, rather obviously, that if the firm does *not* cover its fixed cost, then it will make a loss.

If the firm can sell as much of its product as it wishes at a 'going' price—as often happens with agricultural products and other basic materials—receipts per unit of product are constant whatever the level of output. If, at the same time, variable cost per unit of product (what economists call average variable cost) is constant, we have the situation shown in Figure 8.4a. Here, price per unit of product is *OP* and average variable cost is *OC*. The convenient thing about this situation is that, since price and average variable cost are each constant at every level of output, we can easily define contribution.

However, we must distinguish two meanings of the word 'contribution'. Contribution per unit of output is the difference between the price of a unit of output and the average variable cost incurred in producing each unit of output. This is often known as the 'contribution margin' or 'unit contribution'. In Figure 8.4a it is *CP* per unit. So, if the variable cost of producing each unit of output is 6p and each unit can be sold for 10p, unit contribution is 4p. Because we are making our simple assumption that both price and variable cost per unit of output are constant, then, in Figure 8.4a, we can define price. (*OP*), average variable cost (*OC*) and contribution margin (*CP*) unambiguously. They are the same at every level of output between zero and *OM*.

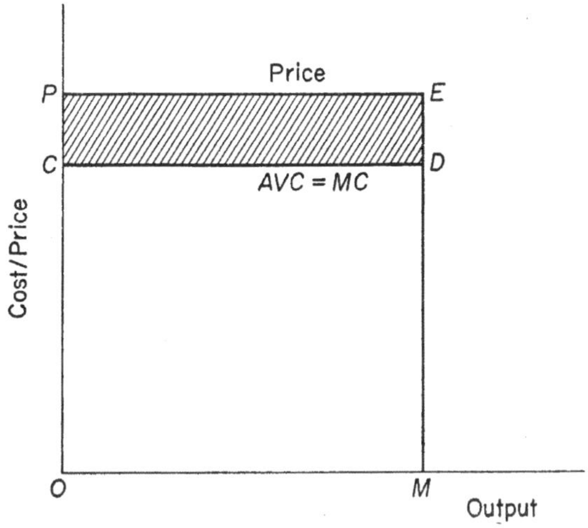

FIGURE 8.4a

Difficulties arise in the more normal situation where price falls as output rises and where variable cost also changes with output, as happens in Figure 8.4b. Unit contribution can then be calculated accurately only if the cost and revenue functions are known, and if great care is taken in working it out. Unit contribution will also be different at different levels of output. It is usually much more useful to think in terms of total contribution from the whole output of a given product, rather than contribution per unit. This is especially the case where the revenue and variable cost functions are not linear. In Figure 8.4a, total contribution is *CDEP*, with sales of *OM*. In Figure 8.4b, it is *RSTU*, with sales of *ON*. Whether these amounts of contribution are big enough to cover fixed costs will depend on whether fixed costs exceed *CDEP*, or *RSTU*, respectively. If not, a profit will be earned in each case.

We have explained that, despite its advantages, there was resistance to the use of marginal costing by both managers and accountants in the firm we studied. One can see that average costing has great attractions for firms in comfortable competitive positions, where there is no difficulty in earning the desired rate of profit; it is so easy to use. Yet, even here, marginal costing would allow more

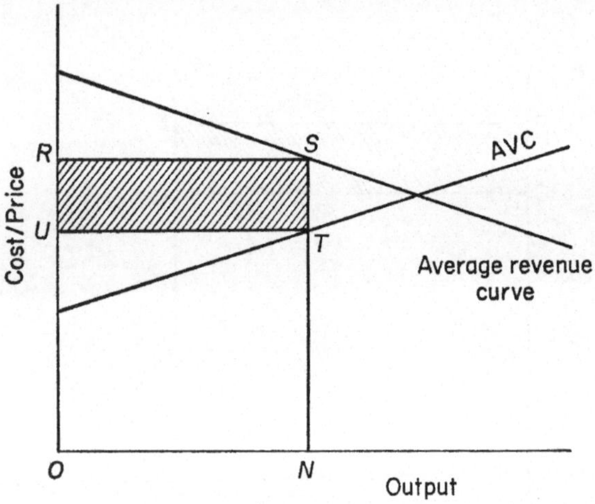

FIGURE 8.4b

flexibility in pricing. What is puzzling is the failure of one or two firms, which genuinely did want to increase their profits, to use marginal costing. Its major advantage is that it allows flexibility in pricing and this is what firms which want to maximize their profits need.

Marginal costing and contribution pricing are too often seen as last ditches for defence rather than as first lines of attack. Our firms often calculated marginal cost only when there was a difficult order to price, or where there was extremely keen pricing, usually in a market in recession. Otherwise, average costing, with indirect costs allocated to individual products, was used. Managers in our firms therefore tended to associate marginal costing with dumping, slumps and price wars. It was rarely understood by managers and usually seen as too difficult by accountants.

8.11 USING MARGINAL COSTING

We now discuss two firms we studied where marginal costing was introduced voluntarily—with no market problems imposing it.

8.11.1 Wensum Engineering Ltd

We have mentioned that Wensum Engineering Limited had difficulty in introducing marginal costing. The story is instructive. Wensum started to think about using marginal costing when a young man who was very enthusiastic about it joined the company as deputy accountant. About this time, the assistant accountant of the parent firm was thinking about introducing marginal costing, although he was aware of its difficulties and drawbacks. He was loath to let the whole group use it, in case some subsidiaries let price fall too far towards marginal cost. However, he felt that Wensum's management was advanced enough to use marginal costing for a trial period. If the trial was successful, he hoped that marginal costing could be extended throughout the whole group.

Initially, the managing director of Wensum accepted the idea of introducing marginal costing and the assistant accountant prepared a highly-technical report on it. However, this did more harm than good. Several people, including the managing director, said afterwards that they 'could not make head or tail of it'. The accountant of Wensum, too, said that, on reflection, he realized that he should not have allowed the report to be circulated in its original form, not least because it contained a very complicated explanation of marginal costing taken from a research paper.

The assistant accountant's document began, 'It has been assumed in this report that the decision to go ahead with marginal costing has been taken, so that no attempt has been made to debate the advantages and disadvantages.' Yet almost every manager in the firm still had to be persuaded to accept it. After proceeding to give the description of marginal costing from the research paper, the report ended with details of the changes required in the accounting system if marginal costing was to be used.

The man who was acting as marketing manager in the company at the time was not keen on the adoption of marginal costing, and the works manager was hotly opposed to it. One of the latter's main arguments was that, under the new system, stock would be valued at a figure that excluded overheads. He said that this would make it impossible for him to compare his department's current performance with that in earlier years. He, and others in Wensum, also argued that the temptations of marginal costing would soon become only too clear to salesmen. To justify accepting orders at reduced prices, they would now be able to use the excuse that the orders were still 'making some contribution'. In applying marginal costing, the accountant had tried to split factory overheads into their fixed and variable components, but had come to the conclusion that more and more costs were fixed in the short run, especially since the firm had become increasingly reluctant to dismiss any of its employees. Furthermore, if Wensum had valued inventory at marginal cost, regarding all overheads as fixed, this would have meant writing down stock and work in progress by half a million pounds. Wensum's accountant had almost persuaded the deputy accountant of the parent firm to accept this writing down, when the marginal costing approach was abandoned because of the resistance to it within Wensum.

The accountant of Wensum said he had tried to discover other industrial firms which were using a marginal costing approach to pricing, but could find none. He felt that the real reason why the attempt to introduce marginal costing had failed was that Wensum's top managers did not really understand it, and so did not work for its success. However, he doubted whether it could have been successfully introduced, even in the most favourable situation, because the chief accountant of the parent firm still had his worries about allowing marginal costing to be used in other divisions. He still feared that difficult market conditions might lead salesmen from these divisions to quote prices very near to marginal cost in order to keep business.

What happened in Wensum may be an extreme example of the problem of introducing marginal costing, but it does show that educational (or at least persuasive) activities are often part of the businessman's job. Since few businessmen would claim much expertise in this kind of activity, there would be a good deal to be said for seeking outside advice. A great deal of effort would have been required in Wensum to prepare managers at all levels to accept marginal costing. Yet no real attempt was made; the report simply referred rather bleakly to the 'complete change in thinking required'.

One interesting point is that once marginal costing had been abandoned, Wensum's accountant wanted to drop the reporting of contribution margins. The works manager (originally, it will be recalled, strongly opposed to the adoption of marginal costing) now said that he had got used to them. Largely for this reason, they continued to be used in the company's reporting system even though marginal costing had been abandoned.

8.11.2 Universal Corporation

We have already noted the use of marginal costing by Universal Corporation, where it was introduced successfully. Physical production conditions favoured its introduction in Universal Corporation, because marginal cost was increasing at every relevant level of output. Average cost was therefore also rising, though less rapidly than marginal cost. Universal Corporation had previously calculated its desired price per unit directly from figures for average cost at the forecast volume of sales. However, if sales exceeded the forecast level, Universal suffered a loss on the extra units sold because the price of those units was below their (increasing) marginal cost. Universal Corporation had made a study of the probable behaviour of marginal costs over the next few years, to discover how they were likely to alter—given the forecast growth of demand, technological developments and planned capital expenditure. This study indicated that, once the capital investment projects that were in hand had been completed, marginal cost at relevant levels of output was unlikely to differ significantly from current levels of average cost. In view of this, it was decided that a system of prices based on marginal cost could best be introduced if Universal Corporation moved fairly slowly towards the new system.

8.11.3 Introducing Marginal Costing

Our conclusion must be that not all firms find it easy to introduce marginal costing, though if difficult trading conditions force them to do so they can usually introduce it perfectly successfully. There are two main problems. First, how can the firm ensure that marginal costing is sufficiently understood by its own management to be accepted? Second, how can it make certain that some prices are not cut too far, especially where individual salesmen are left to set prices? There is always the danger that they will cut them with the excuse that 'we are still making some contribution'.

8.12 OPPORTUNITY COST

We have already mentioned the concept of opportunity cost. None of our firms made specific use of it. Yet it is often useful to look at opportunity cost, explicitly, as one of the ways of measuring the cost of using the resources needed for any one contract, product or customer. Opportunity cost measures the cost of a given course of action in terms of the opportunities sacrificed. The sacrifice occurs because, if the given course of action is taken, some alternative course of action cannot be taken. So, for example, the opportunity cost of introducing Product X is the 'contribution' on Product Y, which will have to be forgone. For if Product X is introduced Product Y cannot be. The problem over opportunity cost was that the accounting systems of the firms we studied were not designed to calculate it.

The firms where the notion of opportunity cost was most obviously relevant were Heavy Technology and Medlock Engineering. Because plant was being operated well below capacity, the opportunity cost of taking any order was usually zero; no sacrifice at all was implied if a given order was taken. No alternative work was available. Indeed, in very depressed times, opportunity cost might even have been negative. If the business in question were not obtained, the firm might think it essential to go on paying some wages solely in order to keep the labour force together. Taking the contract would therefore prevent losses being as big as they would otherwise have been. This does not mean that it will always pay to take business at less than variable cost if opportunity cost is negative for a given order. For example, it may be feared that to do so would mean setting off a ruinous price war so that, for succeeding orders, there would be even bigger losses. However, opportunity cost is still the relevant cost to consider. Most managers in the firms we studied were looking at opportunity costs, at least in their important decisions. But they did so as individuals, and not as part of a formal pricing procedure.

Perhaps the simplest use of opportunity cost is in 'make or buy' decisions and in transfer pricing. The cost of making the product, or component, oneself is the contribution to profit one loses by forgoing the opportunity of making something else. In Heavy Technology of course, the alternative was to make nothing. With the alternative opportunity of earning no contribution at all, opportunity cost is obviously zero. Transfer prices can also be based on opportunity cost. If one did not make a product oneself, one would have to buy it in. The value of a product made by one's own firm can therefore be measured by the price one would have to pay if one bought in the alternative.

Opportunity cost, in a pricing decision, more usually means the contribution forgone by setting one price instead of another, or by taking one order instead of another. The correctness of estimates of opportunity cost is very hard to test in practice. This is because, when any given action is taken, all the alternative actions are automatically ruled out. Any estimate of their effects is, at best, uncertain. Probability theory and statistical techniques may have something to offer in estimating opportunity cost in future, but they offer little at present.

8.13 SUNK COSTS

The final cost concept which must be mentioned is that of 'sunk costs'. Once a cost has been irretrievably incurred, and cannot be recovered, then it becomes irrelevant to any decision taken subsequently. So, for example, once a railway track has been laid, its cost becomes irrelevant to current decisions on rail fares. Only out-of-pocket costs incurred in maintaining the track in the present are relevant. This is not to say that the firm should fail to recoup its sunk costs out of price if it can do so. Nor, indeed, is to say that a firm which frequently incurs large amounts of sunk costs, and then fails to recoup them in the prices it charges, can be happy about the position. It may well go bankrupt. All we can say is that the profit-maximizing (loss-minimizing) course of action must be taken irrespective of the amount of sunk cost which has been laid out.

A good example of this was given in Section 8.5.2. in our discussion of Fourways Engineering. In calculating the cost of the product we studied, Fourways included a large amount of cost incurred in designing it, tooling up for its production, making development models, and carrying out the original market research and sales promotion. It is true that it would have been best if the price could have been set high enough to cover these costs. It is also true that if Fourways consistently failed to cover these design, tooling, and launching costs on many of its products, it would face big financial problems. However, once incurred, all these were sunk costs. What Fourways had to do (what it perhaps tried to do, though rather half-heartedly), was to maximize the contribution from the product.

By definition, no product can do better than that. Yet, including sunk costs within the calculation may well lead to a total cost per unit, and therefore price per unit, higher than the profit-maximizing price. Sunk costs are always irrelevant to current pricing decisions.

8.14 OTHER INTERNAL INFORMATION

We have spent a great deal of time discussing the cost information required for pricing, partly because it is important and partly because there is much disagreement among managers, accountants and economists about how cost information can best be presented to those taking pricing decisions. However, other information from within the firm is also important for pricing, and we end this chapter with a brief discussion of the other internal information which our firms provided for price setters.

In our firms, most of this information was provided through the control accounting system. We saw in Chapter 4 that most of our firms prepared budgets quarterly. Figures for actual performance were then circulated to managers at least monthly. Often, at least part of the information was provided more frequently. In this section we consider the main elements of this control information—information about production and inventories; sales turnover (revenue); and profit.

The value of this kind of internal information lay more in showing when, and in which direction, prices should be changed rather than by what amount. For example, sales turnover and profit figures showed how actual sales and profits compared with forecasts and therefore whether higher or lower prices, and more or less marketing effort in general, was needed in the rest of the year to achieve the budget. This highlights two important points. First, it shows how easy it is to 'satisfice'. If sales are ahead of budget, the tendency is to relax and to regard having reached the budget as an adequate performance. Second, it shows the tyranny of the calendar. It appears to be a common temptation to increase or reduce sales effort *for the rest of the year*, if sales are below or above budgeted levels, whether or not a year is the right unit for determining sales effort.

Similarly, the relationship between actual and budgeted profit was an important factor in determining whether prices needed altering and/or whether the company could be more selective in putting in tenders. Usually, it was only if actual profit was below budgeted profit that action was taken. Again, we can see how easy it is to slip into satisficing patterns of behaviour.

8.14.1 Production and Inventory Information

For our firms, production and inventory information was less important than profit and market-share information in determining whether prices needed altering. However, production and inventory information did have some influence, especially through the effects of levels of production or inventory on cost and price. In five cases, the percentage of capacity being used at relevant points of time had a considerable influence. It affected the cost figures used in deciding whether to quote, and at what price to quote, for particular business. These firms were: Dee Plastics, Heavy Technology, Medlock Engineering, Wessex Timber and Clean Engineering. In these firms, estimated costs were based on the anticipated level of demand rather than on the percentage of capacity currently employed.

Levels of inventory, and of the cost of holding inventory, had a similar influence. The consumer good manufacturers (Alpha Ltd, Gamma Ltd, Basic Foods Ltd, and Epsilon Ltd) produced for stock, but with fast-moving branded items they were able to tailor their production closely to demand. Only four of the industrial good manufacturers produced for stock. These were: Dee, Wensum, Fourways, and Wessex. Wensum had run into problems. Its stocks were too high because it had overestimated the size of the market for its products at the prices it charged.

8.14.2 Revenue Information

Strictly speaking, revenue information should perhaps be regarded as external rather than internal information. However, since a major role of the control accounting system has always been to monitor profits, and since profit is equal to revenue minus cost, we shall deal with revenue and profit information here.

Actual revenue figures for past months or quarters were available to managers in all our firms as part of control information. However, as with costs, price setters were less concerned with past than with future revenue. In each firm, revenue forecasts were made by multiplying estimates of sales volume (market information) by current or projected prices. More time and care was taken in doing this in firms with clear marketing and sales-value objectives. These included all the consumer good firms, as well as the Surgical Instrument

Company and Wessex Timber. Indeed, in all our consumer good firms, detailed proposals for price changes were drawn up, and revenue information formed part of these. In other cases, it is less clear that prospective revenue was adequately taken into account. For example, the arrangements for Wensum's price review did not allow detailed calculations of sales turnover at different prices to be made. They were postponed until any revisions caused by changes in price were made in the budget. In other firms, again, like Heavy Technology and Clean Engineering, we were concerned with the effect that individual orders, taken at particular prices, were having on the turnover of the whole department for a year, or a number of years. Probability theory can help here. It can show what the 'expected value' of turnover for a future period will be, even before it is known which individual orders will be obtained. All a firm needs to know is the probability of each individual tender being accepted.

8.14.3 Profit Information

We have already emphasized the important role of the level of profits in determining the time at which price changes were considered and the degree of effort put into marketing.

All firms kept a check on operating results and on current profitability by providing management with regular cost, profit and sales reports. Projections of future profits were made by all firms. These projections were made monthly, as well as whenever price changes were being considered. Among the industrial good manufacturers, profit projections were normally made for longer periods as part of the budgeting process, as well as for particular pricing decisions. These profit figures were important where firms attempted to monitor the effect of pricing decisions on profitability.

It is true, of course, that price setters were interested in the effects of their decisions on future rather than past profits. Calculations of such effects were usually made by price setters themselves, or in proposals put to them, on the basis of the kind of cost and revenue information discussed in this chapter. As we have seen, because only five of our firms calculated marginal cost, few of them worked in terms of contribution. A number, unwisely in our view, attempted to calculate the 'profitability' of individual products.

We were rather surprised by one fact. Most managers in our firms seemed to think that errors were likely to occur in calculating (and more especially in allocating) costs for individual products or product groups. They accepted that cost figures were unlikely to be accurate to more than 5 per cent or 10 per cent. Yet, despite the fact that the profit figures were based on these cost figures, managers treated them as being more accurate than the costs from which they were calculated. This puzzled and worried us, though of course it is most important where profitability figures for individual products, or orders, are arrived at by allocating large amounts of indirect cost to these individual products or orders. It is less important where one is concerned with the profit of a product group, department, or firm. Cost can more accurately be allocated to a department than a product group; and to a product group than to an individual product.

8.15 CONCLUSIONS

Those responsible for pricing need information presented in a form which shows which costs are relevant to a particular decision. They need information which shows clearly which costs will be affected if one price is chosen rather than another, and by how much. Where profitability needs to be improved, and/or where a flexible pricing policy is needed, it is important to separate fixed and variable costs—that is, those costs which will, and those which will not, be affected by a decision to change prices, and so output. Where 'absorption' costing is used, and overhead costs are allocated to individual products, this is rarely possible. In several of our firms, the allocation of overheads to individual products bedevilled pricing by implying a need to recover allocated overheads, and even sunk costs, in the price of each product.

The price setter's main need is rather for information about the 'contribution' which each product makes individually, and all products make in total, to fixed costs and, once these are covered, to profit. The information given to price fixers must therefore ensure that they can see the effects which their decisions will have on current profitability. It must put them in a position to estimate these effects on future profits. In other words, it is important that price fixers should be provided with information which makes them fully aware of the implications of their decisions for cost, revenue, profit, production and inventories. Management accounting systems should be organized to provide this information, and both managers and accountants should be educated to appreciate the value and the pitfalls of marginal thinking.

In most firms, improvements in the supply of information are hampered by the separation of information-gathering and information-using activities. Accordingly, we found a tendency for information gatherers to supply only information which was available, or which could easily be made available, through established operating routines. Conversely, some price setters required information which was not readily available to information gatherers, and hence not supplied by them.

There is no obvious remedy for this situation. It is not possible to combine information-gathering and information-using activities, because different specialisms are appropriate to each. Better communication between the collectors and users of information is highly desirable. Each can then appreciate more fully the needs and difficulties of the other, and gain a better insight into the costs and benefits of improved information systems. Improved communications should at least ensure that accountants do not, as we found in one firm, refuse to hand over detailed accounting information to price setters because they cannot see its relevance to pricing. They would also make the task of educating managers and accountants to think marginally more meaningful to both.

In the near future, a large number of firms will be installing integrated information systems. This will have two advantages for pricing. First, there will no longer be the split between the collection of market and cost information that we found in our firms. Second, the fact that these will be computer information systems will mean that the emphasis will be on the provision of information about *relevant* (usually marginal) costs. This will be partly because more mathematicians, operational researchers, etc., will be employed in designing information systems. For pricing, the introduction of computer information systems is likely to be an unmixed blessing, though it will clearly lead to problems elsewhere in the firm. For example, firms will have to decide what the role of accountants is to be. Many accountants will have to be re-trained to understand computer systems and the thinking associated with them.

CHAPTER 9

The Pricing Decision

9.1 RECAPITULATION

At this point, we must remind ourselves what we have done so far. First, we looked at business objectives and, in particular, identified the objectives which our firms pursued in their pricing decisions. We went on to consider information for pricing decisions. We distinguished between the information firms would have in an ideal world and the information they actually had.

We shall continue to make the same distinction in looking at the pricing decision itself. In this chapter, we shall consider how pricing decisions would be taken in an ideal world. In Chapter 10 we shall look at the actual process of decision-taking in the firms we studied. We shall comment on differences between the actual and the ideal in Chapter 11.

In this chapter, as in the check list, we shall say little about objectives. We saw in Chapters 5 and 6 that pricing objectives are usually multiple, so that there are often conflicts between different pricing objectives. We saw that the difficulties which this would cause even for a one-man business are increased in larger firms because different individuals and departments have their own objectives and, within varying limits, they are able to pursue them. They try to sub-optimize and sometimes succeed. The problem of setting objectives is therefore often a difficult one, but at the end of Chapter 6 we suggested some ways of reducing it.

We argued that, in an ideal world, conflicts between objectives would be identified and different objectives given appropriate weights. We went on to suggest that the firm was unlikely to go so far as to establish a 'goal index' which would give precise weight to different objectives and so provide a basis for pricing decisions. However, this is a future possibility that should not be forgotten. We argued that at present all one could do was to rank pricing objectives in a way that would allow the firm to give roughly the intended weight to each of them in pricing decisions. Finally, we suggested that the firm should ensure that each individual responsible for pricing decisions, at whatever level in the firm, needed to be absolutely clear what objective(s) he was expected to pursue. Only in this way could sub-optimization (or indeed non-optimization) be kept to a minimum.

The first step in any pricing decision is therefore to go through the steps set out in Sections A and B of the check list. The person responsible should ensure that the product to be priced and the nature of the pricing decision are identified, and the objectives clearly understood by everyone concerned with the decision. The second step is to obtain the optimal amount of relevant information, as suggested in Sections C and D of the check list, and to analyse it on the lines we discussed in Chapters 7 and 8.

9.2 THE ALTERNATIVES

We now move on to the decision itself and things become more complicated still. We are no longer concerned separately with the way in which, say, costs alter with changes in output, or in output per man; or by how much the amount sold is increased by reducing price. We are concerned with cost and demand factors at the same time. We have to look at the effects which a change in price has on both demand and output, and so on costs and profits. If advertising, or other sales promotion activities alter too, even more variables have to be watched. We are concerned with relationships between a number (perhaps a large number) of interrelated variables.

The result is that we have to tackle a problem touched on briefly in Chapter 1. The pricing decision becomes very difficult for human beings to take. The manager must therefore think of using a computer. The human brain cannot work simultaneously in more than three dimensions at most. It is true that we often succeed in solving problems involving many more than three variables, but we do so by breaking the problem into a number of small parts, in each of which only two (or perhaps three) variables are involved. The point is not so much that managers who try to solve multi-dimensional problems are likely to get the wrong answer; though this is possible. The point is that it is nowadays no longer necessary for human beings to try to solve them. The computer is ideally suited for analysing relationships between large numbers of variables, so that it is foolish not to use it where this is practicable. The computer will not necessarily solve the problem outright. But, even if it does not, it will analyse the information the firm has more quickly, and probably more fully and usefully, than will a human being. Those responsible for pricing decisions still have their own contribution to make; they will have to take the decision itself. But their decision-taking will now begin from the computer print-out rather than ending with it.

The complexity of the relationships met with in pricing makes it important for us to understand what the relevant variables are, before we begin to look at the way they are interrelated. What we have done first, in Section E of the check list, is therefore to identify the most important variables. We have done this, not simply for pricing decisions, but for marketing decisions generally. We begin from price because this is the decision variable we are primarily concerned with in this book. We want to know how well the firm would achieve its objectives if it charged each of a number of different prices. Once it knows what the volume of sales will be at each of these prices, the calculation of total sales receipts—what economists call total revenue—is a matter of simple arithmetic. However, if the volume of sales at each price level is not known, a more lengthy process is needed. The first step is to calculate what total receipts would be at each price on the assumption that various possible levels of sales are achieved. At the same time, it may be necessary to establish known (or possible) relationships between a number of alternative levels of promotional and advertising expenditure and the levels of sales—and so of total sales receipts—which the firm would achieve at each of these levels of promotional outlay.

In the check list, we went on to explain that the firm would then need to decide what levels of output these calculations implied, making allowance if necessary for increases or decreases in inventories of the product being priced, at some or all levels of sales. The firm could then work out what were the identifiable costs associated with each level of output. This would allow it to calculate 'contribution', as defined in Chapter 8, for each of these levels of output. Assuming that profit is the important objective, the different amounts of 'contribution' to profit which would be earned if the firm were to charge each of the alternative levels of price open to it, can then be compared.

At the same time, the firm can discover what percentage of its capacity would be employed at each alternative level of price. Keeping activity at or above a given proportion of capacity, is often an important objective; we have seen that it often was in the firms we studied. Any other necessary calculation about levels, or changes in levels, of production, inventory, etc. can be made too. For each level of price or advertising expenditure being considered it will also be necessary to calculate what will be sales volume, profitability, etc.

There are often what economists call complementary or competitive relationships between the products of the firm. Increased sales of product X will increase the sales of product Y if they are complements (like transistor radios and batteries). Increased sales of product X will reduce sales of product Y if they are competitive (two similar kinds of electric motor). It is therefore important for the firm to estimate the full effects on its overall profitability of a change in the price of one product by taking these complementary and competitive relationships into account. The firm must try to judge how far the change in the price of the product being considered will alter the sales of the firm's other products, and so its total sales turnover and total profitability.

All this information should be used to estimate the effect of the price change on the firm's ability to provide itself with finance. Will the price change make it easier or harder for the firm to generate from within the cash it must have in order to carry out its operations? Will it make it easier or more difficult for the firm to raise new funds from banks, shareholders or other lenders? All these effects should be calculated as accurately as possible.

Turning to the outside world, the firm will need to calculate what will be the effect on the rate of growth of its sales, and so on its market share, if the various possible price changes are made. Similarly, the firm will have to estimate the effect of the price changes on its competitive position and, especially in oligopoly, on the pricing and marketing policies of its competitors. These effects may be difficult to judge, but an attempt must be made. Otherwise the problem of how to set optimal prices is impossible to solve.

The firm will have to calculate the effects on its own sales volume, price, promotional expenditure, etc. if each of the likely reactions occurs. Nor will even this be the end of the calculations. The firm must go on to decide what would be its own reactions to the changes which any decision of its own has induced in its competitors' price policies. There may well be a whole series of events to consider if a chain reaction begins when the firm changes its price. The whole series must be considered, not just the first step. We have already expressed our doubts about how far sophisticated techniques like game theory can at present help the firm to predict the whole chain of events which will follow a price change in oligopoly. However, a watch should be kept on developments in this field, since they could prove important over the next few years. Unless and until there are such developments, judgement and hunch will be the most important skills demanded by pricing. Whatever method is chosen, however, it is important that the best possible predictions should be made of what competitors' reactions will be in oligopolistic markets.

Anyone who previously doubted whether we were right to emphasize the complexity of the calculations required in looking at the implications of charging different prices should by now be convinced. Yet, unless all relevant alternatives have been considered in this way, a good decision is impossible. With the information outlined above, correctly analysed, those who have to take pricing decisions will find them almost automatic. Indeed, if *all* the relevant factors had been included, one could programme a computer to take the decision itself. Usually, it will be desirable for the price fixers to take the computer print-out (or figures produced by human beings) as a starting point and make their own decision. They will want to be sure that no obvious mistakes have been made and that any factors not allowed for in the computer programme are taken into account. But this is all. The pricing decision should be taken in as rational a way as possible, with managers relying on the computer where they can.

Logic is easiest to apply where the firm's objective is to maximize profit and where the relationships relevant to the decision are known. We begin with the simplest case, where the problem is to set the most profitable price, leaving advertising and sales promotion expenditure constant, where the firm knows the shape of the average revenue curve and where there is no interdependence between the prices of different firms—as in oligopoly. Such a situation is shown in Figure 9.1. We now have to bring demand and cost factors together. For simplicity, we have used a horizontal average variable cost curve, though not implying that such a curve will be found in practice, We have also used a straight-line and downward-sloping average revenue curve. This implies that the firm is operating in monopolistic, rather than oligopolistic, conditions. Let us suppose that the firm is considering which of three prices to charge—*OP*, *OR*, and *OS*. The corresponding scales would be OM_1, OM_3 and OM_2, respectively. We have already argued that one should work in terms of contribution, so that the question is which price will give the biggest rectangle, like PP_1WT, between the average variable cost curve and the average revenue curve. In this particular example, it is clear that PP_1WT is the biggest possible rectangle. The profit maximizing price is OP, with sales of OM_1. Prices OR and OS would give smaller contributions—would have smaller rectangles. We may add at this point that if one drew in the marginal revenue curve, showing the addition to total revenue from selling one more unit of output, this would cut the marginal cost curve at an output of OM. For, as we already know, the average variable cost curve and the marginal

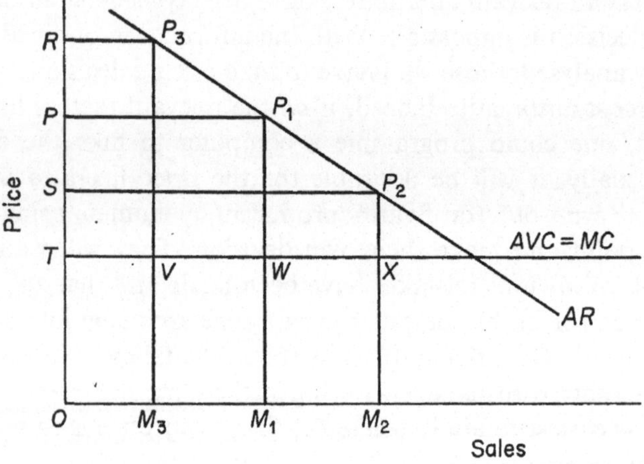

FIGURE 9.1

cost curve will coincide when the former is horizontal. The text-book rule, that marginal cost will equal marginal revenue in the profit-maximizing situation, holds. However, since firms will rarely know the shape of the marginal revenue curve, looking for the profit-maximizing rectangle is a much better procedure to follow.

Perhaps it is worth explaining why it is that maximizing contribution in Figure 9.1 will also maximize profit. We have split costs into fixed and variable costs, and have shown variable costs in the average variable cost curve. Although, if we have made this split, we shall know the total size of fixed costs, we have not shown fixed costs in Figure 9.1. If fixed costs really are fixed, then maximizing contribution must maximize the difference between (constant) fixed costs and contribution. As we have already seen, it is the difference between contribution and fixed cost which represents profit. A rectangle like PP_1WT is equal in area to total revenue (price multiplied by quantity sold) minus total variable cost (average variable cost times quantity sold). This is what we mean by total contribution. In this example, it is clear that PP_1WT is the biggest of the three rectangles—PP_1WT, SP_2XT and RP_3VT. *OP* is the profit-maximizing price.

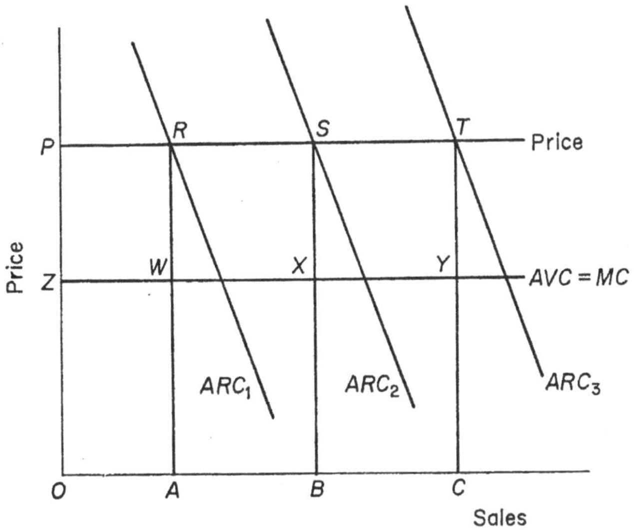

FIGURE 9.2

A similar analysis can be used to show what is the most effective scale of advertising. For simplicity, let us suppose that the firm has decided to charge a given price (*OP*) for a product, but is choosing between three different amounts to be spent on advertising. This situation is shown in Figure 9.2.

At the (given) price of *OP*, the average revenue curve is, say, ARC_1, if there is no advertising. At this point, contribution—shown in Figure 9.1—is *PRWZ*. If the firm now adds £10,000 to its advertising budget, the average revenue curve becomes ARC_2. Total contribution is increased by the rectangle *RSXW*. The question now is whether this rectangle represents more or less than £10,000. If it represents more than £10,000, then the increase in advertising will be worth while. One can then go on to ask whether it would be worth adding another £10,000, to move the average revenue curve to ARC_3. If one does this, contribution will now be increased by *STYX*. One can again ask whether this increase in contribution is worth more than £10,000. If these are the only alternatives the firm is considering, it should make its choice by discovering which of these two amounts spent on advertising gives the biggest increase in contribution over and above the amount spent for advertisement. If both increases in contribution are less than what has to be spent on advertising to obtain them, no advertising should be done.

However, all this is already becoming very complex and, if one allowed for more than one price at the same time as more than one amount of advertising, it would become more complicated still. This adds point to our claim that most of the calculations our firms made were too simple. Of course, if one added other forms of sales promotion then even more complexity would be introduced.

Since we are concerned with pricing, we shall concentrate on the problems of pricing and look at them in a little more detail. Even with pricing, there is still a big question. The main unknown is the shape of the average revenue curve. Is there anything one can do to pin this shape down? One can often do more than businessmen imagine. One can, for example, use the kind of bracketing process described in our study of Basic Foods to settle the estimated size of particular variables. For example, what one needs to know, in order to define the average revenue curve, is what quantity of output will be sold at a particular price. One way of attempting to decide this is to ask whether a particular level of sales appears too big at a given price, and whether a different level appears too small. Continuing this bracketing process, one may well be able to agree on a particular level of sales.

A similar way of proceeding is to use the analysis shown in Figure 9.3. The price of the product here is *OP*. Again, we assume that the average variable cost curve is horizontal and therefore identical with the marginal cost curve; but we do this only for simplicity. Sales at the existing price of *OP* are *OM*. The firm is considering reducing its price from *OP* to OP_1. The firm can now ask one key question. This is: How far would sales *have* to rise for us to be no better or worse off, having reduced price from *OP* to OP_1? The answer is simply a matter of geometry. All the firm has to do is to find a rectangle, which turns out to be P_1TYV, equal in size to the area *PRXV*. Both of these areas represent contribution, although at two different levels of price. We need to know nothing whatever about the shape of the average revenue curve in order to do this. However, the firm can now go on to the second question. This is: Do we think sales will, in fact, rise by more than *MN*? If not, then we should leave things alone, because we can do no better. However, while this method tells us nothing we do not already know, it does enable us to ask these

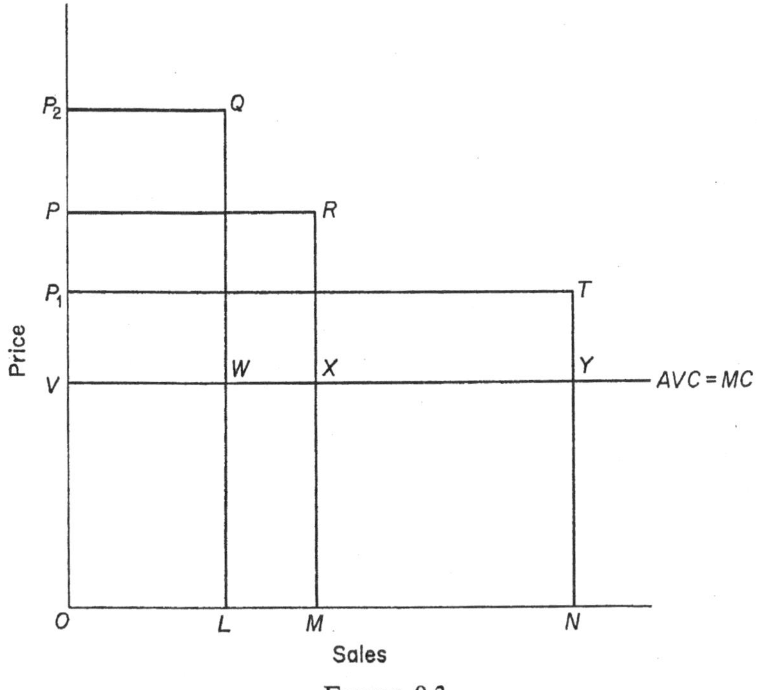

FIGURE 9.3

important questions. If the firm cannot answer the question: 'Do we think sales really will rise by the amount needed to keep contribution at the present level?', then there is no logical way of setting price at the profit-maximizing level. However, the analysis does, for example, enable one to be sure that such a level of sales is technically possible. One can make sure production capacity, support facilities, etc. are adequate, to produce and distribute it. Firms have been known to discover that the level of price they were considering would have had to lead to a level of sales that was beyond their capabilities, at least in the short run, if profit were to be maintained.

Similarly, of course, the analysis in Figure 9.3 can deal with the situation where the firm is considering whether to raise prices. For example, in Figure 9.3, should prices be increased from *OP* to OP_2? Again, this analysis gives one the right question to answer. One has to find the output (in fact *OL*) where the area of P_2QWV is equal to that of the area giving the present contribution of *PRXV*. Again, one can go on to ask: Will sales, in fact, fall by more than *LM*? If they will, then one should not alter the price. Again, if one cannot answer this question, there is no rational way of deciding what price to charge. However, even if an answer is given, one may have to look at other factors—like the administrative cost and inconvenience of changing prices—or put these into the diagram in the first place. Of course, one can also use arithmetic or algebra rather than geometry. Indeed, in business, one would almost certainly do so. However, in our present discussion, geometry has the advantage of being more easily understood.

Another way of tackling the same problem is somewhat more complicated. One can use probabilities. Suppose, for example, that a firm is wondering whether to change from a price of £0·50 to one of £0·40. With a price of £0·50, unit contribution is £0·25. Total contribution, with sales of 10,000 units, is therefore £2,500. The question is, what will it be at the price of £0·40? Suppose the firm is not certain what its sales will be, but it is able to assign probabilities to certain possible levels of sales. For example, suppose it thinks that there is a 20 per cent probability that sales will be 13,000 units; a 50 per cent probability that they will be 14,000; and a 30 per cent probability that they will be 15,000. It can now work out what is known as the 'expected value' for sales. Well-established principles say that it has to multiply each possible level of sales by the probability of that level of sales being reached. If it then sums the results, it has the expected value of sales.

Here, one has:

(1) *Probable Level of Sales*	(2) *Probability of being Achieved*	(1) *1 × 2*
13,000	0·2	2,600
14,000	0·5	7,000
15,000	0·3	4,500
Expected value of sales = 14,100 units		14,100

Suppose that unit contribution, with a price of £0·40 and sales of 14,100, will be £0·15. Total contribution will therefore be £2,115. The result of the reduction in price from £0·50 to £0·40 is therefore that net contribution falls by about £400. Provided the firm believes that the probabilities are correct, the price cut should not be made. Of course, the firm may not be certain that, at the original price, £0·50, sales *will* be 10,000 units. However, the firm can use probability theory in just the same way to obtain an expected value for the initial level of sales. Similarly, it can compare more than two possible prices, using probabilities to get an expected value for sales at each level of price. All that is necessary is that the firm *should* be able to assign probabilities to different possible levels of sales at different possible prices.[1]

If the firm feels that it has too little information to use any of these methods, there are only two ways out. First, the firm could attempt to improve its information. This is why, for example, Epsilon Ltd used test marketing to work out the likely levels of sales of 'Epsilon' at various levels of prices. It will be remembered that this exercise showed Epsilon that elasticity of demand, total revenue and profit was highest at the highest price. Second the firm could simply abandon any attempt to use rational processes in pricing, but it should *only* do this after convincing itself quite conclusively that none of the methods shown above, or any variants of them, is of any use.

However, while any price is set at a moment of time (and often for a relatively short period of time) pricing should be seen in a wider setting. If the long-run trend of cost is downward, because of the benefits of 'learning' with experience, the firm must have a pricing strategy which allows for this. It is likely that after looking at the effect of 'learning' it will want to reduce price, certainly in real terms, over time. Indeed, it must allow for the fact that the higher the level of sales is in any period of time the lower costs will be. It must take this into account in determining pricing policy from the beginning. And it must do this while also taking account of the likely product cycle for the product. While the firm will take a decision to set price for a relatively short period only, it must do this with the long-run strategy in mind. Several of our firms, especially Fourways and

[1] For a fuller discussion of the use of probability theory in pricing and market, ing decisions, see D. C. Hague, *Managerial Economics* (London, 1969), Chapters 6, 13 and 14.

Wensum, had given far too little thought to these dynamic elements. The firm's aim must be to set price, and so quantity sold, to take advantage of costs which fall with experience. One has to look farther ahead than the immediate period, and consider the whole set of pricing decisions over the life of the product rather than the immediate one. This is likely to require discounted cash flow methods, because the timing of costs and revenues now becomes very important.

So far we have assumed that the firm has a single objective. However, one could use the same kind of analysis for other objectives. If the firm has only one objective, it is likely to be a profit objective. However, the firm may be interested in both profit and market share. As we saw in Chapter 6, if the firm is able to say that, for example, a price of £0·60 per unit will give a market share of 40 per cent then there is no problem. Price can be set at this level and the 40 per cent market share obtained.

If not, the likelihood is that the firm will put more emphasis on one objective than on another. Indeed, we have seen that often firms will operate by making other objectives a constraint on the main one. They will maximize profits, subject to, for example, maintaining the current level of employment. Over longish periods, profit is likely to be the most important objective, unless the firm is very lucky indeed in its products and its markets.

This, of course, leads back to satisficing. There is little more to be said about satisficing here. If the firm is concerned with earning a given level of profit which is fairly easily obtained, that is the end of the problem. The firm may wonder whether to increase or reduce prices if it is necessary to raise profit to reach the aspiration level. Otherwise, the rigorous analysis set out above has little to offer. However, we should remember that our studies suggest that even firms that 'satisfice' over other aspiration levels may seek to maximize profit when pricing. The analysis outlined above will help these firms.

Before leaving this section we must emphasize the complexity of the relationships involved in pricing—if this is necessary after the last few paragraphs. Formal, perhaps computer, models are needed more often than we think. This is especially the case when we allow for the effect of pricing on the product's market share, level of output through the accumulation of experience in its production. For, as we have seen, this carries through into costs and profits.

9.3 A CLASSIFICATION OF THE FIRMS WE STUDIED

So far, in this chapter, we have ignored organizational constraints. We have discussed pricing decisions as though there was nothing which would prevent a price fixer from setting whatever price he thought best in given circumstances. Perhaps the biggest lesson for those of us who carried out this research was how human and organizational factors can prevent prices being set as efficiently as they might be, at the level which pure logic would suggest. Most of those who worked on this project had been trained in economics or accountancy. We had learned to see price fixers deciding on what price was to be charged by taking relevant information about costs, revenues, etc. and using pure logic to decide which decision would best reach the firm's objectives. It was not long before we saw that this did not always happen.

We shall introduce these issues briefly by classifying the firms we studied in two different ways.

Our first classification looks at firms in terms of the numbers of people concerned with price fixing. At one extreme, there were firms where one man (with varying degrees of supervision from above) set the price of some or all of his firm's products. At the other, groups of people—either the Board itself or groups of managers—took pricing decisions.

It goes without saying that where one man was wholly responsible for setting price, then human perversity or fallibility alone could prevent the decision being as good as the information available would allow. Perhaps the price fixer was unwilling to pursue the firm's objectives. Or perhaps he might not have collected enough information; or he might not have analysed or understood it correctly, so that the wrong decision was taken. Or perhaps the data was accurate and relevant but the price fixer drew the wrong conclusions from it.

It is also obvious that, where prices were set by a committee, the problems usually associated with group decision-taking must have arisen. Even if detailed written information, on which the decision was to be taken, had been provided for every member of the group, no one could guarantee that the decision would follow logically from the data. Some or all members of the group may have wanted to pursue different objectives, or may have interpreted the information differently from other members. Some members may have been more important, or more dominating than others, so that their views prevailed. No member of these groups could have been quite sure what assumptions and interpretations any other was making, or what the other members' objectives were.

The decision which was taken therefore depended on exactly how the group behaved on the particular occasion. Often (perhaps always) the group did not have all its objectives clearly stated, and all relevant information available in detail, and in writing. Again, some or all members of the group may have had different objectives and/or different pieces of information. The likelihood that the 'right' decision was taken was then even smaller. And, however much or little information was available, we cannot assume that everyone perceived it in exactly the same way.

The most important effect of this double classification was on the clarity of our findings. We soon came to distinguish between those firms where the decision processes were easy to identify—and to observe—and those where it was difficult to be sure of the actual, as distinct from the formal, decision processes. In some firms, especially Alpha Ltd, Basic Foods and the Surgical Instrument Company, it seemed to us as though we were attacking a mass of foam rubber. Not only was the way the organization behaved hard to see; our attempts to push into the mass, to get more detail, rarely revealed anything sharply defined.

As one would imagine, we found most difficulty at the two ends of the spectrum. Where one man set prices, only an ability to observe his thought processes could have enabled us to be absolutely sure what kind of decision processes he was using. Similarly, where the decision procedures brought together large numbers of people, in both formal and informal meetings and at different levels in the firm, it was difficult to be quite sure where and how the vital subdecisions were being taken.

Between these extremes came firms like Wensum, Fourways, Heavy Technology, Clean and Medlock where the decision processes seemed to us to be crystal clear. More than one man was involved, so that information had to be exchanged in meetings; but only a handful of key individuals took decisions and their various roles in the pricing process could be fairly easily identified. Indeed, in Wensum, our researcher was able to sit in on the whole of the annual price review meeting and take detailed notes. Similarly, in Clean Engineering, two of us observed one pricing meeting. This makes our studies of pricing much more revealing, interesting and perhaps more useful in firms like Clean and Wensum than in firms like Alpha.

The result is that out studies are best classified in terms of two characteristics: (a) the number of people concerned with pricing decisions; (b) the size of the organization. We have not distinguished explicitly between the size of an organization and the number of levels of its management involved in pricing. This is largely because, in our studies, larger organizations always had more hierarchical levels concerned with pricing than smaller ones.

This classification is intended only to allow us to present the case studies in a rational order. We shall give what seems to us the most important information from each of the case studies in Chapter 10, including comments on the four cases which we have not been allowed to publish in the Appendix. In Chapter 11, we shall go on to consider what our case studies tell us about the economic, human and organizational factors entering into pricing decisions.

CHAPTER 10

The Pricing Decisions

This chapter looks at the pricing decisions we studied in our thirteen firms. We have classified them in the way outlined in Section 9.3.

10.1 ONE-MAN PRICING: SMALL FIRM (DEE PLASTICS LTD)

To describe this case as one-man price fixing is perhaps slightly misleading. The commercial manager himself took day-to-day pricing decisions. The managing director was, however, consulted on very difficult (or very important) decisions, so that the commercial manager did not have complete freedom to set prices. At the same time, while the commercial manager drew up Dee's list of prices, individual salesmen went out to negotiate prices with customers. They were given limited authority to set a different price for each customer, taking into account the amount Dee sold to him and the size of the particular order. This apart, the commercial manager did not delegate price setting.

The price fixer's task in Dee Plastics was not easy, because he was expected to reconcile two incompatible objectives. He had (a) to earn the rate of return on capital required by the parent firm; and (b) to maintain or increase Dee's market share. Dee had one very large competitor, who effectively determined the level of prices that Dee could charge. At the time of our study, prices were quite simply too low to allow Dee to earn the required rate of return.

The pricing procedure was first to discover the price charged by the major competitor, and we have seen that the most important single step here was to obtain a copy of his price list. Because its capacity was limited, Dee had to make sure that it obtained the most profitable business it could—knowing that even so it could not earn the required rate of return. An important factor persuading customers to give business to Dee was their unwillingness to rely solely on one supplier—the major producer. Discounts were often given in order to obtain business, so that the freedom salesmen had to offer discounts—and the way they used this freedom—were important both in obtaining business and in determining the rate of return Dee earned.

The aim was to obtain a gross margin over 'full' cost of 25 per cent of selling price (33 per cent of costs). However, the price often had to be set below this in order to obtain business, and so allow Dee to obtain the highest possible sales revenue from its limited output. Dee had to judge: (a) how far it would be necessary to increase discounts to obtain a given order; (b) how much 'contribution' this would bring to Dee; (c) whether it would be better to take particular business at once, or to wait to see if other business would be available later at more profitable prices. Since Dee did not carry out detailed written analysis of these issues, and indeed since no one could be quite certain that prices were not cut farther than was absolutely necessary to get the business, we could not judge how successful its price fixer was.

10.2 ONE MAN PRICING: LARGE FIRM (SURGICAL INSTRUMENT CO. LTD)

In the Surgical Instrument Company, the price of each product was set by the marketing manager. We have seen that in this firm each product was judged by the rate of return on capital which it earned. A new product, like the scalpel, would receive little consideration if it was not thought likely to provide the minimum required rate of return. This rate of return was converted back into a gross margin on sales income. As a new product, for which no investment was needed, the scalpel was expected to earn a gross margin of 50 per cent on sales income. The information which the price setter had to work with was of two kinds. For costs, a standard form put together estimates of all costs incurred in making the scalpel, except general overheads, depreciation, packaging and distribution. This gave the lowest price that could ever be charged, though so far as we know, such a low price never had been charged with a new product. The aim was to earn the largest possible gross margin—in total, not per unit.

There was no sign that fixed and variable costs were separated in the Surgical Instrument Company, and indeed the figure for general overheads was an allocated one. The marketing manager made all the calculations he thought necessary in order to discover what level of price would maximize the (total) gross margin, but we do not know how far he made a distinction between fixed and variable costs in doing this. All we can say is that attention was concentrated on the gross margin, from which overheads, depreciation, etc. had to be deducted later. This probably helped to bring the firm nearer to the price that the 'contribution' approach would have suggested than would have happened if all costs had been allocated in detail. But it might well have been better to work explicitly in terms of contribution.

On the demand side, the marketing manager obtained a good deal of information from what we judged to be a good market research department. This information included estimates of sales at various levels of price. However, the marketing manager was himself responsible for obtaining whatever information he needed about the price that competitors were charging for scalpels.

The marketing manager was subjected to a number of organizational pressures as he took decisions. There was pressure from all levels above him to charge the profit-maximizing price, which was usually thought to be a high one. There was also the fact that his department would be given fewer funds for new products than other departments if its products were significantly less profitable than others. Loyalty to his department, requiring him to ensure that ample funds continued to be made available to it, seems to have been an important factor causing him to try to maximize profit. However, this profit-maximizing procedure had to be carried out in the face of the current prices for competing products. In the case of the scalpel, these were low enough to keep its price lower than most of those concerned with the scalpel would have liked.

Almost the whole responsibility for pricing lay with the marketing manager. He set the list price for the scalpel and also decided whether a lower price could be accepted from any particular customer, especially in the export market. So, a one-man price fixer was here responsible for a number of products within the same product group. However, he was not called to account by anyone higher up in the firm. This was not because he was the chief executive; in a general way he was responsible to a director and a Board.

Since the scalpel was a new product, the information available to the price fixer consisted of research, technical and accountancy reports, a market survey and his own data about competitors' prices and sales. In a sense, he did not 'fix' the price at all, but accepted the cost estimates as not being too high. Since the company could vary prices from day to day, it was company policy to allow market forces to establish a more permanent price level than the initial one. However, the price of the scalpel was carefully watched during its first year, and it would have been dropped altogether if that had seemed desirable.

Once a product was established, the price fixer was left to strike what he judged to be an optimal balance between profit and market share. We have already explained that the difficulty with such private and personal compromises is that they can never be fully observed by outsiders like ourselves. Indeed, we are uncertain quite how the price fixer in the Surgical Instrument Company was judged. It seems that responsibility was devolved to him because he was a man of considerable experience in his firm, and no one had the knowledge or the wish to interfere with what he did. The firm appeared to set no minimum price for an individual product, and it seems that the price fixer himself decided when, or if, a product should be dropped.

We cannot help doubting whether this was the whole story. Yet, there certainly never seemed to have been intervention from above on the ground that a decision made was not optimal. Consequently, there was no evidence to show whether, or where, there were limits to the price fixer's independence. There must have been some limits; if he went mad, someone would presumably have acted. Our belief is that either the firm was satisfied that a reasonable balance between profit and market share was being achieved for each product; or the price fixer was judged by the profitability of the whole group of products for which he was responsible, and not by that of any individual one. If the latter was the case, then the overall profitability, for all the department's products, must have been considered satisfactory.

10.3 SMALL GROUP PRICING: SMALL ORGANIZATION (WENSUM ENGINEERING LTD)

Wensum and Fourways both come into the category of small organizations, and in both we were able to study the pricing process in detail. We begin with Wensum, which we regard as our most successful study. Because it is a study where the human and organizational problems met with in pricing were considerable, a warning is necessary. This was a particularly clear and detailed study and we shall devote a good deal of space to it. No one should deduce that Wensum's problems are typical. We simply do not know whether they are or not, although many managers from firms selling technically-advanced electrical, electronic and engineering products, who have attended courses at the Manchester Business School, think that their own firms operate similarly.

It will be remembered that we were studying an annual price review for all Wensum's products. Prices were fixed by a small group of people—especially the commercial manager, the accountant and the home sales manager, with the export sales manager less involved. Formally, the accountant and commercial manager had the same degree of seniority in the firm, and the home and export sales managers were both responsible to the commercial manager. It is important to remember that the commercial manager had only recently been appointed, and that the home sales manager had previously been acting as commercial manager, though without the title.

A number of problems arose because of human and organizational factors at work within Wensum, though we do not believe that they significantly altered the prices finally fixed. They lengthened the pricing process a little, and may have led to some individual prices being different, but we doubt whether the overall percentage increase in prices was affected much, if at all. These problems certainly led to conflict between individuals, some at least of which could have been avoided, and this may well have led to further conflict after we finished our study.

10.3.1 The Participants' Views

We observed Wensum's annual price review, in detail, from beginning to end, and began by asking the principal participants what events led to the annual price review. There was some disagreement about this. The accountant said that he started the process by telling the commercial manager that it was time to review prices. However, the home sales manager claimed that he began the review himself. The commercial manager, having been with the firm for only about six months, said that he did not know what the procedure was but that he expected that he would sit down with the home sales manager and accountant and put forward his views on likely price increases.

All three of them did agree that every product would be examined in the price review. The accountant went on to say that they would be looking for both price increases or decreases. The home sales manager agreed with this, explaining that the firm liked to find one or two products whose prices could be reduced, in order to avoid the impression given if all prices were raised. The accountant said that that there would be no separate meetings between any two of the three people most directly involved in the review. He would collect what information he felt was relevant from his viewpoint. Once this had been done, he would see the commercial manager and call a meeting of all three. When the price list had been agreed by this meeting, it would be put before the managing director and would go no higher than him. It was thought that in some years the managing director had not even looked at the proposed price list. When he did, he gave the impression that he was rubber-stamping the committee's recommended price changes. The managing director himself said that, before the annual price review, the accountant fed information through to him, 'like the fact that there is no gross profit on one range of products we make'.

The commercial manager told us that he wanted to discuss the likely price changes with the home sales manager before he met the accountant. He said, 'We have to get together, and I will be relying on his knowledge to find out where prices can be increased'. This meeting, he felt, would be 'personality' discussion. Once it was over, the next stage would be to discover from the accountant what was 'the pressure from costs' for each product. The commercial manager felt that the export manager should sit in on the final meeting and be allowed to give his views. This would be a departure from the traditional procedure. Previously, the export sales manager had been consulted after the price revisions had been tentatively decided upon. In fact, as we shall see, the export sales manager did not attend the pricing meeting for more than a short time. Immediately before the pricing meeting, the home sales manager said that there had been no preliminary meeting between him and the commercial manager. Indeed, he claimed that any preliminary meeting was to have been between the commercial manager and the accountant.

The export sales manager confirmed much of this, saying that the home sales manager usually put up suggested prices which he could react against if he felt that they would interfere with total overseas business. He said that, in commenting on proposed price increases in this way, he would be influenced by how the sales of any product were divided between home and export markets. For example, if 75 per cent of the sales of a product were made within the UK, he would be more likely to let a price increase go unchallenged than if 75 per cent of sales were overseas.

One man who did not attend the meeting was the works manager. He felt strongly that the company should make a profit but contended that some of those concerned with pricing did not understand what pricing was for. As he put it, 'the *pseudo ad hoc* method of pricing used is very subjective'. He said that what was done was to sum costs and revenue for each product at the existing price; and at an 'ideal' selling price. The price fixers then attempted to make up the difference between the two by increasing the price of particular products. He argued that so many calculations were made before prices were set that it was very difficult for him to be certain what works cost he was intended to meet. The works manager said that, until a few years before our study, he had taken the gross selling price of such product and reduced it by the 2·2 formula, described in Section 8.4.4, to give him an 'ideal' works cost to aim at. However, he claimed that since then there had been so much vacillation over selling prices that he had abandoned this approach. The works manager accepted that he was not directly involved in pricing, but claimed that he played a role in pricing 'by interference'.

10.3.2 The Background

Several explanatory comments are needed now if one is to understand Wensum's pricing activities fully. First, the fact that the commercial manager had only recently been appointed seems to have been an important factor in determining exactly what happened. It meant that he knew less than did the others concerned with the price review about what had been done in earlier years. It also meant that his exact position in the firm was both less clear and less fully accepted by his colleagues than it would have been if he had been there longer.

The appointment of the commercial manager seems to have had most effect on the behaviour of the home sales manager. As we have seen, the latter had effectively been commercial manager for the previous two years. Either because of this, or more probably in addition to it, he had established himself as the firm's leading 'price fixer'. When the commercial manager arrived, the home sales manager was clearly disappointed because he had not been appointed to a post which he had occupied, in fact if not in name, for the previous two years. He therefore seems to have behaved as most of us would have done in these conditions. He was determined, at worst, to show that he was still the firm's chief price setter; at best, he wanted to demonstrate that he was quite capable of carrying out the role of commercial manager.

We think that the home sales manager persuaded the export sales manager to stay away from the pricing meeting. We also think that he did this largely because of his wish to show that he was the firm's main price fixer, not only for home sales, but for export sales too. It will be remembered that the export sales manager explained that, while acting as commercial manager, the home sales manager had also assumed the role of overall price fixer and had reduced the part that the export sales manager played in pricing. Keeping the export sales manager away from the pricing meeting perpetuated this situation. So did the fact that the home sales manager dominated the price review meeting itself. So too, did the fact that the home sales manager independently made further price increases, after the end of the price review meeting. What is not clear is whether this last move should also be seen as an attempt to usurp part of the role of the commercial manager.

The fact that the relative status of those taking part in the price review meeting was uncertain must explain why the price review meeting operated as a leaderless group, with no one taking the chair. This raises the question of what should have been the role of the managing director. Should he have played a major role in the price review meeting? Pricing policy is always a major determinant of profitability, so it is arguable that the managing director should always have attended the price review meeting. In this particular year, since he was under pressure from his parent firm to increase profitability, it is certainly arguable that he should have been at the meeting. This would not only have enabled him to take a leading role in ensuring that the increase in prices was sufficient to raise profits to the desired level; it would also have provided the meeting with an acceptable chairman.

All these are interesting examples of the human problems that can affect pricing processes. We have said that we do not believe that, in the end, Wensum's price review would have reached significantly different results if these problems had never arisen. However, both the immediate and long-term human relationships within the firm would have been improved if they had been avoided—with time saved and perhaps money. If the managing director was not prepared to play a leading role in the price review without persuasion, the commercial manager could have tried to bring him in as a way of establishing his own position. As for the works manager, his exclusion from the pricing meeting must have been linked to the fact that he had such strong views on pricing. What we cannot say is which was cause and which effect.

Quite apart from all this, three changes in the procedure at the meeting would have improved its value. First, the meeting did not group similar products together and look at each group as a whole. If this had been done, time would have been saved. The danger that some of the factors affecting the pricing of a particular group of products might be forgotten when some individual products from that group were being priced would also have been reduced, if not eliminated.

Second, it would have helped if there had been agreement before the meeting about exactly which information was to be supplied by whom. As we saw in Chapter 8, our own research added confusion to Wensum's pricing meeting, because the home sales manager and the accountant had both provided figures for costs and calculated selling prices. The home sales manager's assistant seems to have provided his set of figures largely to impress us. However, the fact that we caused this duplication is not what really matters. Wensum should have had a procedure for ensuring that such confusion could not arise—even with us on the premises.

The third problem was how Wensum should link the annual price review with its budgeting procedures. Wensum produced budgets four times a year—in January, March, July and September. The January and July budgets were worked out in great detail, while the others were merely regarded as 'exercises in loading the factory'. In recent years, the Board had asked for the order budget for the following year during August. Thus, discussion of the order budget for the next year had been completed two or three weeks before there was any discussion of prices.

Both the accountant and the home sales manager said that the people most concerned with preparing the budget were also those most concerned with the price review. Yet both of them thought that none of these people had a clear idea how what happened in constructing the budget might, or should, affect his attitude towards pricing. They divorced the two completely.

The procedure used in preparing the budget was for Wensum's area managers in the UK and the regional managers in its export markets, to estimate what they thought the next year's orders were likely to be. The forecasts were collated by the accountant and were seen by the home and export sales managers. After this, the figures were passed to the commercial manager for his views and to the production department for its comments on the work load that was implied. Finally, the budget was submitted to the managing director and so to the Board.

The budget divided the output of each product into three categories. These were: Category A, made to stock; Category B, made to special order; and Category C, made with the authority of the managing director. Category C usually contained products which were no longer in 'normal' production. Budgeted sales of all products were shown for each geographical area of the UK for the USA, and (in one sales figure) for all other countries in Wensum's export markets. All these figures were included in the budget for the quarter and for the year, and all estimates of revenue were shown net, after discounts.

When the budget was being prepared, about three months before the price review, no allowance was made for the possibility that prices might be altered in the price review. It was presumed that any price changes would be so small that they would make no difference to the budgeted quantity of each product likely to be sold in the next year. The accountant said that the budgeted value of sales would be altered, after the price review, if any price were changed by more than about 5 per cent. He agreed that if the budgeted value of sales for the next year were altered, the revision would be circulated within Wensum, but not shown to the Board.

10.3.3 The Price Review Meeting

We now turn to the price-review meeting itself. This was held in two parts, each lasting about three hours. The commercial manager, accountant and home sales manager were present for both meetings, and on the second occasion they were joined for a short time by the export sales manager. The following documents were taken into the meeting.

1. Current price lists.
2. Calculated selling prices (using the formulae mentioned in Section 8.4.4).

3. Budgeted sales volumes for the next year.
4. Sales trends for each product in recent years.
5. A document comparing Wensum's products with those of competitors.
6. Recent copies of competitors' sales leaflets.

In the review meetings, documents 1, 3 and 4 were referred to continually. So were the home sales manager's figure for works cost multiplied by 2·2. (It must be remembered that these were produced only because our research upset normal routines.) Documents 5 and 6 were ignored, and the other cost-plus formulae prepared by the accountant rarely referred to. However, we have seen that since the home sales manager's assistant had not used the latest cost figures, the home sales manager's calculated prices were wrong in a number of cases. They had to be amended as necessary, by the accountant, when each product was being discussed.

The documents taken to the meeting by particular individuals, and those referred to by them, varied. The commercial manager simply had a copy of the home sales manager's calculated prices and a copy of the next year's order budget. He referred to these repeatedly. The accountant had his own calculated prices, the home sales manager's calculated prices, the next year's order budget and the existing price list. The home sales manager had with him his own calculated prices, the current price list, the order budget for the next year, the document about competitors' prices, sales trends by product over recent years and some of the sales literature issued by competitors. During the discussions, the home sale manager made continual reference to his list of calculated prices, to the order budget, and to the existing price list. He made less reference to sales trends over recent years and no reference at all to the documents about competitors, or to their sales literature.

At the beginning of the meeting, the accountant suggested that they were looking for an increase in price of about 3 per cent overall, as this would be 'a nice increase to achieve'. The accountant said little during the meeting and for the most part merely recorded the decisions that were taken. Each product was taken in turn, according to its reference number, and looked at individually. There was no suggestion that the meeting might deal with all the products in a particular product group at the same time. For each product, the usual procedure was for the meeting to look at the relationship between the calculated price and the current list price; to determine what competitive products there were, and what prices these were being offered at; to look briefly at the sales trends in the current year for the product in question; and to look at its budgeted sales for the following year. The pricing decisions came mainly from discussion of these factors. For individual products, price increases were usually between 2 per cent and 5 per cent, although the prices of some products were left unchanged and some were increased by as much as 17 per cent. In no case was the price of any product reduced, despite earlier suggestions that one or two token reductions would be made.

In the meeting, there were significant discussions of 68 products (out of a total of 92). For these 68 products, we made the following analysis.

	No. of products on which item was discussed
Cost-plus formula	51[1]
Competitive prices	31
Trend of actual sales	31
Next year's sales budget	38
Special considerations: e.g. factors affecting Government orders, or the size of Wensum's current inventory	21

[1] The cost-plus formulæ were referred to for each product; but they were discussed fully for only 51 of them.

There was a quite long discussion on one group of products. This centred on what the basic company policy towards these products should be. Should it continue to produce any of them; or only some of them? In the end, nothing was decided either about what range of products would continue to be sold, or at what prices. It was agreed that a separate study was needed.

It is not easy to be sure what factors were taken into account at Wensum's price review meeting. The discussion was not very sophisticated. Our records show that, for each product, an attempt was made to judge what would be the most profitable price—given relevant factors like the budgeted level of sales, the prices of competing products and costs of production. However, the judgement on how the demand for any product would be related to its own price and other characteristics, and to the characteristics and prices of competing products, depended very much on the individual and collective judgements of those taking part in the review. We have already seen that costs were not clearly divided into their fixed and variable elements. We believe that, at the least, a more careful division of costs into their fixed and variable components should have been made. Besides allowing more-relevant calculations of the effect which changes in price were likely to have on 'contribution', it would have improved the efficiency of the price review. However, it is questionable whether more refined estimates could have been made of the relationship between the various possible levels of Wensum's prices and the resulting levels of sales—of elasticity of demand.

Our original impression was that the commercial manager was the leader of the meeting—the discussion on each product was usually begun by him. However, after discussions with Professor John Morris, one of our colleagues in the Manchester Business School, we changed our view. We now think that the reason why the commercial manager played such an active part in the meeting was that he was continually trying to initiate price changes rather than have these suggested by the home sales manager. Our earlier discussion of the relative positions of the two men suggests that the commercial manager was using the price review meeting to try to establish his position and that the home sales manager was doing the opposite. In fact, the meeting was dominated by the home sales manager, who did not initiate many of the discussions on individual products but usually had his own price recommendation accepted.

10.3.4 Postscript

When the price-review meeting was over, we thought this was the end of the work on the company's annual price review. However, on a later visit to Wensum, we were given a copy of the company's new price list. We compared this with the list of prices agreed at the meeting. Of the 92 products which appeared in the price list, the published list price of 25 was higher than the one agreed at the review meeting. The difference was hardly ever more than £10, and most of the increases were for one group of products.

We had great difficulty in discovering exactly why these changes were made, although everyone in the firm agreed that there had been no more pricing meetings. It turned out that the home sales manager had decided on the further price increases in the light of full information about likely increases in costs in the next year. It will be remembered that although the works manager had told the accountant that there was likely to be an increase in wages of about 4 per cent, accompanied by cuts in overhead costs, no account had been taken of changes in wages in the pricing meeting. Assuming that elasticity of demand was zero—that no change in the sales of any product took place as a result of the alterations in price made at the review meeting, or of the home sales manager's own changes—the complete set of increases made during and after the pricing meeting raised the firm's turnover by about 4½ per cent. The price changes agreed on at the meeting raised it by about 3 per cent. The three principal personalities involved in the price review meeting, after having spent a good deal of time collecting information for that meeting, and after having met for about six hours to discuss price changes, achieved an increase in turnover of about 3 per cent. It seems curious to us that the home sales manager, by himself and in a very short space of time, was allowed to increase turnover by about half as much again as the amount achieved in the whole price-review process.

10.4 SMALL GROUP PRICING: SMALL ORGANIZATION (FOURWAYS ENGINEERING LTD)

In Fourways, we studied the pricing of a single new product. This task was the responsibility of the firm's product pricing committee—a committee with the following members:

managing director (chairman);
accountant;
commercial manager;
works engineer;
engineering manager;
research manager;
technical services manager;
chief engineer.

The committee was provided with all the necessary information about the development, manufacture and pricing of any product, before it was marketed. On pricing and marketing questions, the views of the commercial manager probably carried most weight, since he spoke not only for himself but for the home sales manager and export sales manager as well. This avoided the kind of difficulty observed in Wensum's price review meeting. The man with greatest influence on questions of product policy was probably the engineering manager, both because he controlled research and development expenditure and because product-policy issues were predominantly technical ones.

No very precise objectives were set, partly because the managing director was chairman of the committee and could interpret the firm's overall policy to it. However, to the extent that Fourways had an objective for new products, it was that each should cover all costs that could be attributed to it and make an 'acceptable' contribution to profit. Discussions about pricing in the committee therefore normally centred around giving an operational meaning to the non-operational term 'acceptable'. The committee usually thought in terms of a particular gross margin for each product group, over and above material cost, labour cost and commission. The price for each new product was looked at in terms of the average gross margin which that product would give, relatively to the average gross margin for the whole of its product group.

As can be seen from the case study itself a detailed procedure, which was to be carried out in Fourway's product pricing committee, had been worked out by a consultant. As we shall also see, however, market information was not always as carefully collected or fully presented as this procedure would require.

Information about the product we studied had been collected over a period of about a year before the pricing decision had to be taken. As we saw in Chapter 8, a large number of estimates of this product's cost had been made. The estimate had fallen, during 1962, from a figure of £269 to one of £210.

However, what mattered was not cost but price, and even with the works cost of £210, this was about £410—much higher than a 'tenta tive' price, based on the prices of competitive products, of £350. Late in 1963, the same calculations were made again, by which time, as we saw in Chapter 8, the initial investment had risen by some £6,000 and estimates of sales during the first few years of its life had fallen to half the size assumed a year earlier. The result of this second exercise was to show that while the tentative figure for selling price, based on competitive products, had risen to £390, the 'calculated' selling price showed that to achieve the desired return, the product would have to be sold at £442. Once it became clear that there was this difference, a third set of calculations was prepared. In these, an attempt was made to see how far the cost of the product, and thus its calculated price, could be reduced by removing some of its less-essential features.

The market information used contained a full review of all products of this type already on the market—including their specifications and price. It was from this information that a tentative price of £350 was initially decided on. However, there seemed to be no rigorous examination either of overall market size, likely market growth, or the market share that this product could expect to reach.

This seems to be one case where the price finally decided upon was very much determined by market conditions. As yet more time passed, the estimates of the cost of manufacturing the product became firmer, and it seemed clear that to achieve the desired rate of return it would have to be priced at about £500. However, it was apparent to those concerned that it would be dangerous, if not impossible, to market the product at this price in the face of competitive products being sold at between £350 and £400. For this reason, when the product first appeared in the company's price list it was priced at £390. The price remained at that level for several years afterwards. Because of competitive pressures, the company did not feel able to increase this price. No doubt part of the reason for this was that, even at £390, the product was not selling as well as had been expected.

As can be seen from the case study, late in 1963, Fourways carried out an exercise, to discover what sales of this product would be at various different levels of price. This exercise led to the conclusion that the home market was very price elastic at prices between £250 and £300, but much less price elastic around £450. Fourways therefore calculated that the most profitable price was round about £350. The report went on to say that, since it was necessary to recover as much as possible of the money spent on developing the product, its price should be reduced—in order to minimize this loss. Unfortunately, the accounting department had used the wrong figures for material and labour costs, but it was not until later that anyone discovered that they were wrong. As a result, the exercise and its conclusions were ignored and the price of the product was left unchanged. There was no attempt to recalculate the figures given in the case study, using the correct costs. This is another example, although on this occasion not one caused by our researchers, of wrong costs leading to confusion—or, in this case, inaction.

10.5 SMALL GROUP PRICING: LARGE FIRMS (HEAVY TECHNOLOGY LTD, MEDLOCK ENGINEERING LTD AND CLEAN ENGINEERING LTD)

We shall consider these three firms together, though pointing to the differences in their pricing procedures. Though Heavy Technology and Clean Engineering were pricing a much more complex product than Medlock Engineering, both were selling in a depressed home market, while Medlock was selling in a highly-competitive export market. All three firms entrusted pricing to a small group of people—with the sales manager taking overall, and ultimate, responsibility for pricing in each firm.

In each case, too, because of difficult trading conditions, the problem had become that of making the biggest profit (smallest loss). In the short run, at least, it was not technically possible to reduce employment significantly—especially for staff—below what had been predicted as the profit-maximizing level. Because all three firms tendered for their business, it was difficult for them to know how to maximize profits. Tenders had to be put in before manufacturing began, usually a long time before. It was only too easy to make a bad prediction of the amount of business that would have been obtained by the time manufacture started, and so to tender at too low or too high a price.

In each of the three firms, once a customer had asked the firm to quote for a given order, the design staff worked out which design would satisfy him and could be produced economically. The design was passed to the accounting or estimating department, as the case might be. A 'total' cost was then worked out. In Heavy Technology, the practice, for some time before we made our study, had been to use the formula:

$$\text{Total cost} = \text{material cost} + \text{labour cost} + 25\,\%.$$

This was regarded as the minimum, marginal, price at which business could be taken. In more normal times, profit had been added on. Similar calculations were made in Medlock Engineering and Clean Engineering. However, at the time of our study, all three firms found it difficult to make much profit.

In each firm, the organizational structure was relatively informal and it was not easy to be sure exactly how pricing decisions were reached. In each case, the final responsibility for deciding on the tender price lay with the sales, or commercial manager. He had regular discussions with a number of other executives who were concerned in various ways either with the pricing decision, or with supplying information for it. Each individual contract was considered in detail, in one of these discussions, to see if it was worth taking. In Clean Engineering we sat in on one discussion, where managers' opinions of what had happened were discussed, rather than the facts. As we have seen, managers do not always go to basic sources of information to check exactly what the facts are. Some of the discussions of possible prices for tenders took place in informal committees; others occurred during informal talks between two individuals. Those most usually involved in such meetings in Heavy Technology were (in addition to the sales manager):

general manager;
works manager;
commercial manager;
market research officer;
chief costing engineer;
chief designer.

The arrangements in Medlock Engineering and Clean Engineering were similar.

All three firms used similar information for pricing decisions. The written information available for pricing decisions in Heavy Technology was as follows:

1. Details of estimated labour and material costs provided by the estimating department.
2. Details of the overheads to be allocated to the contract. These were obtained from a manual provided by the estimating department.
3. The area representative's reports about the contract, including any information he had been able to obtain on the customer's intentions and wishes.

Other information which was available for determining prices, but was not necessarily written down, was as follows:

4. The price at which the last contract of the same type had been given. This was currently the most important factor, since fierce competition made it essential for the firm to work to the price level dictated by its competitors.
5. Information from salesmen about the particular customer requesting tenders, including information about any idiosyncrasies which would make it worth giving special attention to particular points in preparing any tender.
6. An assessment of how fully occupied competitors were in producing this type of product. This assessment was based mainly on a view of how full competitors' order books were, and on estimates of whether they were likely to be seriously interested in obtaining business from this contract.
7. Information—usually from the area representative—about whether the potential customer had been satisfied with the firm's service in the past.
8. The anticipated level of activity in the firm at the time when it was expected that the item would be in production if the tender was successful.
9. The balance of production in the factory—i.e. did the firm need an order for this product to keep a balance in its production.
10. The potential customer's assessment of the firm's capacity. This was usually obtained from personal contact with the customer. If the customer thought that Heavy Technology had as much business as it could handle, it would not be keen on giving it more.

The arrangements in Medlock and Clean Engineering were similar to these.

It can be seen that, apart from obtaining relative cost figures, the most important thing for all of them was to work out what was the probability that they would obtain each contract. Heavy Technology was developing complex procedures for attaching probabilities to the likelihood that a given contract would be obtained, and Clean Engineering was beginning to work in the same way. As for the cost figures, while the way these were presented might suggest a 'full cost' approach, difficult market conditions had forced all three firms to distinguish clearly between fixed and variable cost, and they had learned to do so very successfully.

Quite often, the commercial manager of Clean Engineering would take the decision himself but one decision we observed was taken with two colleagues.

In the end, however, the decision had to be taken, either by the commercial or sales manager, or by him and one or two others. In the difficult market conditions facing the three firms when we made our studies, pricing was far from easy. In the process of forming a judgement on the probability of any order being obtained, he (or they) had to decide two important things. First, were competitors likely to be charging even lower prices than they did on the last occasion when tenders were put in? Second, given the answer to this question, would it be desirable to tender at a lower price this time, and if so, how much lower? Or could the price now be held?

The pricing decision in these three firms was complicated by the fact that information was required not only about prices, but about the way customers would react to various technical, or design, features of the product. This was one factor making it difficult to decide on the probability of obtaining a given contract in competition with the assumed prices (and known or unknown technical features) of competitors' products. It was also important to know what view each customer took of the likelihood that each supplier's delivery dates would actually be met; the firm's technical abilities compared with those of its competitors; prices, discounts, and so on. Only then could the probability of obtaining the contract be estimated.

We have seen that Heavy Technology worked out the probability that particular business already tendered for would be obtained. What we could not discover was whether the firm ever made a list of the contracts with a high probability of being offered for tender in the near future. To have known this, would have enabled Heavy Technology to decide whether to tender at a realistic price for a contract now, or whether more attractive business was likely to be offered soon. It is important to emphasize that, at the time of our study, the use of probabilistic models in these firms was in its infancy. Considerable progress has been made since then in all of them. Nothing seems to be more effective in forcing firms to use marginal costing and probability theory effectively than a depressed market.

One thing that puzzled us was that none of these three firms had calculated the cost of preparing a tender. We found this surprising, since all three firms sometimes put in tenders in order to obtain market information, or for prestige reasons. We feel that a procedure was needed to ensure that the firm decided as early as possible whether it was seriously interested in obtaining a particular contract. If it was not, then surely the cheapest possible method of putting in a dummy tender should have been used.

One other point needs making. In Clean Engineering, the level of price was so low, at the time of our study, that no individual producer was willing to take the initiative in reducing tender prices further. Instead, manufacturers were using an elaborate and, so far as possible secret, system of rebates and discounts. They tried to attract customers and persuade them to order large amounts of the product, by offering what were effectively lower prices.

Finally, it must be mentioned that in Clean Engineering and Heavy Technology, if the price for a new tender established a new 'low', the tender was fully discussed with the general manager before being sent to the customer.

10.6 SMALL GROUP PRICING: LARGE FIRM (WESSEX TIMBER INDUSTRIES LTD)

In Wessex, pricing decisions were taken in two stages. First, as a basis for all detailed pricing decisions, there were quarterly meetings of senior executives where the performance of the previous quarter was compared with the budget. Variances were carefully studied to see whether they meant that the budget for the next quarter should be altered. These discussions led to a forecast of output. As we have seen, shortage of labour was the main problem.

The meeting then looked at profitability. The aim in Wessex was to earn $12\frac{1}{2}$ per cent on capital (before tax) and the meeting sought to ensure that the forecast output could be sold at prices which would give this rate of return. The works manager reported likely changes in cost for each kind of timber, on the assumption that output targets would be reached. A target price could then be built up, and this was done at Wessex's head office. A major cost was raw material, which was included at replacement cost, with an allowance for waste. Every item of cost was calculated per unit of timber—usually per foot. Standard labour and packaging costs per foot of timber were then calculated, and an adjustment was made to allow for the amount by which actual costs were expected to diverge from standard costs. The cost of distribution per foot of timber was added—to cover costs of carriage, salesmen, etc. Overheads were added too. Finally, the return on capital of $12\frac{1}{2}$ per cent had to be allowed for. The absolute amount of profit required from each mill was budgeted quarterly and allocated to products in proportion to their total cost.

This led to the second stage of the pricing operation, where the salesmen had to sell the mill's output. The calculations would already have given a target selling price. If the salesman could have charged this price for each order, the mill would have earned its budgeted return on capital. Salesmen were therefore judged by whether they earned the budgeted amount of profit, though Wessex accepted that a salesman might have failed to sell the volume of output required of him because of shortage of labour for production processes, a fall in demand for timber, and so on. Salesmen were given a long training in timber processing and in the uses of timber. One salesman was responsible for the output of each mill, and worked closely both with his own mill manager and with Wessex's head office. It followed that he was expected to keep close and friendly relations with customers and to know the main trends in their industries, in order to have a good idea of the prices he could charge. Clearly, the right man had to be appointed as a mill salesman; otherwise Wessex would not have earned as high a rate of return on capital as it might. The importance of this was emphasized by the fact that neither the head office nor the works manager of the saw mill could be sure that a salesman really had obtained as good a price as he could for a particular sale. Wessex did not pay any bonus or commission to salesmen, but made a periodic judgement on their efficiency when increasing salaries.

We have seen that the salesman was given little discretion in setting prices. He could, if he saw fit, lower price if a valuable customer was finding business difficult to obtain, so keeping the customer's goodwill. He could raise or lower prices if there were booms or recessions in the customer's industry. However, Wessex allowed its salesmen to alter prices in this way only within plus or minus one per cent above or below the target price.

In fact, more than half of Wessex's output was sold to its parent firm, which had a number of divisions that used timber in their products. There was a problem of transfer pricing—of the price at which timber should be transferred to other parts of Wessex. The principle Wessex had established was that it would take timber from its own sawmills only if it could do so on as good terms as it could obtain from other timber suppliers. Salesmen could not expect to get business more easily, or at lower prices, from other parts of

Wessex than from other firms. The whole of their business had to be done in open competition with other firms in the timber industry.

Most of the information which the salesman had to help him in agreeing the price of a contract with a customer was non-quantitative, and the product of his experience. He kept records of customers and knew, in fair detail, how their businesses were currently running. This gave him a sound basis on which to negotiate.

Other information could be obtained from Head Office—about general trends in the industry and perhaps about actions of competitors of which the salesman was not aware. This information was usually given to him at one of his weekly meetings with Head Office executives. Of course, he knew what business he had himself done previously with any customer and at what prices.

From what has been said so far, it can be seen that the mill salesman was given the task of obtaining a particular return on capital (12½ per cent) but only limited discretion to change prices. This might or might not mean that he was attempting to maximize. He might be trying to maximize if market conditions made it hard for Wessex to earn the 12½ per cent return—as had usually been the case in the two or three years before our study. He would not be maximizing in more favourable market circumstances, if he merely aimed to earn the 12½ per cent. Even where the salesman was trying to maximize profits, he was doing so in a situation where there was considerable uncertainty about what price a customer really was prepared to pay for a particular order. The job of negotiating prices required shrewd bargaining ability; the job of judging the success of the salesman required great perception.

This is not quite the whole story. We were unable to find any market-share objective which Wessex pursued. Since Wessex was permanently short of labour this is not surprising. However, the salesman kept in touch with the works manager to make sure that the mixture of types of timber he was selling was in line with production capacity of the mill—both in total and for particular products. This was a constraint on his pricing activities. He tried to earn the required return on capital, subject to selling a mixture of timber which fitted in with the mill's production capacity.

As we have seen, earning the 12½ per cent had been difficult. Salesmen had gone out to set the prices—hoping that the actual return would not be much less than 12½ per cent. This fed back into pricing procedures. When the target price was set by Head Office, current price trends were carefully studied. Prices were then set on the basis of cost figures from the accountant and of market factors. However, there was still room for negotiation over each individual contract, as has already been explained. As with the one-man price setters in Dee and the Surgical Instrument Company, our problem was that we could not be sure how far individual salesmen had maximized profit—given the output constraint. Our impression is that they might have set higher prices. Perhaps they 'satisficed'.

10.7 LARGE FIRM PRICING: LARGE GROUP (EPSILON LTD)

Perhaps the most important fact about 'Epsilon' was that we were here concerned with the pricing of a new product which Epsilon Ltd was persuaded to sell by its parent firm, partly because one Board member pressed for it. It is not certain whether Epsilon Ltd would otherwise have been so enthusiastic or persistent. With this new product, detailed plans were made. They were made with different objectives for each of three different time periods:

1. Test-market objectives: for years one and two.
2. Short-period objectives: for an unspecified period, beginning in year three.
3. Long-term objectives: for a 'normal' period, beginning after the short-period was over.

Some of the test-market and short-period aims were identical. However, we were told that short-period and long-period aims would have been altered if experience during the test market exercise had shown that this was necessary.

The broad objectives for the test market and short period were to establish the brand image of 'Epsilon', to discover the most profitable level of advertising and sales promotion support for 'Epsilon' and to find how big a percentage of its sales was made at the expense of Epsilon Ltd's existing brands of similar products. In the long run, the objective was to establish 'Epsilon' as the leading brand in the premium part of the market and to discover other profitable ways to exploit the brand name 'Epsilon'. Finally, it was intended to ensure that customers regarded 'Epsilon' as an attractive product compared with its competitors.

These broad aims were made more explicit when more-detailed objectives were set for 'Epsilon'. For the text market, Epsilon Ltd set precise objectives—especially for market share and for the scale of distribution through retailers. These objectives were extended into the short period. The test-market aim of finding what proportion of 'Epsilon's' sales came from existing brands sold by Epsilon Ltd was there supplemented by the objective that no more than 30 per cent of 'Epsilon's' sales should be at the expense of other Epsilon Ltd products. Since the short-period objectives implied that 'Epsilon' would be successfully launched on a national scale, precise levels of sales were set initially for the first three years. Similarly, objectives for the long period were set in terms of a rate of growth of 'Epsilon's' total sales turnover, and a 'contribution' of a specific absolute amount—after deducting advertising expenditure.

We have seen that quite sophisticated market research was carried out, including calculations of the elasticity of demand for 'Epsilon' (all other prices being assumed constant). From such data Epsilon Ltd calculated how sales, market share and profits were likely to respond to changes in the price and specification of 'Epsilon' and of competing products. These calculations showed that conflict between market share and profit objectives was possible. The highest profit was at a price of 3s 10d, while the biggest market share was at one of 2s 6d. It was also shown that for years three to seven, other individual products of Epsilon Ltd could be expected to lose as little as 2 per cent, and as much as 25 per cent, of their sales to 'Epsilon'.

Detailed cost figures were worked out. First, before 'Epsilon' was launched, Epsilon Ltd predicted its costs and profit in years one to six. Later, towards the end of year one, further calculations showed considerably lower profits than originally expected.

Both sets of figures were presented in the same way. Total sales receipts were shown first. From them were deducted production and distribution costs—to give figures for gross profit before advertising. Advertising and sales promotion expenditure was then subtracted to give gross profit after advertising. Finally, an allowance was made for profit lost on other Epsilon Ltd brands, whose sales would be reduced because of the introduction of 'Epsilon'. Fixed and variable costs were not explicitly separated from each other and contribution was not shown. The calculation made in year one showed that 'Epsilon' was not likely to break even until after year five. The main reason for this was that the national launch was now to be delayed until year three. In years three and four, there was to be heavy advertising and other sales promotion for 'Epsilon'. It was to be twice as big as all sales promotion expenditure at the time of the national launch, falling somewhat later.

Epsilon Ltd used a considerable number of aids to decision making. For example, a good deal of information was collected during the test markets. In year zero, 'Epsilon's' elasticity of demand was tested (as we saw in Chapter 7) by sales at different prices at different times and in a limited number of areas—care being taken to isolate any spill-over. Epsilon Ltd therefore had a great deal of market information both of this kind and from its own and other market researchers.

A number of market research methods were used to assess the potential market for 'Epsilon'. Apart from the experiments designed to discover its elasticity of demand, market research was carried out to identify the kind of consumer at whom 'Epsilon' was aimed. A number of papers were written within Epsilon Ltd covering various aspects of the marketing strategy to be adopted for 'Epsilon'. These led to a detailed proposal for test-marketing 'Epsilon'.

As for the pricing decision itself, well before the test market Epsilon Ltd laid down the product specification, selling policy and price range for 'Epsilon'. Epsilon Ltd emphasized that the decision process for 'Epsilon' was a continuing one which would persist even after 'Epsilon' was established.

Up to the time of our study, most decisions on 'Epsilon' had been aimed at discovering ways of implementing the basic decision to market it—especially during the test market and the subsequent national launch. Because 'Epsilon' was a new product, predictions of its performance had to be made on the basis of the assumptions rather than facts. However, its newness also meant that there was no cost/profit information about competitors, except on advertising and sales promotion. This made it difficult to reduce the uncertainty facing the management in selling 'Epsilon'.

As with most of our cases, there was more internal than external information about 'Epsilon'. Even though a good deal of this was cost information it did little more than limit the uncertainty facing those taking marketing decisions. As with market information, a good deal of the cost information represented assumptions about future costs rather than firm figures.

There was a good deal of informal discussion of 'Epsilon's' progress within Epsilon Ltd, not least because it was still in its test-market phase. However, the product manager for 'Epsilon' was responsible for presenting formal proposals about its pricing and marketing, with the most important decisions taken by the Marketing Committee.

10.8 LARGE FIRM PRICING: LARGE GROUP (GAMMA PRODUCTS LTD)

It will be remembered that our study in Gamma Ltd was concerned with the introduction of a battery-operated razor introduced to help sales of Gamma's batteries. The firm was divided into three sections, which dealt with sales, production and technical issues respectively. Any study of new products was primarily the responsibility of the sales department. The product manager in charge of battery razors was responsible to the product group manager who in turn was responsible to the sales director of the Board.

The product manager was made responsible for collecting and evaluating information about the razor project, but any proposals he made had to be passed by his product group manager and by the Board before they could be implemented. There was considerable informal contact between these three levels. Part of the product manager's job was to collect relevant technical and production information about the battery razor. Naturally, at Board level, the technical and production directors were involved.

As we saw in Chapter 7, the price fixers in Gamma had (not very reliable) information about the size and growth rate of the markets, both for batteries and for battery-operated razors. We also saw, in Chapter 8, that preliminary cost estimates had been obtained from manufacturers able to supply the battery-operated razors. These showed that the company could have its razors manufactured at least as cheaply as any competitor.

The product manager produced several sets of estimates. These were based on combinations of the following possibilities:

(i) that the number of battery-operated razors in use would rise to 20 per cent or to 40 per cent of all razors used, in the next ten years;
(ii) that Gamma's share of the battery razor market would be 10 per cent, 20 per cent or 50 per cent of the total market;
(iii) that Gamma would allow retailers a 50 per cent margin (a) on razors alone, or (b) on razors plus batteries.

From these figures, a range of profitabilities was obtained. Over five years, profit estimates ranged between *y* thousand pounds and 10 *y* thousand pounds depending on the combination of assumptions used.

Gamma found a neighbouring firm that was able and willing to manufacture the razors. It turned out that, taking net manufacturing cost and adding, first, distribution and selling costs and, second, retailers' margins and discounts, it would be difficult to compete with other products if a 50 per cent margin was allowed. With a 25 per cent margin, Gamma would be able to undercut its competitors. However, the product manager proposed, and his superiors agreed, that the list price of the razor should be set assuming a 50 per cent margin, with the aim of selling at this margin through barbers' shops.

The idea was that when Gamma sold razors through electrical shops, it could allow a 25 per cent margin and so make price cuts. This would keep the price of Gamma's razors in line with those of competitors. It was felt that where razors were sold at a 50 per cent margin (i.e. in barbers' shops) there would be little effect on sales of Gamma's batteries. Where they were sold at a discount, in electrical shops, battery sales would be helped. Of course, the main reason for launching the battery razor had been the feeling that more of Gamma's batteries would be sold if it introduced a razor bearing its own name. No one in the company saw any need to change the price of razor batteries.

Gamma ordered a restricted number of razors for a test-market experiment in a limited area. It was decided to use Gamma's established distribution channels at this stage, namely electrical shops, rather than barbers' shops. To help sales, Gamma offered a set of batteries which would last a year with each razor. These were sold through the company's normal outlets on a 25 per cent margin, and the price of the razor plus batteries was 15 per cent to 20 per cent less than that of competitive products being sold through barbers' shops.

Within two or three months, it became clear that the total numbers of razors needed to meet demand, even for this test-market operation would exceed all expectations. By the end of six months, the number of razors that had been ordered had reached six times the budgeted production figure. Unfortunately, Gamma's supplier could provide only some 60 per cent of the razors needed at this stage. There was naturally considerable dissatisfaction in electrical shops. Electrical retailers remained happy to handle Gamma's batteries, but refused to have much to do with the razor. During this period, Gamma had made some efforts to sell more razors to barbers, but they were not very successful. The barbers wanted 50 per cent margins, refused to consider price cutting for an introductory offer, and thus gave Gamma's razor no advantage over competing products.

This episode caused considerable heartsearching within Gamma and made it necessary to reconsider the whole exercise. Originally, the idea had been that the razor could be marketed at break-even price, if necessary, in order to increase the sales of Gamma's batteries. Now it became clear that this was unacceptable because the demand for razors was so big. The need to take measures to make a satisfactory profit on razors became obvious when it was discovered that the sales of batteries did not follow the sales of razors. Market research conducted after the trial-market period confirmed that, once they had bought Gamma's razors, customers used many other manufacturers' batteries. The hope for loyalty to the company's batteries was not realized.

As for Gamma's batteries, these had been priced in accordance with Gamma's normal concepts. Of these, the most important was Gamma's belief that its image was as a producer of high-quality products, giving it an ability to risk competition from lower-price substitutes. Although this view was correct for many of Gamma's other markets, it was not so true either of the razor or the battery markets. This was the main reason why Gamma's batteries were relatively unsuccessful.

When our study ended, Gamma felt that, for both batteries and razors, it had to choose between different courses of action. With batteries, it might price its special razor battery at a price equal to the prices of competitive products of the same type and quality. Or it might sell its razor batteries at the same price as cheaper products, possibly reducing quality to do so. Second, the razor—still seen as tied to Gamma's batteries—could be sold at the same price as competitors' razors selling through barbers' shops. Or, in view of its success, it could be sold at a higher price. The price of the razor in electrical shops needed to be reconsidered for the same reasons.

Gamma felt that the original arrangements made for the test-market, where its batteries were more expensive than those of competitors and its razors cheaper, could not continue. Among its reasons were these:

(i) the size of the market for razor batteries had been over-estimated, and its composition misjudged;
(ii) batteries, being distributed largely through electrical shops, competed with cheaper batteries also sold through these shops. Against them, Gamma's products faced an impossible price disadvantage;
(iii) the razor-battery market, being relatively simple to enter, was open to all-comers;
(iv) as the long-term prospects for razor batteries were promising, the bigger the foothold Gamma obtained in the early stages the better its long-term prospects would be.

All this led Gamma to decide that the price of its batteries should be reduced. Gamma also decided to raise the price of its razors. The size of the battery-razor market had originally been underestimated. This was why Gamma had decided to market the razor virtually at break-even cost, in the hope of capturing a good share of the razor market and obtaining a large number of loyal buyers of Gamma's batteries. When its mistake was recognized, it became obvious to Gamma that this was a case of expecting the tail to wag the dog. During the period in which Gamma's razor was on the market, some manufacturers had introduced very high-quality models, and others simplified and cheaper versions. This indicated a widening of the whole price range, so that Gamma felt free to increase the price of its razors.

Gamma had considerable information about its main markets, representing about 95 per cent of its total sales. Information on quantities sold, market sizes and market shares, and growth rates for Gamma's staple products, were available for a number of years. Information about the smaller sectors of the battery market, and about some spheres of activity outside it, had not previously been thought significant enough to be worth collecting. It would therefore be unfair to judge the standard and quality of the firm's market information for other products by the information available when it was looking at the battery-razor or battery markets.

The collection of information about the razor and battery markets was very much left to the product manager. It was logical for Gamma to extend its activities into selling razor batteries and both the product group manager and the Board supported the idea—if it would be profitable. However, the idea of developing this market by selling the battery-razor was alien to Gamma's normal ways of operating.

Because Gamma felt that the success or failure of the battery razor project would have little effect on its total activities, there was less opposition to the trial market idea than there might otherwise have been. Although it was recognized that market estimates were unreliable, the product group manager and the Board accepted the profits they implied as reasonable. The expected profit was small by Gamma's normal standards. However, as the whole razor project had been conceived to help Gamma's battery sales, the absolute profitability of the project was regarded as relatively unimportant.

The procedures Gamma followed in deciding to sell the battery-razor followed normal practice. The Board of Gamma had always relied on its operating management to scrutinize and evaluate proposals before they were submitted. The original launching of Gamma's batteries had been accomplished successfully through its normal distribution channels—mainly electrical shops. The introduction of the razor was complicated by the need to consider an extra system of distribution to barbers. In addition, the fact that the demand for razors was underestimated, because of a shortage of market information, led to a great deal of customer and retailer discontent.

This is an example of a pricing decision where objectives were not clear and where market forecasts were bad. Gamma was uncertain how far its aim was to make a profit from its razors and so charged too little. Nor had it seen how hard it was going to be to increase battery sales, even with the razor. The lesson of how important it is to be clear about objectives is one all firms should remember.

10.9 LARGE FIRM PRICING: LARGE GROUP (UNIVERSAL CORPORATION)

It will be remembered that our study of Universal Corporation was concerned with a change in its whole method of pricing—towards a system where more prices were linked to marginal cost. This new price list was the culmination of a long process which began in the early sixties. Pressure for a change towards prices based on marginal cost was exerted throughout by Universal's parent firm, which was impressed by the fact that firms in the same industry in Europe had moved in this direction. Indeed, they gave Universal a great deal of information about their experience in doing so. In addition, the Chairman of the parent firm had been trained in economics and was influenced by his own ideas on the usefulness of linking price to marginal cost and by the ideas of other economists. At the same time, changes in production methods made marginal costing more appropriate. The first move away from average costing was made in the early 1960s. After two years, a conference was held within Universal when it was agreed that the movement away from average costing should be continued. The conference went on to look at a number of ways of doing so. One group of customers, which took part in the conference, was particularly keen that Universal should introduce a pricing policy on roughly the same basis as was finally accepted.

In the early 1960s, it was suggested that Universal Corporation might be charging its two main groups of customers prices that did not reflect the marginal costs of supplying each of them. The suggestion was that because one group tended to make a bigger proportion of its purchases at periods of peak demand, it might be paying too little for what it bought, and be subsidized by the other group. While the study showed that both groups were paying prices that *did* cover the long-run marginal costs of supplying them, this episode strengthened the hands of those in Universal who wanted to move to marginal costing.

It will be remembered that Universal Corporation was a satisficing firm, with the clearly-stated objective of earning a certain rate of return on capital employed for its whole operations. We also saw, in Chapter 8, that Universal worked out very carefully how total cost and marginal cost would change as output altered, both in the aggregate and for particular customers. The task of drawing up a price list based on marginal cost was a complex, but clearly-defined one. The detailed work was the job of the commercial department. An engineer in a section of this department was responsible for collecting output forecasts and cost information. In collaboration with the head of his section, he worked out proposals for a new price list, using this data. There was no formal set of procedures or directives to limit the way in which the section did this. What was done therefore depended very much on what had been done on previous occasions, on how things had worked out then, and, of course, on the objectives—especially the return on capital objective—laid down by Universal's Board. Within these limits, the pricing section, and the head of the commercial department, were free to make to the Board what recommendations they thought best.

Proposals for the price list, which came into operation on the first of April in each year, were worked out towards the end of the previous year. Universal's full Board had to approve the price list before it was published. The proposals were presented to the Board by the financial director after he had discussed them, and perhaps suggested final changes, with the heads of the commercial department and of its pricing section.

Formally, only the Board could decide on the price list. However, in practice, there was a good deal of informal discussion among those concerned. As well as forming the channel for passing pricing proposals to the Board, the financial director and the head of the commercial department kept in touch with the Board members and, especially during periods when the price list was being reviewed, were told of any changes in the Board's policies and requirements. There was therefore a two-way movement of information, ideas and broad proposals between the Board, the financial director and the two managers most closely concerned with constructing price lists.

At an early stage in the process of considering the new price list for Universal, a decision had to be taken about the main types of charge to be made. Universal had previously built up its price list from three elements. First, there was a production charge. This had previously been closely related to the average cost of production. In view of the fact that it had now been decided to link price to marginal cost, it was decided that production charges would have to be based on the running costs of marginal equipment. However, this at once led to a problem. Universal's marginal machinery was less efficient than its new plant. As a result, marginal production costs were well above average costs. Universal therefore decided to delay relating its production charge very closely to marginal cost until more new equipment had been installed. When that had been done, a system of production charges closely linked to marginal costs could be introduced.

To avoid introducing a very complicated price structure, Universal had identified three different kinds of production period and associated a different kind of production charge with output produced in each of them. There was a peak period charge, at times when Universal was exceptionally busy; a normal production charge, for periods when trade was brisk but there was some spare capacity; and a slack-period charge, for times when Universal was working well below full capacity.

Once its total output for the next year had been forecast, Universal was able to use its computer programme to forecast the amount of output which would be produced in each of these three different kinds of time period. We have seen that this was a computer-simulation programme, which separated variable cost from the remainder of total cost and so identified the marginal cost of producing the output made in each of these three different types of period. The only problem was that production was not constant within each kind of time period. Marginal cost was therefore different at different times, even within one kind of time period. This was so, even though the three kinds of time period had been carefully chosen to keep such cost variations to a minimum. Strictly speaking, this meant that marginal cost had to be an average over the range of output associated with each of the three types of time period. The computer simulation programme forecast what would be the level of demand, and so which marginal plant would be in operation, at any time in the next year. This could be done quite easily, because the marginal cost of operating each machine was known.

The two other elements lying behind Universal's price list were two kinds of capacity charge. Universal met marginal demand during peak periods mainly by using rather old machines. For the remainder of its output, Universal could afford to install new ones. While these had much lower variable costs than did marginal machines, they also had higher fixed costs. Universal had found, in previous years, that only during peak periods was it working beyond 90 per cent of its total capacity, and it did not expect this relationship to change much in future.

The new price list, whose introduction we studied, included two capacity charges. First, there was a peak-period charge. Each year, Universal worked out with its customers what the highest level of output it was going to have to produce would be. Universal defined peak-period capacity as the capacity required to produce the top 10 per cent of its output. The total peak-capacity charge was, therefore, one which Universal thought sufficient to keep the capacity needed to produce one unit of output in existence, multiplied by 10 per cent of the maximum demand agreed with customers.

There was also a charge for the remainder of capacity. In principle, this was intended to cover the remainder of the fixed costs which Universal had to meet; these were the costs incurred in keeping the remaining 90 per cent of its total plant in existence. In practice, it was calculated as the amount which Universal must earn in order to meet its estimated costs for the year, after deducting the amount expected to be raised from the production charges and the peak-capacity charge. Total 'costs' included an amount which would give the rate of return on capital required from Universal by its Board. If the output produced was the one expected, Universal would meet all its costs and would earn a profit of the size required by the Board. At the same time, the peak capacity charge would have recovered the amount of money needed to keep open the plant required to meet demand in peak periods.

10.10 LARGE FIRM PRICING: LARGE GROUP (BASIC FOODS LTD)

One of the most important documents leading to any initiative to change prices in Basic Foods was the quarterly review of performance. This gave all managers figures for output, sales receipts, costs, profit and return on capital. Once a year, more detailed information was given—including data on the market shares of Basic Foods and its competitors, on Basic Food's unit production costs, unit marketing expenditure, unit contribution, and so on. Comparative data was given for all these items. It compared performance in the current year with that in the previous year; performance in the current year with the plan for the current year; and performance in the current year with the estimate for the next year. Quite detailed analyses were made for individual products.

When a price change was seriously being considered, a thorough analysis was carried out. Basic Foods calculated what would happen if various possible prices were charged—including what would happen if no price change was made at all. Basic Foods rightly emphasized that what mattered was the *difference* between the results of pursuing each of the various possible courses of action, so that alternatives were compared by looking only at those aspects of each alternative which would differ if prices were altered. Factors which would affect the firm's final profit, but which would not be altered by the price changes, could also be ignored. Thus, for example, a price change was being considered by our study, at a time when Basic Foods was in the process of changing its distribution system. It was agreed that the effects of this change in the distribution system on Basic Food's market share would be the same whatever the level of price was. It did not need to be taken into account when Basic Foods was making the pricing decision.

In the end, of course, only one of the possible lines of action could be followed, but Basic Foods considered all realistic ones. Since Basic Foods was operating in an oligopolistic market, account had to be taken, in some way, of the fact that each different alternative set of prices would lead to a different response by competitors. No very sophisticated procedures were used in doing this.

However, the success of any such exercise depends on the assumptions made and on the quality of the data used. It does not seem to us that Basic Foods could have improved on the information it had about the reactions of competitors—short of engaging in industrial espionage. When we studied it, Basic Foods was mainly concerned with how to respond to possible price changes—which later occurred—by a major competitor. With smaller competitors, Basic Foods knew the prices of their raw materials and the prices at which their final products were sold, so that it could quite easily work out their costs and profits. With bigger (and therefore more diversified) competitors this was harder. Basic Foods therefore fell back on the assumption we found being used in several of these studies—that the costs of competitors were similar to its own. Basic Foods felt that unless its price were lowered it would lose market share—if only to smaller suppliers selling through cut-price stores. It was not prepared to change retailers' margins.

Some of the other assumptions were even harder to decide on. One example, in the year when we were studying Basic Foods, was how to decide what would be the size and timing of any fiscal change which might affect its products. In fact, the nature and size of a change in taxation was predicted quite accurately, but it took place four months later than had been anticipated. It was also hard to know what would happen to the sales of each of Basic Foods' products. As the incomes of its customers rose, there was a relatively bigger increase in the sales of the more expensive of Basic Foods' products. What happened was also affected by the ending of resale price maintenance and by lower prices for its raw materials.

While accepting that mistakes could be made, Basic Foods believed that, provided similar methods of estimation and analysis were used throughout, a good comparison of the effects of alternative courses of action could be obtained. As we have emphasized continually, it is comparisons between alternative courses of action that matter.

What did not seem to be done in Basic Foods was to make sure which were the crucial elements in each problem. For example, how important was it to be right about competitors' reactions? Was this more important than to be right about how far customers were switching from cheaper to dearer products? Obviously, time was limited, and not all possible alternatives could be considered. As a result, Basic Foods may be one of the firms we studied which could have benefited from using a computer to make such complicated calculations quickly. The computer would have enabled it to carry out the kind of sensitivity analysis we shall discuss in more detail in Chapter 11.

One problem was that Basic Foods did not think that its assumptions could be checked by test marketing. Its market was so fluid at the time of our study that it felt unable to be sure that a given effect was the result of a given cause. This was especially true with pricing. It was thought that price cuts in test markets were very unlikely to lead to the same results as price cuts on a national scale. It is important to remember that this objection is not equally valid if the test marketing is carried out to find the effects of local rather than national price cuts.

The detailed calculations made by Basic Foods were as follows. First, calculations were made for the current year and for up to five years ahead for the 'no change' case. At this stage, calculations were made of: (a) the total market; (b) the market shares for Basic Foods and for its competitors; and (c) the financial implications of 'no change'.

Fixed costs were assumed to be the same for all alternatives, so that changes in costs were concentrated on raw material costs and other variable costs. The firm argued, correctly, that fixed costs determined only whether it was profitable to trade at a given price, and not which was the best of a series of alternative prices. The calculations for the relevant alternatives were made one by one, the aim being to get estimates that were reasonable and cautious. Thus, for example, if the proposal included producing a new quality of product, questions like these were asked. Would this reduce sales of Basic Foods' other products? Would it reduce sales of competitors' products? A 'bracketing' procedure was used. Is *X* too much? Is *Y* too little? A consensus figure was then reached, by reducing *X* and/or increasing *Y* until there was agreement. It was obviously important that each step in each calculation, for each alternative, should be consistent with each other step. The aim was that, at the end, the figure for each alternative would be reasonable, given the figures for all the other alternatives. With no computer used, Basic Foods depended heavily on the judgement and experience of those concerned. One calculated, the results could be checked against known factors. Thus, when Basic Foods introduced a new type of product, it found it possible to take the market share held by a similar product made by a competitor, estimate Basic Foods' likely market share if it went into the market and so estimate the result of adding the new product to Basic Foods' range.

The translation of changes in the volume of Basic Foods' sales into money terms was relatively simple. As compared with the 'no change' case, the increase or decrease in sales for each type of product could be multiplied by the new selling price, with an allowance for loss or gain of revenue from lower prices on existing sales. From this figure could be subtracted changes in variable cost, giving a change in profit. Having made these calculations, it was possible for Basic Foods to compare each alternative with the 'no change' case and with each other alternative.

At this point, Basic Foods' calculations for all of the alternatives were presented to the general manager in charge of marketing, with a recommendation about what should happen to prices. The figures and the recommendation were discussed. At this stage, and at all subsequent stages, it was possible for variants of any alternatives to be asked for and calculated. This was a possible source of error, because the calculations usually had to be made very rapidly to meet deadlines. They could, of course, be complex.

The final recommendation was likely to be the one that gave the best long-run increase in profit, as compared with the no-change case. This recommendation was then presented to the marketing director. There was further discussion and, perhaps, re-calculation. The same happened with the vice-chairman. It was in these discussions with the marketing director and vice-chairman that wider implications had to be considered. For example, how would a change in the price of this product affect Basic Foods' operations for other products and markets? What would be the effect of the recommendation on Basic Foods' overall profitability? There was some feeling in Basic Foods that the wider implications of pricing decisions for its operations were not always considered sufficiently fully.

10.11 LARGE FIRM PRICING: LARGE GROUPS (ALPHA LTD)

More than any other firm in our study, Alpha Ltd emphasized that pricing was never considered separately, but as one element only in the whole marketing mix. This was largely because Alpha was selling consumer goods in a market where advertising and other forms of sales promotion were important.

The formal organization structure of Alpha Ltd was complicated. The chairman of Alpha Ltd was responsible to the parent firm. Below him, there were three executive directors—concerned with commercial, marketing and technical matters. The commercial manager supervised the financial and accounting staff. The marketing director had a sales director, an advertising director and a number of product group managers below him. The sales director was responsible for the sales and operations staff and the advertising director for advertising. Each of the product group managers was responsible to the sales director and had a number of product managers responsible to him, as well as a technical liaison manager. The latter worked with the staff of the technical director and his senior colleagues—namely, the production director, the technical liaison director and the development director.

However, Alpha used a product group system which cut across this hierarchical structure. Each product group was made up of a product group manager, a deputy product group manager and a product manager. The product group also included managers from finance, market research, sales and advertising. These four provided specialized services for the group, while remaining responsible to their own superiors in the managerial hierarchy.

The reason why Alpha Ltd used the product group system was that this made communication easier than would have been possible if it had used the normal lines of communication in the formal hierarchy. A large amount of information was exchanged within Alpha Ltd, and it was thought that using marketing groups reduced the possibility of delay and misunderstanding. In other words, Alpha Ltd had introduced product specialization for information.

To understand the decision process in Alpha Ltd, one has to look at another organization structure. The chairman of Alpha Ltd was responsible to the parent firm. The board of Alpha Ltd included the chairman, three executive directors and the four directors of sales, advertising, production and development. In fact, the board of Alpha Ltd was not the most important body in its decision structure. By the time matters reached it, they would have been fully considered by its product or technical sub-committees. The board's job was to determine policy for the next one to five years, in fields like marketing, investment and research and development.

From our point of view, the most important body was the product sub-committee. This consisted of:

executive marketing director (chairman);
sales director;
advertising director;
product group managers

and perhaps the deputy product group managers and product managers. This committee met every fortnight and dealt with each of three product groups in turn. Each group was therefore dealt with every six weeks.

Below this, meetings of product groups were held immediately before each meeting of the product sub-committee. The product group was not given any formal task to perform at these meetings, but dealt with matters of current importance to the group. The product group manager could also call meetings to discuss the problems of individual products when he thought this necessary. When called, such a meeting would have included:

product manager;
product group manager (chairman);
assistant product manager;
technical liaison manager;
market research officer;
sales manager;
promotion manager.

There was also a technical sub-committee of the Board, under the technical director. This met fortnightly and reported on technical matters to the full Board.

Even the fairly flexible structure just described was often superseded, in practice, by an even more flexible and informal one, with frequent contact between product group managers (representing product groups) and the executive marketing director. Pricing decisions within Alpha Ltd—including decisions on product specification and sales promotion—fell into four stages. We must now look at these. First, however, we must remind ourselves of the objectives of Alpha Ltd. It will be recalled that, for short periods, usually the next year, any conflicts between objectives were eliminated during the budgeting process. This left Alpha Ltd with specific budgeted objectives, for sales, profit and market share. For longer periods, conflicts between objectives were possible, though in the case of product 'Alpha' the procedure had been to set objectives for the next five years by specifying a given absolute amount of money profit and a given market share which were to be achieved.

With these objectives, the decision processes for 'Alpha' were set in motion if a change in one or more of five factors occurred. These were as follows.

First, and most important, there was the competitive situation. This was the whole competitive situation, including the market position and marketing mix for 'Omega' as well as for 'Alpha'. The most important elements in the competitive situation were: the competing brands and their characteristics and their prices, as compared with those of 'Alpha', trends in market development; and the marketing plans, financial position, production and selling capacity of other firms in the market. Significant changes in any of these would trigger off marketing decisions within Alpha Ltd.

Second, there was the revenue, cost and profit situation for 'Alpha' itself, at the relevant level(s) of sales. If the current and forecast sizes of these financial factors moved significantly out of line with their budgeted levels, marketing decisions again became necessary. Third, there was the underlying market situation. Here, those concerned with 'Alpha' had to consider the size and type of market, its likely development and growth, buyers' attitudes and the type of product currently being sold.

Fourth, there was product development. Alpha Ltd was continually monitoring the way all its products were expected to change as a result of technical advances or in response to changes in the market situation or in the competitive position.

Finally, there was the mix of price, product design, sales promotion and distribution arrangements currently being offered to the consumer of 'Alpha', including both advertising expenditure and trade margins. This represented the total marketing mix for 'Alpha'. Changes in price would be made only as part of changes of this total marketing mix.

A change in any one of the five factors listed above would lead to discussions about possible alterations in 'Alpha's' marketing mix.

However, since all these variables were linked, it was likely that any change in the external situation would alter more than one of them.

Now that we have considered the factors which led to discussions of marketing problems within Alpha Ltd we can move on to look at the decision process itself. This was divided into five stages.

(a) *First Stage: Initiation*

One of the distinguishing characteristics of Alpha Ltd was the way that a proposal to alter the marketing mix could be initiated anywhere in the organization from the product manager to the chairman. In practice, an initiative for change most often came from the product manager. Initiatives arising within the product group were in any case channelled through the product manager for the product in question and so become his responsibility. Again, initiatives which came from a higher level normally required the agreement of the product manager, although there had been a few cases where this had not happened. At this stage, no one had more than an idea which was precise enough to be formulated into a marketing (pricing) proposal. The proposal was conceived (though not necessarily written down) in terms of: 'What would happen if . . .?'

(b) *Second Stage: Discussion*

With most pricing decisions, this stage was likely to be both the most important and the most time-consuming. The main tasks were:

1. Giving answers to the question: 'What would happen if . . .?'
2. Discussing the consequences of adopting the proposal in the light of the answers. If the proposal looked unsatisfactory at this stage, it would be rejected. If not, a formal recommendation would be made to the Board. All levels of management in Alpha Ltd took part in these discussions, and the informal nature of decision mechanism meant both that it was very flexible and that it was very difficult for a researcher to observe, in detail, how it worked. The product manager prepared the final proposal. In this, the developments lying behind the proposal were outlined, precise recommendations were made and the results of accepting these recommendations were forecast. Any alternative proposals which had been considered were usually set out, together with the reasons why they had not been accepted.

Alpha Ltd made more use of mathematical models and other aids to decision making than any other of our firms. Obviously, it was at this discussion stage that they were most useful. In particular, Alpha Ltd made a good deal of use of probability analysis and other operational research techniques. It was helped in this by the operational research department of the parent firm.

Besides using these techniques, in the discussion period while pricing changes were under review Alpha also made a good deal of use of regular and *ad hoc* reports asked for by the product group. These were written either within Alpha Ltd, in the parent firm or by outside consultants.

The product group might ask for *ad hoc* reports to help it solve particular problems. Studies were made of particular markets or situations within the context of the current and forecast state of the world or the national economy; of the current competitive situation; of Alpha's plans and aspirations; and of what was known about competitors' plans and prospects. All the known implications of the new situation, and of the various alternative lines of action which might be followed to meet it, were studied before a report was made to management. The effects of these special studies could be cumulative—a series of studies about a particular aspect of a problem might become part of an overall study dealing with that problem as a whole.

The most important report produced within Alpha Ltd, circulated twice a year, was the marketing review. This was the foundation for the budgeting procedure. However, since it provided both an analysis of marketing resutls and a foundation for budgets, it was also useful background information for marketing, including pricing, decisions.

(c) *Third Stage: Decision*

Decisions normally followed discussion of a recommendation from a product manager. They were made either by the Board or by the executive marketing director. By this stage, any proposal would have been intensively discussed within Alpha, so that the product group and product management would be committed to it to some extent. However, a proposal could still be rejected. If the proposal were to be accepted in a modified form, this would be taken as a rejection and the new proposal would be discussed again in detail.

(d) *Fourth Stage: Implementation*

Little need be said here, except that the implementation of any decision was the job of the branch manager.

(e) *Fifth Stage: Review of Pricing Decisions*
Alpha regarded pricing as essentially a dynamic process. Formal review machinery was provided by the half-yearly marketing review. In addition, each product group kept the progress of each of its products under continuous review, watching any changes in market conditions and any changes in competitors' marketing mix. This meant that Alpha had a process which enabled it to observe the way decisions were working out and to suggest remedial action where necessary.

10.12 CONCLUDING REMARKS

We have now looked in detail at all the pricing decisions we studied. In Chapter 11 we shall go on to consider what conclusions we can draw from them.

CHAPTER 11

Conclusions

11.1 INTRODUCTION

In this chapter, we try to bring out what we have learned from our study of pricing decisions. In particular, we try to answer the questions we posed in Chapter 1.

11.2 OBJECTIVES

In Chapter 1, we asked two questions about objectives. Does the organization set itself the objective of reaching satisfactory rather than maximum solutions? Does the fact that the firm is a coalition of individuals, rather than a unitary organism, affect the kind of objective that is set?

Eight of our firms were satisficers rather than maximizers in making the pricing decisions we studied, but this does not prove anything at all about British industry as a whole. First, we know only that the five profit-maximizers attempted to maximize profit in taking the pricing decisions we studied. In taking other pricing decisions they may have satisficed. Nor do we know how far they were maximizers in taking other kinds of decision. One of our important conclusions is that the impact of pricing decisions is felt by customers and competitors rather than colleagues. So, firms seem more likely to maximize when taking pricing decisions (and perhaps when taking marketing or investment decisions) than when taking decisions on levels of production, inventory, employment, etc.

Even so, eight of the thirteen firms were satisficers rather than maximizers and of the five maximizers some appeared a little half-half-hearted. Moreover, even our whole-hearted maximizers could only *attempt* to maximize: none had enough information to be certain they *were* maximizing, given changing external conditions. It is also certain that we had a biased sample, in the sense that four of the five maximizers were member firms of the Centre for Business Research who asked us to study pricing in their firm because there were difficulties over the profitability of the products in question. They thought that we might be able to help them to improve it. Of the maximizers, only the Surgical Instrument Company did not come to us in this way.

There is no doubt that there is a great deal of satisficing in making pricing decisions, and almost certainly much more in making other decisions. However, we must qualify this remark in two ways. First the member firms of the C.B.R. are among the best-known and most efficient firms in Britain, so that they are probably more likely to maximize than industry in general. Second, there has almost certainly been a good deal of improvement in pricing methods in recent years. There is probably more emphasis on profit maximization now than when we made our studies. However, we feel confident that a great deal of satisficing behaviour remains.

As for the effects on objectives of the fact that the firm is a 'coalition', we did not find much disagreement over what objectives should be, or were, except in Alpha Ltd. There, we (but not they) feel there was a difference of objectives between the top management and lower levels. However, some of the consensus over objectives in other firms occurred because, as Cyert and March suggest, many objectives were non-operational. They were so meaningless that they could be easily accepted. We have also seen that the *real* objectives were set in the budgeting process, where disagreement over objectives appeared to be treated as a largely technical matter. With the proviso already made about Alpha, there was less difficulty over reconciling objectives in big firms—and these were the ones where the budgeting process was most efficient. In the big firms, the analysis of pricing problems was written and explicit, and objectives were made clear—except perhaps in Gamma where there was uncertainty over the extent to which the firm did, or did not, want to make profit from the razor as distinct from the battery.

The existence of a coalition could affect the one-man price setter only in the objectives given to him. In our cases (Surgical Instrument Company and Dee Plastics), there was no sign of this. It was less clear what the position was in the medium-sized firms—Wensum, Fourways, Heavy Technology, Clean Engineering and Medlock Engineering. There was little use of written analysis in taking pricing decisions and it was not clear, even in the pricing meetings we observed, how far perceptions of objectives differed between individuals. One man whose perceptions were different was the home sales manager of Wensum Engineering, but we think that this was not so much a result of a difference in objectives as of the fact that he wanted to alter his own role and status in the pricing-decision process.

What the 'coalition' did seem to do, as Cyert and March would have expected, was to lead to a good deal of satisficing.

11.3 INFORMATION

On information, we asked three questions in Chapter 1. Is it possible, in oligopoly for firms to make reasonably scientific assessments of the way in which competitors will react to given price changes on their part? More important, is it possible to say more about the problem, ignored in traditional economics, of how much it is (a) necessary to pay, and (b) worth paying, in order to obtain extra information about reactions of competitors? Can one do anything to devise ways of calculating the costs and benefits of obtaining extra information about markets, costs, etc? In other words, can one put a value on cost accountancy and market research in oligopoly?

On whether it is possible to make scientific assessments about the way competitors will react, we can say only that our firms seemed to be reasonably successful in making such assessments. However, our firms may well not be typical. Only Heavy Technology and Medlock Engineering were beginning to use probability to assess what competitors' tender prices were likely to be, but the process of reaction was a very slow one. It was not usually possible to react until the next tender, so that the whole process was slowed down. There was no attempt at all at scientific analysis of shorter-run reactions. Scientific assessment of oligopolistic reactions may be possible, but our firms, including many leading ones, had not yet begun to tackle the problem seriously.

Nor can we say much more about the other questions. These were clearly issues that greatly concerned our firms, especially Wensum Engineering, but they were not able to answer the questions for us. It clearly would be extremely helpful to be able to put a value on cost accountancy and market research, both in oligopoly and in more simple market situations. However, this is a field where, if success is possible, it appears to lie fairly far into the future. One immediate move might be to use sensitivity analysis (described on p. 260) to show what the benefit would be from acquiring particular information. This would at least put a figure on what the firm could *afford* to pay for given information.

11.4 WHO TOOK PRICING DECISIONS?

We have so far said little about precisely who took pricing decisions in our firms. It may be useful to analyse what we have discovered from our cases. Although each firm had its own pricing organization, there was a common pattern. In every case one or more senior managers was directly responsible for making pricing decisions. They worked closely with middle management (marketing or sales) in beginning discussions on pricing and marketing problems. In every case but one, the whole pricing process had been delegated by the chief executive to subordinates; in Dee Plastics, the chief executive took the final decision in certain cases. In six firms, Alpha, Gamma, Basic Foods, Epsilon, Wessex and Universal Corporation, pricing decisions were made or approved collectively by the Board, after separate or joint studies of possible price changes had been undertaken by the Board and by marketing management. In Wessex, limited authority to vary prices was given to salesmen.

In five other firms, Wensum, Fourways, Heavy Technology, Medlock Engineering and Clean Engineering, pricing decisions were also made collectively by committees of Board members and senior managers. With one exception (Fourways) these committees tended to be dominated by one man—either the sales or commercial manager.

In the two remaining firms, the Surgical Instrument Company and Dee Plastics, prices were set by one man, who had almost complete freedom to do as he thought best. In the Surgical Instrument Company, sales agents had limited authority to vary prices. The marketing manager himself was not subject to any discernible control by the Board. In Dee, the final decision was made by the managing director, if the commercial manager thought that the upper or lower limit of price, within which he was expected to work, was likely to be reached.

11.5 THE ANALYSIS OF INFORMATION

The way in which information was analysed for pricing decisions can be summarized most conveniently by distinguishing three situations. These are where the analysis was carried out: by one man; by a small group; and by a large group.

11.5.1 One-Man Pricing

One man set prices in Dee Plastics and in the Surgical Instrument Company, though in Dee the managing director took over pricing negotiations where these were thought to be particularly important. Inevitably, the one-man price fixer had to rely on his own judgement in estimating the nature of relationships between relevant variables and in forming an opinion about the way competitors would react to any move he made. Dee, for example, was selling in a duopolistic market. The price setter therefore had to judge questions like: how far he would have to increase discounts to obtain a given order; how much 'contribution' this order would bring in; and whether he should take the business at that price or wait. The case for waiting would be strong either if prices were expected to rise later, or if Dee expected its bigger competitor to match any price cut.

However, while our one-man price setters were dealing with oligopolistic markets, these two men usually had little alternative but to accept the prices set by their competitors. This was especially true of Dee. The importance of competitors' reactions in our case studies resulted from our particular sample of firms. We can say nothing about the market situations faced by one-man price setters in general.

The comments that seem worth making are these. Our one-man price setters did not produce detailed, written analyses of the information they used in setting prices, whether about demand, cost or competitors' reactions. This need not mean that their thinking on these matters was unsophisticated. What we can say is that, in both cases, the information they had did not make it easy for them to distinguish between fixed and variable costs. They must have found it harder than was necessary to estimate the effect of any given price change on 'contribution'.

11.5.2 Small Group Pricing

In six of the firms we studied, pricing was carried out by small groups of people, though four of them—Clean Engineering, Heavy Technology, Medlock Engineering and Wessex Timber—were big firms. The remaining two of the six firms, Wensum and Fourways, were smallish subsidiaries of large businesses. This made what was happening much clearer for us than with one-man or large-group pricing,

Because more than one person was involved in pricing some written information was used, though there was no sophisticated analysis. Wensum seems to be a good example of what happened.

We saw in Chapter 10 that, for each product covered by its annual price review, Wensum looked at the existing relationship between the actual price and the 'calculated' price; at the characteristics of competitive products and their prices; at current sales trends; and at the expected level of sales for the next year, as shown in the sales budget. Given the sales-budget figures, and the relationship of the price of each product to those of competing products, an attempt was made to judge the most profitable price for that product. This was not made easier by the absence of information about which costs were fixed and which variable. At the same time, the informal character of the discussions meant that there was no effort to carry out rigorous analysis of the information to see what effect any change being considered was likely to have on output, on costs and so on 'contribution'. To do this would probably have required, at least, the use of a desk calculator. More realistically, it might have meant adjourning the meeting for a day or two until the necessary calculations had been made. This might well have paid off. Even if few individual prices would have been different from those actually set, someone would surely have noticed that the expected increase in wages had been overlooked at the price review meeting.

In Fourways it will be remembered that the problem was that the maximum price that could be charged, given the price of competing products, was greater than the 'cost' of the product. This was an average cost, including an amount for research and development expenditure. Fourways later came to wonder whether it should be working in terms of 'contribution'. It carried out an analysis which showed that a price of £350 would apparently give maximum contribution. However, this calculation was ignored because of mistakes in the cost figures, and the price kept at £390. Although it is not clear why the calculation was ignored, it must have been the result of the way those concerned behaved. A one-man price setter would have been less likely to ignore figures he had himself asked for. Although some members of the group in Fourways that had to price this product were keen on charging whatever price would maximize 'contribution', others must have been more reluctant to do so. Presumably, the latter made the mistakes in the cost figures an excuse to abandon working in terms of 'contribution'.

In Heavy Technology, Medlock Engineering and Clean Engineering, a small number of people was provided with information showing which costs were to be treated as fixed and which as variable. Because market conditions were difficult and prices therefore very unprofitable, fixed and variable costs were clearly separated by the accountant. Cost information was more relevant to pricing decisions than in other firms. The pricing group discussed the cost figures fully, though on one point at least doubts about facts were removed by argument and not by looking up those facts. The big problem was to guess what prices would be tendered by competitive firms and how fully the firm's own capacity would be at work when the orders currently being tendered for came to be produced. This was decided by the pricing group, given the information it had. More recently, Heavy Technology and Clean Engineering have both shown that they were not entirely happy about the results, because they have increased their use of formal decision models, involving probability theory.

In one sense, what happened in Wessex Timber could be more accurately described as one-man rather than small-group pricing. Responsibility for the price finally charged was very much with the mill salesman. In this sense, we are back with all the difficulties of one-man pricing. Indeed, one of Wessex's big problems was being sure whether the mill salesman had obtained as high a price as he might, for any sale. Nevertheless, while the salesman was given discretion to alter prices by plus or minus one per cent around the target price, this price was set by the head office. The mill salesman also had to keep in close touch with the mill manager. This was not really one-man pricing. The price a salesman could quote was closely tied to the figure set by a small group of managers at head office; it was also influenced by the mixture of products the mill was equipped to manufacture.

What happened in Wessex, therefore, was that the group at head office tried to set prices which would give adequate profits—given the combination of lowish prices and labour shortage which Wessex faced. The main question is whether Wessex might have found pricing easier if it had separated fixed and variable costs more clearly. As for the mill salesman's discretionary one per cent, Wessex had to rely on the experience and ability of individual salesmen to judge how far prices should diverge from the target level.

11.5.3 Large Group Pricing

Finally, we turn to large-group pricing—in Alpha, Basic Foods, Epsilon, Gamma and Universal. It was not always easy, especially in Alpha, Basic Foods and Universal, to be absolutely sure where and when pricing decisions were being taken. In all three firms there was a good deal of informal discussion whenever pricing decisions were in the air, with several levels of management taking part. Indeed, in Alpha, different views of some issues seem to have been taken at different levels in the firm, though we doubt whether the prices actually set were much affected by this. With so much discussion, we were not always sure how far the real decisions were taken in formal meetings. Perhaps, as often happens, they were effectively taken in informal contacts among key people between formal meetings. The significant role that an individual can have in such circumstances is shown by what happened in Epsilon Ltd, where one Board member was especially active in championing the introduction of the new product, 'Epsilon'. In Universal, there was a good deal of discussion while the calculations underlying pricing were being made. Once this had taken place, the decision seemed to be almost automatic.

Despite the difficulty of being absolutely certain where and how pricing decisions were taken, our impression is that they were most often taken in the best way where large groups of people were involved. Partly perhaps because of the firms' size, and partly because they always tried to use up-to-date thinking, pricing proposals were written down explicitly. Emphasis was put on identifying those variables which would change as the result of a given decision. This was especially true in Basic Foods.

These were also the firms where modern analytical methods, like probability theory and other operational research techniques, and modern concepts, like marginal cost, were used. Epsilon Ltd had made quite sophisticated calculations of elasticity of demand by selling 'Epsilon' at different prices at different times and in different areas. Universal Corporation was an enthusiastic proponent of marginal costing. Again, probably because of the firm's size, there were clear, well-established routines to be gone through before prices were finally set. Especially in Alpha Ltd and Gamma Ltd, the man responsible for seeing that the procedure laid down was actually followed was the product manager. Despite some uncertainty whether we had really understood everything that was going on in these firms, our judgement is that pricing decisions were most effectively taken in Alpha, Basic Foods, Epsilon and Universal. In Gamma, things did not work out quite so well, even though the analysis was again sophisticated.

11.6 PRICING DECISIONS

11.6.1 Constraints upon Price Fixers

The Managers concerned with pricing in our firms found that there were three main constraints upon their freedom of action:

(i) constraints imposed by the overall and pricing objectives of their firm;
(ii) external constraints; resulting from conditions in the markets in which firms operated, and from other external factors;
(iii) organizational constraints; resulting from human and organizational relationships and pressures within the firm.

We have said a good deal already about the kinds of constraint imposed by objectives, in Chapters 5 and 6. We must, however, say a little more about external and organizational constraints.

11.6.2 External Constraints

The most significant external constraint operating upon managers was the fear of price warfare. This was thought likely in Alpha Ltd, Dee and Epsilon Ltd. Price cuts would almost certainly have reduced profitability very severely in Alpha Ltd and Epsilon Ltd. They might even have destroyed Dee altogether. Severe price cutting had actually broken out in the markets served by Heavy Technology, Medlock Engineering and Clean Engineering. These firms could stay in the market only by cutting their own prices to meet competition (Heavy Technology and Medlock Engineering) or by giving bigger discounts from list prices (Clean Engineering). Again, Basic Foods was forced to cut prices because its major competitor decided to do so. Basic Foods had to follow, given that the products of the two firms were very similar, and the cut in the price of one firm's products had to be followed by a price cut in that of the other.

In two cases where industry-wide price agreements had lapsed, external constraints upon pricing procedures imposed by the agreement had been removed; managers were discovering for themselves how to price in a new situation. In a number of other cases, fears of Government intervention under Prices and Incomes or Monopolies and Restrictive Practices legislation imposed limits upon what managers felt they could do in pricing.

11.6.3 Organizational Constraints

Organizational constraints upon pricing were either formal, through systems of control over price setters; or informal, stemming from contact or conflict between individuals and groups within the firms. There was no clear division between formal and informal arrangements so that we could not always distinguish them clearly.

11.6.4 Formal Constraint

The clearest example of a formal organizational constraint was in Alpha Ltd, where a detailed job description laid down the responsibilities of a product manager under fourteen heads. This degree of detailed control over the individual manager was exceptional. Even Alpha Ltd, while it laid down his responsibilities, did not require particular action from a product manager in any given situation.

Formal constraints on pricing decisions were sometimes imposed. We have seen that, in Wessex, the authority to agree prices was delegated to salesmen, within closely-defined limits. In the Surgical Instrument Company and Fourways, pricing was not subject to any formal constraints except that decisions by the parent company, and by the product committee, committed the firm to develop some new products.

In nine of the thirteen firms we studied, the managerial control procedure depended upon the formal reporting and circulation of operating results within firms. Price setters were then subject to the highly effective constraint of having the results of their decisions made widely known. This appeared to increase the amount of care they took in working out the likely results of pricing decisions before they were taken.

11.6.5 Informal Constraints

Informal constraints on pricing resulted from the interaction of individuals and groups at different levels within each firm. Limits on the freedom of action of price fixers were set by precedent or by the behaviour of superiors. These limits were not normally set out explicitly. Where they were, the constraint was made formal. In the Surgical Instrument Company, no limits at all were apparent once the product committee had taken the decision to produce the product; the marketing manager was in complete control of pricing. In Universal Corporation, the pricing staff had complete freedom of action, subject to the Board agreeing with the recommendations they put forward.

With one exception (Dee), at least one stage of the pricing process was handled by a formal or informal committee. Some committees provided built-in constraints. In Alpha Ltd, for example, product managers were required to justify their proposals in committees which included the marketing director. The need for committee unanimity sometimes put limits upon what could be done in pricing. Wensum provided an excellent example of a firm whose collective decisions resulted in agreed prices which were lower than those which the members of the committee, as individuals, claimed they would have set. This was largely why the home sales manager subsequently increased some prices without recalling the committee.

11.6.6 Pricing Decisions—Our Conclusions

On pricing decisions, we asked the following questions in Chapter 1. How do those who take them deal with the complexity of pricing problems? Do they simplify them, and so obtain tolerably good solutions? Are routines developed which eliminate some alternatives and so simplify the decision? Do organizations, like human beings, devise ways of using two-dimensional brains to solve multi-dimensional problems? If so, how do they do it? Second, what *ought* they to do? Should they use computers? Or should they use simpler methods? If so, are the existing 'simpler' methods good enough? Can one say anything about how far away from the optimal solution the ones reached by these methods are?

We went on to suggest, rather obviously, that one way to simplify pricing decisions so that two-dimensional brains could deal with them was to look at various parts of the problem 'sequentially' rather than 'simultaneously'. Indeed, we think that this is how human beings always have tackled difficult problems. What we wanted to know was how far the results were less satisfactory because the elements in the problem were looked at sequentially.

It was clear that our firms *did* have ways of simplifying multi-dimensional problems—as indeed it was obvious that they must have had, since they did solve them with two-dimensional brains. However, most of our firms did not use complex models, though perhaps some of them should have done. The models used were not always sufficiently complex to ensure that all relevant information was included. Nor were they rigorous enough to ensure that the analysis of this information was always satisfactory. Indeed, these failings resulted largely from the fact that the analysis *was* 'sequential' rather than 'simultaneous'.

This is not to say that all our firms could be criticized in the same way. Universal Corporation, for example, used a complex, computer model, based on very sophisticated analysis, and we would not wish to fault it. Alpha Ltd, and Basic Foods also used rigorous analysis correctly, though we have seen that probably Basic Foods would have benefited from using a computer to ensure that rapid and complex calculations were correct.

It is not so easy to say whether our firms eliminated unsatisfactory alternatives correctly before making serious comparisons. By the very nature of things, this is an extremely difficult part of the process to observe. In many cases, managers will eliminate alternatives, perhaps even almost subconsciously, without making explicit to anyone else which alternatives these were. So far as comparison between alternatives was concerned, Basic Foods, Alpha Ltd, Epsilon and Universal Corporation (all big firms) compared alternatives correctly, though Gamma (another big firm) was less successful. There is no evidence that too few alternatives were compared in the other firms, though we have seen that the analysis of the alternatives actually considered was not always satisfactory. If we had doubts, they would mainly be about Wensum and Fourways.

While we lack satisfactory evidence on the success with which our firms eliminated alternatives, it is perhaps worth expressing the conviction that one of the biggest attributes that any businessmen can possess is the ability to identify quickly which are the right alternatives to compare. It might well pay most firms to make a study of the way in which they generate alternative courses of action and then eliminate those—whether in pricing or other problems—that they do not see as worth serious consideration. Evidence from a business game used in the Manchester Business School shows that members of our Management Course were very much better at choosing between alternative courses of action already selected for them than they were at generating alternative courses of action for themselves. This suggests the hypothesis, as yet untested, that firms may at present be rather good at choosing between what could be the wrong alternatives.

On whether firms should use computers, or whether 'simple' models are adequate, our conclusion is this. Where the 'simple' models worked best—because there was careful and detailed analysis of the problem—the problem was so complex that computers might well have been used. The two firms we have particularly in mind are Alpha and Basic Foods.

In other cases, simple methods were not always adequate. In some cases this was because fixed and variable costs were not carefully separated—especially in the Surgical Instrument Company, Wensum and Fourways. On other occasions, the firms did not take into account all the complexities of the problem—as with Gamma and its battery-operated razor, Wensum and Fourways especially. However, perhaps one should include Wessex and Dee here too.

Reasonably satisfactory analyses had been developed by Heavy Technology, Medlock and Clean Engineering, because of the extreme competition in their markets. Even these firms have shown that they had doubts about their methods, because they were moving on to using probability analysis. Perhaps these firms did not need to use computers, but a rather more explicit model was often needed, which would have included all elements in the problem. Indeed, we suspect that it would be best if such a model was 'simultaneous' rather than 'sequential'. This is partly because this would emphasize the way in which all elements in the problems are interlinked. It would emphasize the danger of forgetting parts of the problem if its elements are treated one at a time.

We therefore see no reason to accept the suggestion in our questions from Chapter 1 that firms should tackle problems sequentially rather than simultaneously. The great need seems to be to move towards a fairly complex analysis which *does* look at all elements simultaneously. Even if there is a case for a sequential approach where human beings are concerned, computer models seem likely to be most successful if 'simultaneous'. And while human beings may do reasonably well on a sequential basis, the result seems to be that they can therefore leave out important parts of the pricing problem. It seems to us that there is no obvious gain from programming computers to use sequential methods which, in the hands of humans, lead to less-than-optimal decisions.

As to whether one can say anything about how far from the optimum the solutions reached by these methods are, the answer is that one cannot be very precise about this from our study. Our judgement is that the decisions we studied came close to being optimal in most cases, but that some improvements would have been possible, particularly in Gamma and Wensum. However, we *have* seen that in some cases, because information was not carefully analysed, or even used correctly, more time was taken and more argument caused in taking pricing decisions than was necessary. We therefore feel that it is important to differentiate between a price which is set at an optimal level, and one which is set at an optimal level but with only the optimal amount of time and energy devoted to doing it. The prices that our firms set seem to have been closer to the optimum than the procedures used in setting them were.

11.7 FEEDBACK FROM PRICING DECISIONS

Feedback is extremely important in pricing decisions. Most of our firms had developed control systems in which operating results were circulated regularly. These provided price setters with feedback from their decisions, enabling them to compare the actual and the intended effects of pricing decisions. Four firms, Alpha Ltd, Gamma Ltd, Epsilon Ltd, and Universal Corporation had reporting systems that provided, each month, indicators of performance in terms of sales volume and value, market share, cost, profit and return on assets. In most of our firms, reports were circulated less frequently or in less detail. Feedback of this sort provided a way of constantly monitoring changing situations, and provided price setters with a way of reacting to developments in a dynamic way. However, we are not sure whether the results of decision-taking by individuals like the one-man price fixers in Dee and the Surgical Instrument Company, or by the individual salesmen in Wessex, were adequately monitored.

11.8 PRICE REVIEWS

Once the introduction of the new products whose pricing we studied was completed, with their introduction to the market, the Surgical Instrument Company, Gamma Ltd, Fourways Manufacturing and Epsilon Ltd, fitted their new products into their normal patterns for price reviews. In the consumer good firms, Alpha Ltd, Gamma Ltd, Basic Foods and Epsilon Ltd prices were constantly under review, with feedback processes of the kind discussed in 11.7 operating. Market research data provided much of the necessary review material. In fact, prices were not changed very frequently.

Three of the industrial goods manufacturers, Wensum, Fourways, and Universal Corporation reviewed their price lists annually, and Wessex did so quarterly. Here again, prices were not necessarily changed as a result of every review. The remaining five firms, the Surgical Instrument Company, Dee Plastics, Heavy Technology, Medlock Engineering and Clean Engineering conducted price reviews only when they were considered necessary. In the Surgical Instrument Company, this could mean one of two things. Either there might be a general price review to offset decreasing profit margins (though not necessarily general price changes), or there might be a special review for particular products in particular markets, because of changes in trading conditions reported by selling agents. In the remaining four firms, general price reviews were not made. Prices were negotiated individually with buyers and the need for higher prices and margins was one of the factors taken into account by firms in their negotiations.

11.9 TRANSFER PRICING

We came across several examples of transfer prices in our cases, especially in Basic Foods. Here, the parent firm had developed an elaborate, and successful, system of indicating to Basic Foods the costs which it had incurred in producing some new materials. The biggest problems met with in transfer pricing were in Wensum. Wensum supplied products to part of its parent firm, as well as to outside customers. As we have seen, Wensum supplied these goods to the parent firm at very considerable discounts from list prices. Since Wensum was under pressure to earn higher profits, this procedure was resented by its managers who felt that the profitability of the firm was being understated by the amount of the discount. What they did not seem to appreciate fully was that, if products had been transferred to the parent firm at list price, the profit expected of Wensum by the parent firm would have been increased.

It is doubtful how much effect, apart from creating annoyance, this procedure had. The way the accounts were set out did not itself affect the profits of the firm as a whole. The reduction in the profit of Wensum was exactly equal to the increase in the profits of the other part of the parent firm. The only question is whether this arrangement altered either motivations, or decisions, in a way that left the firm in a less satisfactory position than it might have been. Did the other part of the parent firm buy from Wensum, when it ought to have bought outside, because Wensum's transfer prices were artificially low? Worse still, did the other division actually charge its own customers prices which were unnecessarily low, because it had been able to buy from Wensum below 'cost'? Did Wensum fail to act in an optimal way, because its business with this other division was not 'profitable' enough?

While we cannot answer these questions, the essential point is to emphasize that transfer prices can, and often do, alter behaviour. Decisions will not be optimal if transfer prices are set in the wrong way. When transfer prices are being set, the key questions are these: What are they intended to achieve? What effects, if any, will they have on behaviour and decisions? Are these the effects we want? There are many ways of setting transfer prices. Some firms, like the parent firm of Wessex, expect their subsidiaries to transfer goods to other parts of the firm at prices established by competition on the open market. Other firms have more or less elaborate ways of estimating what the 'correct' price for the transferred article would be. Indeed, nowadays, linear programming is being used on an increasing scale to do this.

This is all simply an illustration of a more general point. It is now taken as axiomatic by most accountants, and presumably most businessmen, that the way accounting data are presented and the way accounting conventions operate, affect both managerial motivation and performance. The form in which accounting data, especially for control purposes, is presented within the firm should be designed to motivate managers to behave in the way that top management intends. This has been well put by R. N. Anthony[1] in his textbook on management accounting. As he says, one should ask of any accounting system: '(i) what will it motivate people to do in their own selfish interests?; and (ii) is this in the best interests of the company?'

The important thing about transfer prices, therefore, is that they should motivate management in the way that the firm intends. One cannot simply set transfer prices on a mathematical basis. One has to ask how setting them in a particular way will motivate managers in the firm and will affect their decisions. One has to go on to consider whether this will influence performance and profitability in the way that the firm intends.

[1] R. N. Anthony, *Management Accounting* (Irwin), p. 317.

11.10 CONCLUSIONS

11.10.1 Information

Not all the information that was readily available to our price fixers was used. Some remained unused in the firm's files; some was ignored in pricing meetings although it had been taken into the meeting.

As we have seen, differences of opinion over facts were also sometimes resolved by debate and by not looking at those facts. More frequently, we suspect that different assumptions made by different members of a pricing committee were not brought into the open. In fairness, one has to admit that this is difficult to do.

The firm should therefore consider how to make the best use of the information it already has. Failure to do this appears to be as important a problem in pricing as any failure to collect extra information.

11.10.2 The Analysis of Information

The important thing in evaluating information is to establish relationships between relevant variables. For example, one wants to establish relationships between different possible prices, outputs, market shares, profits and so on. It requires a complex process of analysis. In some cases, this will be too difficult for the human brain. One looks to an increasing use of computers to set out the likely results of charging different prices. If this is done, discussion on decisions on prices can begin from the computer print-out. One benefit of this is that it will become much easier to use sensitivity analysis. We suggest that sensitivity analysis should be more fully used, whether or not in association with computers. Sensitivity analysis asks how important it is to be right about particular elements in the analysis. One reworks the calculations for a pricing problem several times, making different assumptions about the sizes of particular variables on each occasion, in order to discover what effect a given change in the size of any one variable has on the outcome.

For example, it may then be discovered that a smallish error in predicting how many customers will switch to other products if the price of the product being considered is raised, will have a bigger effect on profit than if the firm makes a large error in estimating what this product will cost to market. By showing how 'sensitive' the outcome of a price change is to differences in the size of the variables in the problem, one can find how much time and money it is worth spending to improve the accuracy of particular pieces of information. It is obviously much more important to get an accurate figure for a variable if a 10 per cent error in estimating it would lead to a 20 per cent difference in 'contribution', than if a 100 per cent error would change contribution by only 2 per cent. Indeed, one attraction of using computers is that they allow sensitivity analysis to be carried out quickly and easily, so showing which variables in the problem the firm needs to obtain more information about.

Perhaps the biggest problem met with in our study was how to predict competitive reactions in oligopoly. The kind of question continually being asked was: 'If I cut my price by 10 per cent what will my competitor do?' 'Will he change his price too, and by how much?' There was little explicit analysis of this. Instead, most firms relied on their innate ability to predict the reactions of competitors. This ability was, as my colleague Dick Cripps puts it, 'bred by hunch out of experience', although Alpha, Epsilon and Gamma were using probability analysis and other operational research methods to throw more light on oligopolistic interaction. There is obviously room for development here and firms should be on the lookout for any significant advances.

11.10.3 Human and Organizational Factors

In a number of cases, human and organizational factors affected the pricing decision. Decisions which were by their very nature difficult to take correctly were made more difficult. Where a number of individuals are working within any organization, conflicts, rivalries and differences of opinion are bound to arise, though good management will seek to reduce them. It must be recognized that pricing decisions are just as liable to be affected by human and organizational factors as any other aspect of a business. Firms should (a) identify, (b) understand, and (c) try to solve problems of this kind.

11.10.4 Dynamic Factors

One of the most striking features of the pricing decisions we studied was the almost complete absence of a pricing strategy, lying behind individual decisions, that took account of dynamic elements in the situation. Only Universal Corporation paid explicit attention to this problem, in deciding that it would not introduce marginal costing fully until its new plant, with lower costs, had been installed.

Firms need to look at dynamic factors affecting both costs and revenue. As we have argued, the firm should be ready to drop products which have reached a late stage in the product cycle. Pricing strategy should take account of the product cycle to a much greater extent than it appears to do at present. It may well benefit the firm to charge high prices in the early stages of a product's life, while there are few competitors, and allow competition to reduce prices later. At the same time, the firm's pricing strategy should take account of any reduction in costs which is caused by experience. The firm should determine its desired market shares to take advantage of these effects of experience on costs.

11.10.5 Control Procedures

We feel that the need for a feedback process to monitor the results of pricings should be emphasized. It is needed to provide a check on how past pricing decisions have worked out, and to show whether further pricing decisions are necessary. Such control procedures could probably be improved in many firms. The importance of effective control arrangements is emphasized by our research. Where pricing decisions were taken by individuals, there seemed to be little attempt to ensure that the effect of these decisions on profitability was checked and monitored.

Control is especially necessary if any discretion in pricing is given to salesmen. If prices are based on marginal cost, there is a serious danger of salesmen cutting prices too far. Actually *charging* marginal cost without taking total company operations into account is the quickest way to bankruptcy. It is important to distinguish between the short-run and long-run strategies of using marginal cost as a basis for pricing. In the short run it is possible, in extreme situations, to charge prices very little above marginal cost. In the long run, if the firm is to survive, it must earn satisfactory margins, over its whole range of products. Marginal pricing can have wider and more complex effects than is normally apparent to salesmen.

Where marginal cost is used as a basis for setting prices, there must be central control over all pricing. Only thus can the firm discover whether the 'contribution' over and above marginal cost that is being earned to date is adequate. Actual contribution, desired contribution, and price must be constantly monitored and compared in order to keep price, contribution, production and employment at satisfactory levels. This is another task which, in future, is likely to be performed by computers; but where marginal pricing is used it must be performed by someone.

CHAPTER 12

Recommendations

In this chapter, we give briefly the main recommendations which flow from our study, in the form of a number of questions which all firms wanting to improve their pricing arrangements should ask themselves.

12.1 SETTING OBJECTIVES

Is there a mechanism for ensuring that the objectives to be pursued in pricing decisions are as clearly stated as possible?

If there is more than one objective, is it clear how different objectives are to be ranked, or otherwise related?

Do all those concerned with pricing decisions, at whatever level in the firm, clearly understand the objectives which are relevant to them?

12.2 IDENTIFYING ALTERNATIVES

Do those taking each pricing decision identify enough possible courses of action between which to choose?

If not, can more satisfactory methods for identifying sufficient alternatives be developed?

12.3 OBTAINING INFORMATION

12.3.1 Market Information

Is the firm sure that the information it has about its market and its competitors is adequate?

Could it make better use of the information it has, for example, by analysing it more fully or by using it to forecast the future rather than report on the past?

Could the firm make profitable use of more sources of information? Is adequate use being made of outside specialist market research?

Could more help be given to the firm by trade associations? Could the firm make more use of information agreements, while remaining within the law?

12.3.2 Cost Information

Are there figures which give price setters relevant cost information for their decisions?

Do they show which costs will, and which will not, be altered by particular pricing decisions?

Are these costs shown for whatever *future* time period is relevant? Does the allocation of some costs confuse the price fixer rather than help him?

12.3.3 Profit Information

Does the information given to the price fixer enable him easily to identify the effect on profit of choosing each relevant alternative?

Would this kind of information be improved by using the notion of 'contribution'?

12.3.4 Other Variables

Is the price fixer shown what effect his decision is likely to have on production, employment, inventories, market share, etc.?

Are there difficulties because accountants and others concerned with providing information find difficulty in working smoothly with those who set prices?

Should the firm improve communication and collaboration between information providers and information users?

Should more be done to help accountants and managers concerned with pricing decisions to think marginally?

12.4 TAKING THE DECISION

Assuming that objectives are known, that the right number of alternative courses of action has been identified, and that the correct information is available, is the available information fully used?

Are differences of opinion over objectives, alternatives and facts brought into the open where it is helpful to do so?

Does the price fixer correctly relate all the relevant variables in the problem?

Does the information which he has fully represent these relationships or does it show a mere time series of historical events?

If the decision is a complex one, can all the elements in it be adequately dealt with by managers, or should a computer be used?

If a computer is not necessary, is the analysis of pricing problems fully thought through and correctly used?

If a computer is needed, is it used?

Whether or not a computer is used, is sensitivity analysis used, to give more information than the firm already has, and to determine which elements in each decision are the important ones?

Is the firm fully aware of all the human and organizational problems which arise in making pricing decisions?

Has the firm identified, understood and tried to solve problems of this kind?

Is there a long-run strategy underlying pricing?

Does the firm base pricing on the life-cycle of its products?

Are products dropped soon enough, when they reach a late stage in this cycle?

Does the firm look at the effect of 'learning' in reducing costs, as the aggregate amount of any product which has been produced increases?

In sum: are pricing decisions taken as logically as possible with: (1) rigorous thinking; (2) minimum interference from human and organizational factors; (3) allowance for the fact that judgement and prediction is needed about the future not reporting about the past; and (4) within a dynamic strategy.

12.5 ENSURING CONTROL

Are there procedures to ensure that pricing decisions taken by individuals, or small groups, fit into the firm's overall strategy?

In particular, if prices are based on marginal cost, are there procedures to ensure that individuals do not cut prices too far?

Does the firm need a central control arrangement to maintain profitable prices?

12.6 MAINTAINING FEED-BACK

Is there a feed-back mechanism to ensure that all who should know how individual pricing decisions have worked out are fully informed about their consequences?

CASE STUDY B[1]

Surgical Instrument Company Limited

by C. Troughton and R. J. Cripps

INTRODUCTION

This case study was concerned with the introduction of a new product into an established international market for technical products, which was expected to decline in the future. The product was the result of intensive research and development by The Surgical Instrument Company, intended to enable the company to enter a market which, at the time, was blocked by competitors' patents. We have disguised the case by describing the product as a disposable scalpel.

THE MARKET SITUATION

The business had for many years been an international one, with about eight major firms competing in all world markets. The industry grew up with a large number of small family firms making products for local customers. By the beginning of this century, the quality and quantity of product demanded by the industry's customers outpaced the resources and expertise of these small firms. Increased quality demanded by customers caused the remaining firms to spend considerable amounts on research and development, and competition quickly focused on product performance and innovation. Only the largest firms could hope to provide the capital necessary for research, so that all the firms in the market were among the largest in their respective countries.

Given the size of the firms in the industry, and its highly-technical product, it would have been virtually impossible for commercial monopoly to develop. There could have been a technical monopoly in the short term, but this would have lasted only as long as it took competitors to assess the situation and to launch their own products. These would do the job required equally well, but might use different techniques.

One of the Surgical Instrument Company's main problems was to convince customers that its product was superior to that of its competitors. With a product that was judged mainly by its technical

[1] We have not been given permission to publish case studies A, C, D, G, and I.

attributes, this could be difficult when there was already a well-established product on the market. The Surgical Instrument Company's customers merely required a product that would do the job adequately, and cheaply, so they were not attracted by marginal advantages. Though there were some customers who required specialized products of great technical reliability, these were in the minority.

The market for disposable surgical instruments developed when it was realized that the cost of carrying out careful sterilization of instruments each time they were used in the hospital was considerable. If this cost were added to the cost of the time of skilled staff spent on sterilization, and to the initial capital outlay on the sterilization unit, the total cost was very high. Once technology had advanced to the stage of providing plastics with the necessary properties, capable of cheap mass production in almost any shape or size, the disposable surgical instrument industry developed rapidly. The demand for scalpels was directly dependent on the number of operations performed, and could be significantly affected only by the ability of manufacturers to persuade customers of the benefits of using their products. For some time, the market for surgical instruments had been static.

The Surgical Instrument Company had for many years been involved in the manufacture of surgical instruments. When it decided to enter the market for disposable instruments, it found that it was rather late. The attractive section of the industry, concerned with the manufacture of disposable plastic syringes and disposable needles, had been taken over by its competitors. Again, the manufacture of complete scalpels from plastic, which were used once and then thrown away, had been lost to the Surgical Instrument Company through its competitors' early entry. Since the more attractive ideas had already been patented, the only way for the Surgical Instrument Company to enter the market effectively was to add a quite new product to the whole disposable instrument range.

Finding itself blocked, at least in the short run, from using plastics in disposable syringes and scalpels, the company's research staff concentrated on the use of steel and of the metals which it was known had certain attractions to customers. The Surgical Instrument Company soon discovered a process for making a metal scalpel with disposable steel blades. The blade would cost a few pence each, would be sterilized by gamma radiation, and would be packed in aluminium foil wrappers in the factory ready for dispatch to the customer. This discovery meant that the Surgical Instrument Company could enter the disposable surgical instrument market and, indeed, be ahead technically of all competitors in it.

At the time when the Surgical Instrument Company was working on its scalpel, it was known that the total market for surgical instruments was likely to decline because of the spread of preventive medicine and other developments. The Market Research Department of the company found that the scalpel market was not worth much new capital expenditure. This view was based on statistical information and also on experience the company had of other sections of the medical market. However, it was seen that the particular section of the market in which the Surgical Instrument Company was interested would probably expand for some time. If carefully marketed, the disposable steel-blade scalpel could take profitable business away from the all-plastic scalpel.

INFORMATION AVAILABLE

The company had a recognized procedure which was followed when a new product was introduced and this was followed in the pricing of the disposable scalpel. The procedure was as below.

Once it had been agreed by the Surgical Instrument Company's management that further research into the disposable instrument market could be rewarding, time and money were allocated to it. When it had been discovered that fine, precision-ground blades could be manufactured in bulk, sterilized and packed to a standard acceptable to customers, a meeting was held by the executives concerned in the project.

The Surgical Instrument Company fully realized that there was tremendous market potential for the disposable scalpel. Comparisons were made between it and existing products. These showed a distinct advantage for the Surgical Instrument Company's product. However, when relative costs were studied, it was seen that the normal scalpel was being marketed at a price which, at that time, the Surgical Instrument Company could not undercut. Even allowing for the cost of sterilizing and regrinding the all-in-one scalpel did not bring its total cost significantly above that of the Surgical Instrument Company's disposable blades. There would have been little, if any, real incentive for customers to change from the traditional instrument to that of the Surgical Instrument Company. Faced with these facts, the company decided against marketing these scalpels.

Quite soon, however, the Surgical Instrument Company's scientists and metallurgists found a new method of manufacture which radically reduced cost. A further meeting of the company's executives was held, and it was agreed to take the next step in the procedure for introducing a new product. A small number of scalpels and blades was manufactured under expected production conditions, in order to obtain full details of cost and technical aspects of the process.

From the manufacture of the scalpel, manufacturing costs were calculated and a detailed analysis of the manufacturing process undertaken. The accountant drew up as detailed a statement of profitability as he could at this stage of development. Another meeting was held to consider this information. Using the sales Manager's forecast for a five-year period, the net profit and the ratio of net profit to capital employed were calculated. The various reports were satisfactory and the sales forecasts optimistic. It was found that the expected profitability of the product was above the minimum required by the Surgical Instrument Company's Board. So, the decision to begin full-scale production was accepted by the Board.

In taking the decision to manufacture the product, the Surgical Instrument Company gave full weight to the fact that the market would decline in the end. However, the type of machinery which would be used in producing the scalpel was already installed and was either being used in the production of less-profitable goods or left unused altogether. The introduction of the scalpel required little or no capital investment and the Surgical Instrument Company decided that it would be an acceptable commercial proposition.

RESPONSIBLITY FOR PRICING

Pricing of all new products was the sole responsibility of the marketing manager. The sales manager, who was responsible for organizing the sales network, acted as the main channel through which price queries from the company's agents came to the marketing manager. The Surgical Instrument Company's products were sold by accredited agents throughout the UK. These agents might deal exclusively in the Surgical Instrument Company's products or might act on a free-lance basis. As the man on the spot, the agent had some degree of authority to vary the prices of the company's products. However, he was not entitled to go beyond a certain distance above or below the head office's recommended price, without first obtaining the agreement of the marketing manager. The company gave the quantity discounts and credit rebates normal for its industry. In general, the need to deviate from the recommended price was small and usually happened only in times or areas of intense competition.

An organization chart is given below:

main company board (including sales director)
↕
company executives
↕
marketing manager
↕
sales manager
↕
local agents
↕
customer

THE PRICING DECISION

As has been explained, it was the responsibility of the marketing manager to recommend prices for new products. As far as possible, he kept a record of all competing products, their prices in both UK and overseas markets, and a technical and commercial assessment of how they compared with the Surgical Instrument Company's products.

It was recognized that the customers which the Surgical Instrument Company was aiming at would not change their traditional instruments for the new one offered by the Surgical Instrument Company if it would cost them more. There was an upper limit of around *x*/- for the new scalpel. No hospital would pay more. This price set the upper limit for the scalpel. Had there not been this upper limit, the marketing manager would have been under strong pressure to set his price as high as necessary so that, with its superior product, the company could earn as much as possible. It was seen to be much easier to reduce the price of the product if it were initially set too high than to increase it.

The marketing manager also had to consider how big a market share he wanted for the new product. Although there was a temptation to set a high price, this might be misguided. To obtain as high a *total revenue* as possible he should have set a low price and obtained high market penetration. There was also the fact that the highest price available to the Surgical Instrument Company was *x*/-. To get customers to purchase the new product, it had to be priced lower than the traditional one. The marketing manager felt that his colleagues were wrong. To sell the product solely on its technical attributes was not enough.

Weighing the commercial and technical factors, and obtaining the correct balance between them, lay at the heart of the Surgical Instrument Company's pricing decision. If the marketing manager made the wrong techno-commercial decision the product could fail to achieve any significant success.

When the Surgical Instrument Company looked at the technical and commercial aspects of its product from the customers' point of view, it became obvious that it had a distinct advantage over competing products. For example, if a hospital changed over completely to the new scalpel with disposable blades it would make money savings so long as more than *Oy* operations were performed each year. The larger the number of operations conducted the greater would be

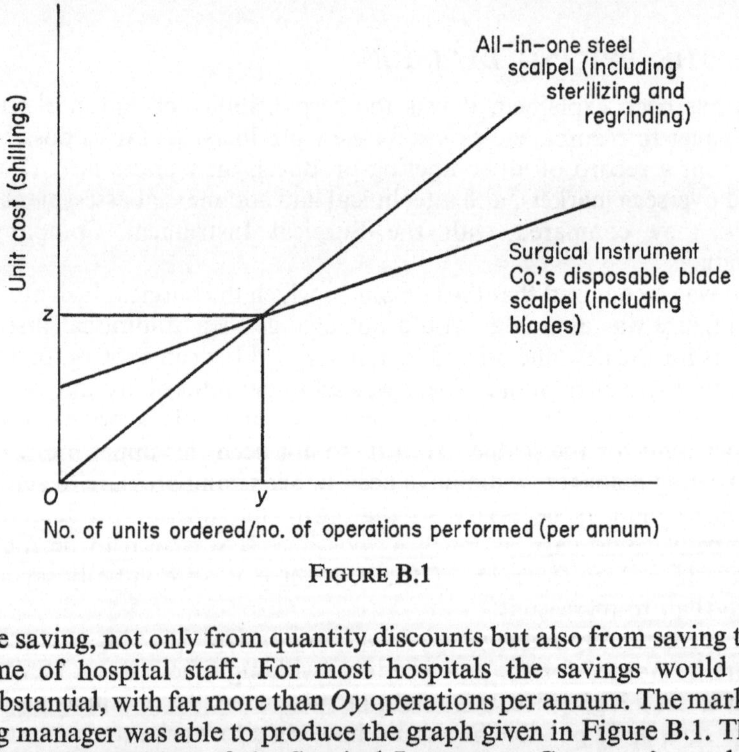

FIGURE B.1

the saving, not only from quantity discounts but also from saving the time of hospital staff. For most hospitals the savings would be substantial, with far more than *Oy* operations per annum. The market ing manager was able to produce the graph given in Figure B.1. This shows the position of the Surgical Instrument Company's product relatively to that of competing products from the customer's point of view.

It was therefore felt that the price of *x*/- could be charged. One could argue that the marketing manager did not 'fix' the price of the scalpel at all. He merely approved the cost estimates as not being too high, because they allowed an acceptable rate of return on capital employed with the price of *x*/- implied by the price of competing scalpels. There was a considerable element of truth in this. The company's initial prices were not necessarily adhered to for long periods. They could be varied when and if market pressures made this necessary. The reaction of the market to Surgical Instrument Company's initial price level was gauged by the agents' ability or inability to sell at that level, as evidenced by the number of requests from them to offer different terms to different customers.

The scalpel was quite different either from the company's other products, or from those of competitors. The information available to the marketing manager consisted of the research and technical reports previously mentioned, the market survey and his own files on prices and sales figures for similar products.

PRICE REVIEWS

Price changes were considered for three reasons. First, and most important, changes were usually made in response to requests from agents to be allowed to raise or lower list prices beyond their discretionary limits. These usually resulted from particular competitive situations. In judging what to do, the marketing manager took into account some or all of the following facts:

The size of the order and of the prospective customer;

The history of the Surgical Instrument Company's previous business with the customer and the terms on which it was done;

The ability of the company to meet the order (stock levels, etc.);

The level of activity in the Surgical Instrument Company relatively to what was desired;

Possible side effects of the order in providing new business, providing an entrée to a customer for other products, etc.;

The amount of cut asked for in relation to profitability;

The bias of the agent (some tend always to ask for more price cuts than necessary . . . etc.).

After taking all these things into consideration, the marketing manager told the agent what amount of cut, if any, he was prepared to allow.

Second, at intervals, the Production Department revised its cost-and-profit estimates. As a result, profit margins altered from their initial level to a figure determined partly by competitors' prices and partly by the way in which agents and the marketing manager tried to set prices that were low enough to gain orders without unduly sacrificing profit.

RESPONSIBILITY FOR THE EFFECTS OF PRICING

As the sole price setter within the company, the marketing manager greatly affected profitability. There was no interference with his decisions by anyone in the Group or on the Board.

We know little about the standards by which the operations of the marketing manager were judged. Because the Surgical Instrument Company had no minimum level of profitability which it required from individual products *once established*, the marketing manager had himself to determine what was acceptable. There had never been occasions in the past when the Board had intervened to raise profitability, so we have no notion of the limits of profitability which it imposed on the marketing manager. This might be either because the profitability of the Surgical Instrument Company had never been low enough to cause anyone to question what he was doing, or else because the Board felt confident that the marketing manager extracted the best terms he could from customers, so that no improvement could be made. However, the marketing manager was in close touch with the sales director, and we presume that it was in discussions with him that the marketing manager determined what rate of return was being required of him.

CASE STUDY E

Wensum Engineering Limited

by David Taylor

INTRODUCTION

This case was concerned not with the 'original' pricing of an individual product, but with a price review for all the products within a particular product group. There was an annual review of selling prices for all the product groups within the company. We shall concentrate on the price review for just one of these product groups.

Within the group, all the products were of similar design, and had very similar end-uses. At home, they were sold both to Government and to industry; home and export sales were roughly equal in value.

MARKET SITUATION—DEMAND

It was difficult to identify either the total British or the total export markets for the complete range of products manufactured and sold by this company; it was even more difficult to identify such markets for individual product groups.

One of the major difficulties in trying to acquire such information stemmed from the fact that published Government statistics were so classified that the products made by the company were lumped together with other slightly different products.

This sort of difficulty affected forecasts of market growth. Since the firm knew that the overall American market was growing by 7–8 per cent per annum, Wensum tended to assume the same rate of growth for the UK. However, there was still the difficult task of making the right assumptions about the growth rates for individual product groups.

The same sorts of difficulties were encountered in assessing the size of the export market and its future rate of growth. If anything, the problems were even greater.

A recent survey of the industry as a whole, to which Wensum contributed, indicated that over the next five years the UK market was likely to grow (in value) by some 136 per cent and the export market by some 123 per cent. However, once again, the broad classification used in the survey covered a wide range of products, whilst Wensum felt that the basic forecasts were over-optimistic.

Wensum's own market research section had not, at the time of our study, become deeply involved in market surveys. Nor had Wensum so far employed outside market research consultants to any significant extent. It was expected that the market research section would be more fully used in future.

It was felt that information about the structure of Wensum's markets could be obtained by normal market research techniques. However, the cost of obtaining this information largely explained why the company had not sought it. Basic information for one major product group would cost the company some £3,000 per major market. Once a major study of that type had been carried out, the cost of collecting statistics about Wensum's market share from time to time, though not so expensive, would still be considerable.

It was therefore difficult, if not impossible, to assess Wensum's market shares. It may well be that this is the reason why the broad aim was to achieve a given percentage return on overall investment rather than a particular market share for each product group.

MARKET SITUATION—SUPPLY

There was much competition in the market for the product group we studied. Competitors could be divided into the very high-quality class typified by two German firms; the high-quality class (including Wensum as well as three American competitors); and the medium and low-quality class (which contained two smaller English firms each producing a cheaper, run-of-the-mill product).

Wensum saw the competition offered by the American companies as the keenest, since these companies were all producing a competing product in the same quality bracket; they were also steadily increasing their interests in this country through subsidiary companies. German competitors, by comparison, were producing products of very high quality, but ones for which market demand was relatively small. They were not, as yet, providing as much competition within the British market as the American companies and none of them had subsidiary companies operating in the UK.

We may note that Wensum is the only British company of any size left in its field.

The product group that we studied in this case represented over one-third of Wensum's sales turnover, and was a field where Wensum had traditionally been the price leader. More recently, especially with increasing competition from the large foreign companies, Wensum's position as price leader was being challenged.

At this stage, we may note that the product group studied was one where there was fairly rapid technological change. The product sold more on technical merit, performance, and suitability for the job as the customer saw it, than on price.

For these reasons, it was also a product group where there was heavy expenditure on research and development, and where production was in small batches.

WHAT IS PRICE?

The review of prices was undertaken automatically each year, usually during November and December, so that any alterations in prices could be incorporated into the published price list, invariably published on January 1st of the following year. With few exceptions, Wensum was reluctant to alter prices at any other time during the year. Thus the annual price review provided an opportunity for Wensum to pass changes in cost that had occurred during the previous twelve months into prices.

The price of each product in the product group was reviewed and the new prices were charged to all customers, subject only to quantity discounts. During the price review there were lengthy discussions on whether a price range, rather than an exact price, should be quoted for each product, thus giving Wensum greater freedom to quote slightly different prices according to the business of each customer. In the end, this idea was not adopted, partly because it was necessary to quote exact prices for certain contracts, and partly because it was felt that each customer would expect to be quoted the lowest price in each range.

Wensum's discount and rebate structure took the form of a quantity discount for all industrial customers, based on the gross annual value of their purchases. The same rates of discount were allowed to all those customers who spent given amounts on Wensum's products, although more favourable discount terms were enjoyed by one or two customers who made separate agreements with Wensum's Managing Director.

RESPONSIBILITY FOR PRICING

The following were directly involved in the price review for the product group we studied in the sense that they were responsible for preparing background information and that they sat down together to discuss ways in which the prices in the product group should be altered: the commercial manager, the home sales manager, the export sales manager and the accountant. However, some of these people played a larger part in the decision process than others.

In addition, the managing director and the works engineer, though not directly involved in the price review, had very definite views on what ought to be achieved. However, there is some doubt whether their views were fully considered by those who had responsibility for altering prices.

Finally, it should be noted that whereas the accountant and the commercial manager were directly responsible to the managing director, the home and export sales managers were directly responsible to the commercial manager.

DIRECTIVES FROM ABOVE

One can divide the directives which were given into two parts. There were directives for the ensuing twelve months which the managing director of Wensum received from the parent company; and there were the directives which he himself then gave to those directly involved in the price review.

Originally, the parent company had asked for a 20–25 per cent return on capital employed. The managing director felt that this was unreasonable and was able to get it reduced to a target return of 17 per cent on capital employed. It should be noted at this point that target return allowed for the fact that Wensum sold large amounts of its products, on very favourable terms, to other members of its group.

Having been given this target, the managing director said that he hoped to achieve it by a 10–12 per cent return on turnover for the company's products as a whole, with capital turnover over 1·5 times in the year. To achieve this aim, Wensum did not intend to rely solely on what could be achieved through the price review. The managing director had already decided that during the following 12 months there must be a 6 per cent reduction in general company overheads. However, it was hoped that the review itself would make a significant contribution towards achieving higher profits, i.e. increasing profits from the 8 per cent in the current year to the 10–12 per cent aimed at for the next year.

Despite this hope, no specific written directives were given to the price reviewers. The managing director said that they already knew what the basic goal was, namely, the 10–12 per cent return on turnover.

INFORMATION AND SOURCES OF INFORMATION

(a) On the Market

As already mentioned, it was extremely difficult for Wensum to obtain market information. It was therefore admitted within

Wensum that apart from the specifications of competitors' products and their prices, knowledge of the market and of competitors was poor. The company's market research section had consistently obtained information from competitors' published catalogues and price lists, and by going to trade exhibitions. However, it was admitted that information on the size of the market in many cases was the result of sheer guesswork. This statement was qualified by the suggestion that once a product or product group had become established, there was a tendency to stop collecting information about market size, market growth and market share.

Further, it seemed that there was an attitude within the company that one could not do market surveys. A similar feeling was expressed by a statistician in the sales department, who said that he had not been allowed to make sales forecasts when he arrived at the company 12 months previously, and that he was still not allowed to forecast the rate of growth of the market by product group.

The recently-appointed commercial manager was surprised that the market research effort over the last five years had succeeded so little in establishing the broad facts about the company's markets. Moreover, he was staggered at the cost of providing what he considered *a priori* to be a normal amount of information about the market for each product. To him, this was one of the real costs of product variety. The commercial manager was soon deeply involved in trying to improve this state of affairs.

In the absence of definite knowledge of the market, perhaps too much importance was attached to individuals' opinions, in the sense that such opinions were treated as absolute facts. Similarly, the company itself was not clear exactly why its products were bought. The company's engineers tried to examine each product as they felt a potential customer would examine it.

(b) Cost Information

By comparison with the dearth of information about the market, too much cost information was gathered before the review meeting. In addition, two people prepared what was reputedly the same set of statistics.

The accountant collected together a series of working papers, which, for each product in the product group, contained the latest works cost estimates both in total, and subdivided into materials, labour and factory-overhead costs. The next three columns for each product represented alternative ways of arriving at a calculated selling price: first, by multiplying the works cost estimate by 2·2. This formula at normal capacity was sufficient to allow for full recovery of overheads and an acceptable contribution to profits. Second, by taking works cost and adding to it 20 per cent of materials cost and 212 per cent of process cost. Process cost was labour plus factory overheads. Third, he took a 65 per cent gross margin over materials plus labour. The final column for each product on these working papers gave the current published list prices.

Unfortunately, unknown to both the accountant and the home sales manager, one of the latter's assistants had also produced a calculated price for each product by taking the latest estimate of works cost and applying the 2·2 times formula to each one. Normally, there would have been no confusion in this duplication. As it happened, the assistant to the home sales manager had not, in every case, obtained the latest works cost estimate, so that in the price review meeting there was some confusion over which of these two series of calculated prices was correct.

Of the major participants, the home and export sales managers had been able to collect little specific information on markets, before the meeting, although they did have a good deal of knowledge based on their past experience. The commercial manager, being relatively new to the company, collected little specific information himself, although he had assimilated a good deal of knowledge from his subordinates. The accountant had prepared his extensive working papers on costs and on calculated prices.

PRICING DECISION PROCESSES

The price review meeting, at which the four major participants would sit down together to discuss price changes, was at the centre of the review process. However, there was a suggestion that before this the commercial manager and the home sales manager would have a preliminary meeting to discuss the price adjustments in general. In actual fact no such preliminary meeting took place, so that the major participants had not exchanged ideas in any detail on the price alterations before the price review meeting itself.

We have explained that the four major participants in the price review were the commercial manager; the home sales manager; the export sales manager; and the accountant. However, when the actual review meeting took place—a meeting lasting for some six hours and spread over two days—the export sales manager played a very minor role. He was at the meeting for about one hour, and then only at a time when prices had already been altered by the other three participants. Thus, he was really asked only to give his formal assent to the decisions already reached. It will be remembered that 50 per cent of the company's sales went to export markets.

However, we were later told that for some time it had been accepted that the home sales manager was the pricing authority within the company and that he had a fairly good knowledge of export prices generally. Further, it was said to be generally recognized in Wensum that price competition did not vary very greatly from one area to another, although there could be substantial price differences on particular products between geographical areas. In the event, the export manager was asked to say whether any of the proposed price increases were likely to weaken the competitive export position seriously.

The following were taken into the price review meeting:

(a) current price lists;
(b) calculated selling prices;
(c) budgeted sales volumes by product for the next year;
(d) sales trends by product over recent years;
(e) a document in which the company's products and those of its competitors were compared directly;
(f) recent copies of competitors' new product pamphlets.

In the meeting, documents (a), (b), (c) and (d) were referred to continually; documents (e) and (f) were completely ignored. Before the meeting, it had been said that the participants would be looking for price increases or decreases. In fact, there was no instance of a product's price being reduced.

The opening comment in the meeting was that they were aiming for a 3 per cent increase in price across the board. Subsequently, each product was examined individually, in sequential order of its reference number. No attempt was made to look simultaneously at all products in a product group.

The usual procedure for each product was to look at the relationship between its calculated price (usually from the 2·2 formula) and its current list price; to determine what competitive products there were and what price they were offered (it should be noted that technical factors made it very difficult to make accurate comparisons); to look briefly at the trend of sales in the current year for the product in question; and at its budgeted sales for the next year.

From a full record of the products discussed, it has been possible to make a brief analysis of the points at issue:

	Percentage of the Products on which the Item was Discussed
(a) Cost-plus formula	75
(b) Competitive prices	45
(c) Trend of actual sales	45
(d) Next year's sales budget	56
(e) Special considerations (e.g. contracts, etc.)	30

N.B. The cost-plus formula was referred to for each product, but discussed fully in only 75 per cent of cases.

It should also be noted that although competitors' prices were discussed in 45 per cent of the cases, these discussions were strictly related to the prices at which competitors were selling comparable products—there was no knowledge of how big sales of competitors' products were at these prices. Nor was there any discussion about the total market size for the product group, its rate of growth, or the market share in that product group possessed by the company in question or by its competitors.

At the end of the meeting the accountant, who had been keeping a record of the agreed prices, summed up. He said that, assuming the price increases would make no difference to the budgeted sales for each product in the next year, the price adjustments had achieved an overall increase in revenue across the board of 2 per cent.

After the price review meeting, our impression was that this completed the work on the company's price review; and all that remained to be done was for the new price list to be published.

Some weeks later, when the new price list was published, it showed that the prices of some products had been altered once again. On questioning the major participants, the only satisfactory explanation for this further adjustment was that the home sales manager had done it 'off his own bat'. This further adjustment, made very quickly as compared with the lengthy collection of information and quite protracted discussion of the price review, added half as much again to the prospective sales revenue for the next year as had been achieved by the price review meeting itself.

In considering the amount of extra revenue that would be earned as a result of the adjustments to price in the annual price review Wensum was obviously assuming that there would be no changes in quantity sold as a result of the price alterations.

The order budget for the next year had been completed in advance of the discussions on price reviews which took place in November and

December. Although the same people were involved in preparing the budget and in the review, they were convinced that the decisions they reached on the budget did not affect their outlook with regard to the price review. When the budget for the next year had been prepared, in August, no allowance had been made for possible product price increases as a result of the review. It was presumed that the price changes, which were usually small, would make no difference to the budgeted quantity of products likely to be sold. Once the price review was completed, the budgeted value of sales would be altered only if the agreed price increases were significant; for changes in prices of less than 5 per cent it would be recommended that the budgets should be left unaltered.

ADJUSTMENTS TO PROPOSED PRICE CHANGES

The proposed price alterations were normally, though not always, submitted to the managing director for his consideration. It was suggested that he merely 'rubber stamped' the recommended price reviews. The managing director virtually agreed with this when he said that he usually accepted the results of the deliberations of those directly involved in the review.

THE COMPANY'S VIEWS ON ITS PRICE REVIEW PROCEDURE

At various points in this product study, we have made passing reference to certain aspects of the review which some of the participants felt to be unsatisfactory, e.g. the commercial manager's surprise at the lack of market information. Further the commercial manager, being a relative newcomer to the company, was inclined to follow the existing procedure for this, his first price review. However, he did express the feeling that in the review at the end of the next year, when he had become fully conversant with the company's activities, he would want to take a more rational look at the price review.

CASE STUDY F

Fourways Manufacturing Limited

by David Taylor

This case study discusses the 'original' pricing of a product. The product was one of a series of similar products which was being marketed, without much success, by the manufacturer.

MARKET SITUATION—DEMAND

It was extremely difficult to make an accurate assessment of the current market demand, or the likely market growth, for this product. Estimates were arrived at largely by keeping an eye on technical and financial journals where competitors' annual sales figures were quoted at intervals. In addition, since product F was used, amongst businesses, by industrial concerns producing one of the country's major 'growth' products, Fourways was helped in making estimates of possible sales. The major growth industry was more than willing to give details of its sales. Since Fourways knew how many units of product F and its competitive products were used with each unit of the 'growth' product, it could make some predictions about market size.

However, this still left Fourways in the position of having to make further assumptions, based on rather vague statistics about current market size, about the market's future growth rate. In these circumstances, recourse was made to American estimates of the growth of the USA markets. The justification for this sort of approach was that the production of the major growth industry's product was begun in America; the American market for this product was far more developed than the market for the product in the UK; and what happened in America yesterday would happen in Britain today and tomorrow. It was on the basis of this reasoning that estimates of the future growth rates of the UK market were made.

MARKET SITUATION—SUPPLY

Fourways faced its most intense competition from American firms (two American firms in particular) for higher-priced versions of the product. Fourways did not produce any really cheap versions, but the cheaper part of the market was already supplied by two smaller manufacturers, both originally British. (One has since been taken over by a third American company.)

At the higher-priced end of the market, one American company produced the equivalent of product F and nothing else. Furthermore, its products were regarded as supreme in their class. The other American company produced an equivalent product, but only as one of a number of other products which it manufactured.

At one time, Fourways had had some protection against the competitive American products in the form of an import duty, and the higher freight charges payable on purchases from America. It is doubtful whether Fourways took full benefit from this sort of advantage; now it was too late. Both the American companies had production plants within the British Isles, thus avoiding the problems and expense of import duty payments. At the same time, they had built up their own marketing organizations in the UK, enabling them to give far more satisfactory service than previously, when they had marketed through agents.

As already mentioned, Fourways had made little impression at the lower-priced end of the market. To be fair, it must be said that to some extent this was a matter of choice, since it was thought that the market for cheaper products (in terms of sales value) was far smaller than for more-expensive ones.

At the same time, two other points should be noted. First, Fourways had been producing products with a similar purpose for many years, and had built up a name for good-quality products. Second, the design, engineering and production staff were therefore engaged in working to high standards, and in this industry it was generally held that one could not mix the design and manufacture of products with greatly dissimilar quality standards. Finally, one should also note that the company went into the manufacture of product F rather late in the day.

PRODUCT F—DEMAND

Probably the best indication of the demand for this product can be gained from a comparison between budgeted and actual sales for the years 1963 and 1964. In 1963, budgeted sales were for 96 units of the product; actual sales were 11. In the 1964 sales budget it was forecast that some 142 units would be sold; actual sales amounted to 38. The company's hopes for the product were far from realized. This is emphasized when one notes that in some background calculations for the 'original' pricing of the product, the range of estimated sales for the first four years of its market life was from 790 to 1,450 units.

To some extent, the low demand for product F was because it was paying for the failings of earlier models within the same product group. The first model of this type produced by Fourways was very unreliable and earned the company a very bad name. A succeeding product was good technically but it, too, had problems in reliability and performance. Product F used a quite revolutionary technique, although it was beginning to be said that the product was not good enough; its price was extremely high. The comparatively low demand for product F has to be viewed against these sorts of consideration.

PRODUCT F—SUPPLY

Before the Second World War, Fourways had developed one of the first prototypes of this type of product in the world. As it was ahead of its time, and had very specialized application, it was not developed further.

In the early 1950s, when business had been fairly static for a number of years, there was a feeling that if Fourways was to expand, it would have to look for, and develop, new product lines. In addition there was pressure on Fourways from the parent company to enter the general field which included product F, largely, because the group was already spending large amounts in buying products of this kind. In fact, demand within the group since that time had been far below expectations, partly because of the unreliability of early versions of product F.

So far as product F was concerned, it was one of only three products of this type being manufactured and sold by Fourways. It was the cheapest of the three, although 'cheapest' in this context is used only in a relative sense. All three were very costly and, because they were of good quality, were aimed at the upper end of the market. The cheapest (and lowest-quality) products of this type on the market were sold at a price 75 per cent below that of product F.

WHAT IS PRICE?

Pricing in this study means the 'original' pricing of the product before its first appearance on the market. The price went into the company's price list and was the price which customers are asked to pay. Separate contracts with individual customers were the exception rather than the rule. However, discounts were given to all customers, the amount depending on the gross value of their annual purchases. Fourways' largest customers, and those of the parent firm, were given rather more favourable terms.

RESPONSIBILITY FOR PRICING

The price of the product we studied was decided by Fourways' Product Policy Committee—a committee which was composed of the following:

managing director (chairman);
accountant;
commercial manager;
works engineer;
engineering manager;
research manager;
technical services manager;
chief engineer.

All information about the development, manufacture, and pricing of the product (before its appearance on the market) was submitted to this committee which took all decisions about new products. In the committee, the commercial manager carried most weight when the marketing and pricing of a new product was being discussed. He spoke not only for himself, but also for his home and export sales managers who were not members of the committee. However, the engineering manager probably carried the greatest overall weight in discussions of product policy, because: (a) the subjects under discussion were technical, and (b) he controlled expenditure on development.

The work of the committee, both in general and for product F, is discussed in more detail below.

DIRECTIVES GIVEN TO THE PRICE SETTER

Since the managing director was the chairman of the Product Policy Committee, it was not given any formal directives. However, Fourways' general company policy was that each product would, at least, carry an initial price that would allow the product to cover the general overheads associated with its production, and also make an 'acceptable' contribution to profit. It should be noted that, for each product group within Fourways, continual reference was made to the gross margin (i.e. gross invoice price minus commission, labour and materials), which each group contributed. The margin was reported to the committee in both sterling and percentage terms. Thus in arriving at a tentative price for a new product, the gross margin it was going to earn was compared with the average margin being earned from existing products in that group.

INFORMATION AND ITS SOURCES

As a general guide to the information (both commercial and technical) which, in theory, Fourways collected and considered for each new product, we cannot do better than quote from a report written three years earlier by an internal consultant attached to the managing director.

(a) **The Theory**

The report read as follows:

(1) *Product Evaluation Proposal*

At this early stage, one is involved in price to the extent that the chief engineer and the commercial manager are asked to quote a price bracket within which the product's price is likely to fall. From the commercial manager's point of view, the price quoted at this stage is likely to approximate to the price of a similar type of product already on the market.

Should it be decided to continue further with the product, then a development proposal is completed.

(2) *Development Proposal*

In broad terms, the chief engineer is responsible for guiding the product through this stage. The technical services manager is responsible for advising the commercial manager on its market potential; on the competition for a product with the sales specification and price proposed; and on any changes which would make the product more commercially attractive.

The project engineer and a team is responsible for working out a basic design and proving it by a 'breadboard' model, together with a space model showing the relationship between major sub-assemblies. Any major deviation from specification, selling price, or development cost, will affect the product's prospect of success, however, and should be reported to the Product Policy Committee by the chief engineer.

The commercial manager, advised by the technical services manager, appraises sales appeal, market potential, and serviceability as follows:

(i) size and distribution of the market (by areas and customers);
(ii) special applications and comments on any special commercial reasons for marketing or not marketing the product;
(iii) competition (including strong and weak points);
(iv) probability of Government and other contracts;
(v) sales restrictions (if any);
(vi) recommended manufacturing approval date;
(vii) acceptability of target specifications to the market;
(viii) serviceability;
(ix) possible selling price;
(x) possible sales promotion plan;
(xi) possible quantities sold in first five years.

The accountant compiles a project profitability analysis on the basis of cost and sales estimates.

(3) *Manufacturing Approval*

The Product Policy Committee require the following reports before giving manufacturing approval:

(a) performance figures taken jointly from the quality control engineer on the whole of the batch, together with the Quantity Control Report evaluating the results;
(b) product specification;
(c) recommended sales specification;
(d) production engineering report;
(e) estimate of works cost from the chief estimator, based upon the production documents and on a prototype;
(f) a sales and service report by the technical services manager based on the prototype, with regard to usability, serviceability, and the sales promotion programme.

(b) **Practice**

The report quoted above outlines all the information, both commercial and technical, which should, in theory, have been gathered and discussed for a new product. In fact, the marketing information did not seem to be gathered as rigorously, or presented as fully, as the report would suggest. The ways in which practice diverged from theory can be seen in more detail by examining the information actually collected for product F.

Since the beginning of 1962, there had been a vast number of estimates of this product's works cost. From the start, it was agreed that the smallest economic batch size was of 100 units, and the first estimate of works cost was £269. Following that calculation, a series of works cost estimates was produced during 1962—estimates which were significantly lower (at about £244). These were based on the assumption, justified by a series of reports, that the price of an important bought-in component would fall significantly before the product was in full production.

As the product progressed through the various stages outlined in the internal consultant's report, estimates of works cost fell even further—to about £210, at which point they remained relatively stable. Adopting one of the measures used by the company for arriving at a rough indication of the selling price, these works cost estimates indicated a price of about £460 per unit.

Such works cost estimates had consisted of estimates of labour, raw materials, factory overheads, and sub-contracting costs. To these were added an alternative series of calculations in which attempts were made to allow for recovering the initial investment in the product (i.e. expenses of product design, tool design, manufacture, market research and sales promotion).

These initial costs were divided by the estimated sales of the product in its first few years to give an idea of the cost per unit of the product which would have to be recovered.

Unfortunately, at this stage in the product's development its calculated price per unit, arrived at by the company's most commonly used method, totalled about £412. At that level, it far exceeded an earlier tentative price of £350 per unit.

Some 12 months later, in October, 1963, the same calculations were made again. By this time, although the figures for the initial investment had risen by some £6,000, the estimate of sales of the product during the first few years had fallen to half the size assumed in the exercise carried out the year before. The result of the second exercise was comparable to the first. Whereas the tentative figure for selling price (based on prices currently being charged in the market) had risen to £390, the calculated gross selling price showed that, to achieve the desired return, the product would have to be sold at £442. This sort of discrepancy led to a third set of calculations. In these, an attempt was made to see how far it was possible to reduce the cost of the product, and thus its calculated price, by removing certain features. It was admitted that this was a clear indication of the difficulties faced by this product.

Some information about every product of this type already on the market had been built up before the product was released. This information included all aspects of competitors' products specifications as well as their price. From it came the feeling that the tentative price for product F should be fixed originally at somewhere around £350, because this was the price at which the most-comparable British product was being marketed.

Very little general market information was collected. There appeared to be no rigorous examination of the overall market size, market growth, or market share that this product could expect to achieve.

PRICING DECISIONS

As already mentioned, the earliest estimate of eventual selling price (based on prices already ruling on the market for this quality of product) was £350. As the product progressed through the various stages of development, and as estimates of manufacturing cost hardened, it became apparent that to achieve the rate of return that was desired product F would have to be priced at about £500.

Although, in theory, this was what was needed, it was apparent to the Product Policy Committee that it would be dangerous, if not impossible, to market the product at this price. For the painful, but none the less unavoidable fact, was that competitors' products of equal specification and performance were being sold at around £350–£400.

When the product first appeared in the company's price list at the beginning of 1963 it was priced at £390. Since that date, its price had remained unchanged. Because of competitive pressure, Fourways had been loath to try to increase its price, not least because, even at £390, the product was not selling as well as was expected. Yet, even at this selling price, the product was not making its 'full' contribution to profits. 'Sunk' costs, in particular were not being recovered.

THE COMPANY'S VIEWS ON ITS PRICING PROCEDURE

A particular difficulty which Fourways had found with all products was the long time lag between known alterations in estimates of the works cost of a product and the transmission of these alterations through to the accountancy staff, who applied the company's normal pricing formula to the estimates of works cost to give a calculated selling price. This could lead, and in many cases had led, to difficulties. The sales managers and their staffs, in discussing a proposed new product with potential customers, had quoted a tentative price. They then found that, because of last-minute notifications of changes in works cost, the final calculated selling price was very different from the one they had been quoting.

One way of showing the extent to which the pricing decisions on product F in particular were felt to be wrong is to describe certain exercises which were carried out after the product appeared on the market.

In December, 1963, an exercise was initiated in which an attempt was made to assess the most economical price for product F. To understand the underlying motive for this exercise one can do no better than quote the home sales manager's letter to his area managers: 'As you are probably aware, we have priced product F at £390, but it appears that the "right" price for the quantity budgeted for sale during 1964 is nearer £600 having regard to standard recoveries. However, this "right" price can vary enormously with quantity, and in order to assess the most economical position I would like you to fill in the attached form.' The alternative questions asked on this form were that each area manager should say how many units of the product could be sold if its price was £250, £300, £350, £400 or £450.

The same questionnaire was sent to the company's agents overseas with respect to the export market.

The results obtained from this exercise were as follows:

Estimates of Total Home and Export Sales[1]

	£250	*£300*	*£350*	*£400*	*£450*
Export	669–839	457–610	241–306	149–174	47–57
Home	617	306	235	145	114
Total	1,286–1,456	763–916	476–541	294–319	161–171

1 For the export markets a range of possible orders was quoted, because there was a possibility of obtaining large orders in some countries, although the exact quantities represented by these contracts were not known at the time.

From this table, the report deduced that the home market was very price conscious at the £250–£300 price end and not so price conscious at the £450 end.

The report on the exercise continued with the following table:

Optimum Price of Product F

Over the next few years and taking the lower sales estimate:

	£250	*£300*	*£350*	*£400*	*£450*
(a) Sales estimate (Qty).	1286	763	475	294	161
(b) Gross turnover £000.	321·6	228·9	166·3	117·6	72·5
(c) Net turnover £0000.	273·3	194·6	141·4	100·0	61·6
(d) Material and labour costs £000.	252·1	149·5	93·1	58·6	31·6
(e) Margin (c–d) £000.	21·2	45·1	48·3	41·4	30·0

The margin obtained would have had to cover fixed costs, such as development expenditure and tooling, as well as production overheads and selling expenses, in so far as these were not fixed. Basing itself on these figures, the report reached the conclusion:

> 'That a selling price of £330 to £340 would provide the largest margin to cover fixed costs and overheads.'
>
> and
>
> 'Since we may as well make some attempt to recover as much as possible of the development expenditure, we should reduce the price of product F, thus minimising our loss.'

Unfortunately, it turned out that the accounts department, which had been responsible for producing the cost estimates for materials and labour for the tables in the report, had made an error. It was not discovered until later that these figures were wrong. Because of these mistakes, the exercise and its conclusions were ignored. The price of product F remained unchanged.

CASE STUDY G

Basic Foods Limited

by R. J. Cripps

Product G was mass produced for sale to both consumer and producer markets. This study is concerned with pricing in the consumer market.

THE MARKET SITUATION

The UK market had grown at an average rate of 8 per cent annually, from 1953 to 1966. During this period, supply grew more rapidly than demand and the market became increasingly competitive.

Basic Foods was the largest firm in this well-established market, which it shared with four significant competitors and a growing num- of others. Basic Food's market share fell between 1953 and 1966, as a number of new firms entered. Although only one of these entrants had become sizeable when we made our study, together they were significant.

The whole group manufactured and marketed many other products besides those now under consideration. It was organized into a number of semi-autonomous divisions, of which Basic Foods was one of the largest.

Total demand for the product was inelastic, so far as could be judged from information and experience available to Basic Foods. However, demand for any product of an individual company was elastic to changes in the prices of other firms' products. For any significant elasticity of demand to be apparent, a price differential at the retail level of 5 per cent was thought to be necessary. In view of this, and the fact that retail prices were not maintained, price cutting occurred on a large scale, even though it was normal for retail prices to be recommended by manufacturers.

Price cutting was particularly common with the products holding the smallest market shares. Elasticity of demand was such that an active retailer, with suitably situated premises, could more than double his sales of a product if the retail price were 10 per cent lower than that generally recommended. Although it was not thought that all retailers could obtain this result (no estimate of elasticity of demand of widespread application was available), it shows what was thought possible by price cutters.

Basic Foods had traditionally been the price leader for these products; in recent years, more-aggressive marketing methods adopted by competitors had whittled away this leadership.

There was a large number of widespread retail outlets. Some were owned by producers, although the majority were either independent or part of multiple chains. There was no discrimination in wholesale prices charged to different types of store, but prices to retailers depended on the quantity ordered. The idea was to encourage the growth of efficient retailers and to help Basic Foods to achieve economies of scale in distribution. Discounts from the wholesale price were given in exchange for exclusive supply contracts, the size of the discount varying with the size of the stores' sales.

COMPANY OBJECTIVES

Objectives for the group were formulated in general terms by the group Board annually, for the following year and the ensuing five years. They were in effect guide-lines for the company, along which it could develop its operating policies.

Company objectives were then set by the Board of Basic Foods, taking into account the general statement of group objectives, the results achieved as compared with current objectives, and factors expected to influence future operations. These objectives, covering the next year and the following five years, were then presented to the group, together with the capital budget. At the same time, approval was sought for the next year's capital budget.

This document listed the known influences affecting the market for the product during the period, and the company's plans for dealing with them. It covered all aspects of marketing effort, together with expected results in terms of sales volumes, sales value, costs, profit, return on capital, and the DCF rate of return for the capital expenditure programme.

It was a statement of intent based upon certain limited assumptions. From it were developed annual plans, targets and budgets for all the company's activities. It was recognized by Basic Foods that in the fluid market situation, where decisions, including price decisions, made by the company and its competitors would directly effect the market situation, the target assumptions about sales, profits etc., might be changed.

Price decisions were made to meet a combination of marketing (i.e. sales volume and market share) and financial (i.e. sales value and profit) objectives. In the existing market situation the prime objective was 'to maintain adequate growth while maintaining profitability so far as this is possible'.

INFORMATION USED FOR PRICING DECISIONS

A considerable amount of market and cost information was available to those setting prices.

(a) Market Information

Actual (historical) data on market size (and therefore market growth) were available each month through an industry information agreement. Basic Foods could work out its market share by comparing its own sales figures with those for the total market from the information agreement.[1] Market shares of competitors were estimated by Basic Foods' marketing economics staff in the same way and with, it was believed, considerable accuracy. Forecasts of future market size, growth and share, for Basic Foods and its competitors, were also made by the marketing economics staff.

Past and current nominal retail and wholesale prices for Basic Foods and its competitors were publicly available. Actual wholesale prices were more difficult to discover. While the general framework of competitors' discounts was known, their detailed operation was discovered by Basic Foods only in exceptional circumstances.

Other firms' prices could be compared with those of Basic Foods only by detailed study of the price and specification for each individual product; different products might be similar in all important respects, but firms might differentiate the products in such a way that differences in retail price were fully accounted for by technical and marketing differences.

From estimates of competitors' sales volume and prices, Basic Foods' marketing economics staff estimated their turnover. Its own turnover figures were available internally.

(b) Cost Information

Basic Foods divided its costs into:

(i) product values[2];
(ii) distribution costs, including marketing costs; and

[1] This information agreement was operated through a trade association and provided data only on market size.

[2] Actual product costs were not available, since the product we studied was jointly-produced with certain other products. Product value was an allocation of joint-costs to each product.

(iii) overheads, allocated to products in proportion to an estimate of each product's contribution to total overhead expenses.

Product values were defined in two ways. They were either:

(iv) average cost per unit of the product at budgeted or actual outputs, or
(v) incremental/decremental unit cost of the product for increments of output above or below the budgeted or actual level.

Product value as defined in (iv) was used in calculating overall company profit.

Product value as defined in (v) was used to assess the profitability of different levels of capital expenditure, output and price. Competitors' costs were assumed to be broadly in line with those of Basic Foods, though where they were known to vary, allowance was made for this.

Closely linked to this information about competitors' costs was Basic Foods' knowledge of their marketing and capital investment plans and their financial arrangements, etc. Good and early information on all this was often lacking; some information, frequently without any figures, could be gleaned from the Press, public announcements, personal contacts, etc. Basic Foods normally had to use its knowledge and experience to make its own judgements about the likelihood of particular marketing moves by competitors, or about the scale and nature of investment plans, etc. In its oligopolistic market, Basic Foods regarded knowledge like this about competitors as very important. A section of its marketing economics staff spent the whole of its time analysing competitors' activities. Basic Foods believed that this information was as good as it could hope for without using industrial espionage; inevitably, it was not as complete as Basic Foods would have liked.

(c) Operating Results

Data on profitability—past, present and future—was derived from turnover and cost figures. Past and present operating results came from the accounting and management information departments. For competitors, and for the future, they were estimated.

Reports on operating results were circulated quarterly within Basic Foods. They covered:

(i) sales volumes and values;
(ii) its own and competitors' market shares;

(iii) average unit value of product;
(iv) direct marketing expenses;
(v) contribution to overheads and profit;
(vi) return on average capital employed.

All these items were given for the previous year, the current year (actual and planned) and the following year (latest estimate).

INITIATING PRICING DISCUSSIONS

Unsatisfactory operating results could lead to suggestions that prices might be changed. Similarly, discussions of capital expenditure proposals, and forecasts of operating results, could lead Basic Foods to decide to consider price changes.

Some other factors might have the same result. Most important among these were competitive conditions, particularly actual or expected changes in competitors' prices. An assessment of market pressures, based upon such competitive factors, could lead to discussions of price changes. These might be designed to forestall changes in competitors' marketing plans, or to bring Basic Foods into line with changes that had already taken place in the market.

Normally, the initiative to discuss price changes was taken by the general manager; this frequently followed discussion with the marketing director. With his department the general manager was responsible for developing proposals for changing prices and for recommending these to the company Board.

PREPARING PROPOSALS FOR PRICE CHANGES

The basis of every proposal for changing prices was a comparison between the effects of choosing one of a number of alternative prices and what seemed likely to happen if no change was made. Although assumptions had to be made about those marketing activities and those competitors' activities which would be common to all alternative prices, the important feature for Basic Foods was the emphasis on comparison *between* alternatives, not so much on the assumptions made. However, the better the assumptions, and therefore the forecasts of market changes and competitors' activities on which they were based, the better would be the forecasts provided for the management of Basic Foods about the results which would probably follow a number of alternative pricing moves. Given the fluidity of its market, Basic Foods did not think it possible to link actual changes in results with changes in any one factor or assumption. For this reason, it did not consider the effects of changing the basic, common assumptions made. For similar reasons, not least the possibility that competitors' reactions might spoil the test, test marketing was not used to prove any of the assumptions.

The first stage in making a price recommendation was to calculate the figures for the no-change case, for as long a period as was appropriate. This would cover the following points:

(i) market size and growth—in total, and for different varieties of the product;
(ii) market shares—own and competitors';
(iii) financial implications, including effects on sales turnover and costs.

The second stage was calculating the predicted effects of choosing particular alternative price levels, and comparing these results with those of the no-change case. In making these calculations, the aim was to produce estimates that were both reasonable and cautious. The important factor in the calculations was an attempt to estimate elasticity of demand with respect to price for each variety of the product, and cross-elasticities between products. The estimates for sales volume were a compromise between the (largely subjective) estimates; they were put forward for discussion because they seemed reasonable. It was considered important that, for each alternative, the estimates put forward should be consistent with one another; they should also be reasonable in the context of the whole series of alternatives. Once calculated, predicted sales volumes could often be checked against past experience; where Basic Foods was relying on judgement and experience, it seemed likely that those factors which *were* known would have the biggest influence upon the estimates adopted.

Translating any estimated sales volume into financial results was relatively simple. As with the no-change case, incremental and decremental sales value and cost data were compared.

Discussions and calculations within the general manager's department led to an agreed recommendation which was presented to the marketing director. There might then be further discussion and calculation before the recommendation was made to the chairman. At this stage, the possible implications of the proposal for the products and activities of the whole group, which included Basic Foods, were taken into account and a company recommendation formulated.

THE PRICE DECISION

The formal presentation of these recommendations to the group Board followed, perhaps preceded or accompanied by informal discussions. The group Board made the final decision. This could be to accept or reject the recommendation, or to call for its modification (and hence the reconsideration and calculation of other alternatives). At this stage, all aspects of the group's marketing strategy and operational performance would be considered, as well as more limited considerations affecting the particular product which had been important during its development.

Once the decision was made, the general manager became responsible for implementing it. This was done through his product managers and operational marketing and sales staff.

There was centralization of pricing authority, with operational staff allowed to vary prices only within narrow limits laid down in discount scales. This was partly due to the impossibility of obtaining accurate product costs in a firm producing joint products. Basic Foods believed that to keep overall control of profitability in its joint-product/joint-cost situation, it needed centralized control over costs and prices to determine how much all products collectively would be contributing to profit.

CASE STUDY H

Heavy Technology Limited

by R. H. Vause

This study was on the pricing of an established product manufactured by Heavy Technology, using the latest technical knowledge and extremely sophisticated production methods. The finished product was sold to large organizations for use as a capital asset. Whilst remaining basically the same, the product was being developed considerably with advances in scientific knowledge and new manufacturing methods.

THE MARKET SITUATION

Total sales in the market amounted to several millions of pounds each year, and the market was highly competitive. The industry contained about ten companies which competed for the UK business; in fact this was more than the market could profitably sustain at that time. The relatively large number of firms in the industry had been brought about by the fact that the return which the companies could obtain in the early years of the industry had been high and so had attracted many firms, particularly as it had seemed obvious that the industry was going to expand rapidly.

The skills needed to manufacture the product were very high, calling for experts in mechanical and electrical engineering as well as craftsmen in wood and metal. Though the customers of Heavy Technology would order a particular model, they would often wish to have alterations or additions made to it, which called for top-class technical designers.

With technical skill, expert knowledge and very expensive equipment needed to manufacture the product, it is not surprising that most companies in the industry were very big. Quite large amounts had to be spent each year on research and development by the various companies in the industry. This required substantial amounts of capital which only a large organization could supply. Of the companies in the the industry, four accounted for roughly 60 per cent of sales in the UK.

The product had to work continuously for long hours if the purchaser were to recoup his capital outlay on it; it had to be as reliable and require as little maintenance as was possible. Customers put great emphasis on the reliability and quality of the product when placing orders. Only by meeting these requirements, could orders be won. Delivery dates were also important in influencing the customer in placing orders. Late delivery could upset a complex timetable and throw a whole section of his activity completely out of phase.

The market for the product had been steadily increasing until the time of our study—when an economic squeeze hit the industry's customers. It was unfortunate that the squeeze came when it did from the industry's point of view, for it was just at this time that its customers were trying to assess the long-term demand for their product in order to plan further capital investment. The squeeze reinforced the customers' conclusion that a steady demand increase was not certain, and orders were cut back. The result was that there was less business for the industry to compete for and prices fell. Indeed, competition became very fierce, with prices close to marginal cost. When we ended our study, there was no clear indication when customers would again increase the amount of business they were offering. The position had been further aggravated by the fact that one firm had begun to dominate Heavy Technology's customers, taking over most of the smaller firms. By 1965, the equipment manufacturers were faced with what amounted to a monopsonist—a sole buyer.

There were strict standards for the manufacturing processes and materials to be used in Heavy Technology's product. These standards had largely been imposed by the purchasers of the product who had to consider their customers. This had resulted in some standardization of designs. Each contract for equipment was based on these minimum requirements, but manufactured to suit the customer's wishes for the particular contract. Most of Heavy Technology's competitors had used similar designs to its own, but with differences in material, production techniques and ancillary equipment.

The name of the manufacturer of the capital equipment was not usually known by the eventual users of the product. Consequently, all advertising and marketing was very technical, aimed at Heavy Technology's customers—especially the monopsonist. It was thought that with a highly-technical product, advertising had little effect on the buyer; it was kept to a minimum. More reliance was placed on building up Heavy Technology's 'name' by the technical excellence of its product.

There was little foreign competition for British manufacturers, since to be able to export to the UK other countries would have had to possess at least equal manufacturing ability and scientific know-how and in their field many did not. These countries' labour costs were similar to those in the UK so that they could not export to Britain at much of a price advantage. There was also the fact that the main customer of the industry preferred to buy British products, although there was no obligation that it should do so.

The demand for the product was geared to the amount of capital available to the monopsonist as well as to the general economic situation, which affected spending on its product by the public. Changes in these factors could have relatively rapid effects on the customer industry, and orders could be cut back and the latent excess capacity of Heavy Technology's industry uncovered. Heavy Technology had found it difficult to forecast the demand for the product, not least because it was hard to predict changes like those mentioned above.

QUOTATION PREPARATION

Heavy Technology's customers had found that the best way of getting good terms from Heavy Technology and its competitors was to put contracts out to tender. The usual method was for the prospective customer to send his supplier details of his needs and to request a quotation from each of them.

The manufacturers then each studied the contract specifications, drew up a design and assured themselves that the customer's delivery date could be met. They sent in their quotation after having the design costed to make sure it would be sufficiently profitable to be worth manufacturing.

As far as we could discover, the criteria that the purchasers of the product applied in awarding contracts were:

(i) the quotation price;
(ii) the likelihood that the delivery date would be met; and
(iii) their satisfaction with previous contracts given to the manufacturer.

What we could not discover was the order in which the above criteria were ranked, but it probably depended on factors beyond the control, and indeed often knowledge, of the producer.

PRICING RESPONSIBILITY

The responsibility for pricing Heavy Technology's tenders lay with the sales manager, though he spent a good deal of time discussing pricing problems with the commercial manager. The sales manager made the final decision about what price Heavy Technology would quote on a contract. He also had regular discussions with a number of his colleagues who were involved in the pricing decision, or in supplying information for it. At one or more of these meetings each individual contract currently under consideration would be discussed in detail to assess its likely profitability and to decide what price for it would fit in with Heavy Technology's overall objectives. These discussions could take the form of a committee meeting or of informal talks with an individual. The people with whom the sales manager spent most of his time in these discussions were:

the general manager;
the works manager;
the commerical manager;
the marketing research officer;
the chief costing engineer;
the chief designer.

These men provided the sales manager with information about customers' requirements, competitors' activities and market shares, and about how important the contract under consideration would be to Heavy Technology in keeping production capacity employed and maintaining profitability. Some effort was also put into trying to assign a probability that the tender would be accepted at a number of possible prices. All this information helped the sales manager and the commercial manager in pricing. The general manager discussed the general policy of the company with the sales manager and, together with the sales manager, set the overall pricing and sales policies within which prices were decided. The general manager was responsible for the overall profitability of the company and so was intimately concerned with the success of pricing and other marketing activity.

INFORMATION FOR THE PRICING DECISION

Although the sales manager had discussions with the other executives mentioned above, the actual pricing decision was not a committee decision: it was his alone. Three main sources of information helped him in arriving at the price to quote.

(a) The Costing Section

This section provided information on the estimated costs of producing the product and of installing it on the customer's premises. The job was carried out by a staff with expertise in both engineering and accountancy.

Material and labour costs could be predicted with reasonable accuracy from previous contracts. The calculation of likely indirect expenses was more difficult: they were allocated according to the level of activity expected when the contract would actually be on the shop floor, and according to the value of the order, using well-tried formulae. These were applied to individual contracts by the sales manager's staff who thereby obtained a detailed understanding of the costs included in any contract. This helped them in pricing.

All costing was done on the assumption that the product would be assembled on the customer's premises, and taking into account any special requirements in the order.

(b) The Sales Force

The salesmen provided up-to-date information on the customer's requirements, and about any of his idiosyncrasies which might affect the probability of Heavy Technology being successful in its quotation.

The salesmen were able to pick up information from various personal contacts within the customer's firm, and were used to providing Head Office with regular reports on their areas. This was a very useful source of information about the market and, on occasion, about competitors because some employees of customer firms would give hints about Heavy Technology's performance or price, by comparison with a competitor. This was particularly liable to happen when Heavy Technology had recently been unsuccessful in a contract, but only just so, through quoting too high a price.

Salesmen visited all customers' offices regularly and were able to pass on information to the sales manager in one of the regular meetings each of them had with him. Meetings with any individual salesman were more frequent when business was being quoted for in his area. He was then expected to provide as much information as he could about customers' intentions.

(c) The Market Research Section

This section provided information on the activities of both customers and competitors. Customers' ordering methods and trading strategies were predicted by the section from their annual reports. These gave details of their future plans and requirements, in general terms. Any other relevant publications, as well as past orders, were also studied.

Information was also collected about the order books of Heavy Technology's chief competitors. This was useful because, if it was known that a competitor had enough business to keep it working at capacity, it would be unlikely to try very hard to obtain more business. Heavy Technology could then afford to raise the price it was quoting. At the time of our study, of course, there was too little business for this to happen.

Work was being carried out to see if the sales manager could assign an accurate probability of getting any particular contract at a certain price—given known and possible actions by competitors. The sales manager played a part in this as he had personal contacts with his opposite numbers in various competing firms. His assessment of the activities of competitors could be vital for Heavy Technology in obtaining business by tender. In coming to his decision the sales manager put considerable emphasis on getting an idea of competitors' pricing policies and of trends in their pricing by studying records of the past prices at which both Heavy Technology and other manufacturers had been successful in getting business.

An attempt was also made to discover what the customers thought of Heavy Technology. Such information came mainly from the sales force, who were in the best position to see customers' reactions. If a customer had been satisfied in previous contracts with Heavy Technology, then it was likely that they would prefer to deal with Heavy Technology again. This last point was important because it suggested that Heavy Technology saw price as only one criterion being used by its customers to decide which company should be given business. It also made the sales manager's task that much more difficult.

PRICING OBJECTIVES

Heavy Technology had no formally-defined set of objectives, but the general philosophy of the company could be summed up as being to use the latest scientific and technical knowledge to ensure that its product was the best on the market. At the same time, it wanted to provide the Board with the highest possible return on capital employed in the depressed market and to maintain an acceptable market share while doing so.

It was for the general manager and sales manager to formulate the pricing objectives to fit in with the general company philosophy. In the existing market conditions, it was difficult for them to do as well as they would have wished; they were being forced to reduce prices to obtain business.

One of the most important objectives in pricing was to try to ensure that sufficient revenue was obtained to finance research and development so that Heavy Technology could keep ahead of its competitors by offering new techniques and better performance to its customers. Ideally, Heavy Technology would have liked to earn a return on capital employed of 15 per cent but we have seen that this was impossible at the time of our study.

THE PRICING DECISION

The sales manager, having obtained all the information he thought necessary, had to prepare the quotation. He had to decide how vital the contract was to the company. For a large contract he would be able to offer a discount to the customer. The work would keep the company busy for some time to come and, in existing market conditions, this was very important.

The costing information provided by the chief costing engineer was vital, since it enabled the sales manager to discover what price he must obtain in order at least to cover the variable expenses incurred in manufacturing the product. Traditionally, a formula had been used: the price should cover material and labour costs, and add a further 25 per cent. In the past this had been sufficient to cover any indirect expenses, and had been regarded as the minimum price at which any business could be taken. With strong price competition existing when we were carrying out our study, this price could not always be obtained by the sales manager. The costing engineer had therefore begun to study costs more carefully and to identify exactly what variable costs would be for any particular contract. The sales manager paid a great deal of attention to the price at which the last contract for this type of product had been awarded. This was the basis for his calculations, and any further adjustments would be made in the light of differences in specification for this product, or the known intentions of competitors on the prices at which they would tender.

After the sales manager had met the people mentioned above as being concerned with pricing, either in committees or as individuals, he had to take a decision. At the time of our study, this meant either following the market price for the last contract given for this type of product, or moving below it. If any individual decision appeared to mean a change in the normal pricing policy of Heavy Technology, then the sales manager would meet the general manager to make sure that the latter agreed with what he was doing.

Once the decision had been made, it was communicated to the customer in the normal way, together with the company's design drawings and working specifications.

CASE STUDY J

Medlock Engineering Limited

by R. H. Vause

This was a study of the pricing of a capital good being sold in international markets by Medlock Engineering Ltd, under conditions of fierce competition. The product was manufactured on very expensive machinery with highly-skilled labour. It was an established product, but was constantly developing to take advantage of the results of scientific research. Much of the development was by Medlock itself, for it had a large research and development section. One measure of progress is that one of today's products can do the work of ten of those of twenty years ago.

THE MARKET SITUATION

It was known that the market was worth many million pounds each year. Beyond this, it was impossible to arrive at an accurate estimate of the total world demand. Demand for the product was related to a country's economic development. To use it, a country must have reached a certain level of technical expertise, as well as an ability to invest capital in such expensive equipment. Medlock Engineering tackled the problem of discovering world demand by making a series of studies. Each focused attention on one or two countries, and made a detailed investigation of potential demand for the product. This provided information which helped Medlock to decide on the intensity of any sales campaigns and on whether to bid for a contract or not. If a survey showed that one country offered a particularly attractive market to Medlock, the sales manager could ensure that Medlock was adequately represented there.

As with attempts to assess world demand for the product, there was difficulty in obtaining anything like full information about the competitors that Medlock had to face. All of the technologically-advanced countries had an indigenous industry manufacturing the product—though not necessarily making such advanced models as Medlock did. It was also possible to determine which of the larger companies in each country was likely to compete in the international market. Even with this information, the task was difficult. For example, the UK industry contained about eight firms which could compete in the international market if they chose to do so. When this number was multiplied by the number of countries likely to have an indigenous industry, the competitors Medlock might find itself facing for any one contract could be very numerous. The export market for British firms was not as profitable as the home market. This was because British prices were higher. (Our study was carried out before devaluation in 1967.) The reason for low export prices was that companies in all countries with an industry making the product had to sell abroad to keep their capacity satisfactorily occupied. Prices were close to marginal cost. Medlock was no exception in having to sell a proportion of its output in the international market in order to keep its factories satisfactorily employed—even if this meant selling at very low prices. Although export prices were low, export selling had to continue so long as there was too little business in the home market. Medlock's export prices were about 55 per cent of home prices for the same products.

By carrying out business in the international market, Medlock obtained valuable experience in designing and producing advanced products. The main countries overseas to which Medlock sold usually had stricter specifications than did customers in the UK. Once Medlock had built a model which worked satisfactorily abroad, it could introduce it into the home market, perhaps gaining competitive advantage as well as prestige.

MARKET INFORMATION

The chief source of market information was Medlock's agents. They lived in the countries in which they represented Medlock. They were usually 'shared' with other UK companies operating in those countries —though in different industries or with an associated or subsidiary company of Medlock. There was often difficulty in getting agents to collect the right sort of information. This was because they usually had no training in market research. Once this deficiency was overcome, the agent appeared to provide Medlock with valuable information on his particular market.

As has already been mentioned, Medlock had initiated a series of studies on particular countries which seemed to offer good potential markets. These studies were carried out by the Market Research Department under the supervision of the sales manager. All available sources were used in obtaining information on the country in question. What usually appeared was a complete picture of the country as a user of Medlock's product. The study would include information on the technical ability of local manufacturers of the product; probable demand for the product, including a forecast of the growth of the market; an assessment of the economic situation within the country; and any information there was on the company's preferences about which manufacturers it would buy from. For example, it was obviously of little use for Medlock to try to sell its product in a country which would trade only with iron curtain manufacturers. Finally, there was an assessment of the prices of the product in the country. This could usually be made from records of prices quoted on previous contracts. If no business had been done before, or if the information was impossible to obtain, Medlock had to make its own guess. Once an idea of previous price levels had been acquired Medlock could judge whether or not it would be commercially profitable to intensify its activities in the country. With this information, the sales manager could decide whether Medlock could operate there profitably.

The main responsibility for collecting other market information rested with the Market Research Department and the staff of the quotations manager. As much information as possible was obtained on the prices charged for each product by Medlock and by its competitors in all export markets. Where bids were opened in public, this was relatively easy. Otherwise, it was up to Medlock's agent to glean what information he could. It was not practicable to keep a dossier on all major competitors in the international market, but individual executives built up personal files on the companies they met most often, and which were known to be interested in the same type of product as Medlock. For it was they who usually quoted for the same contracts. In addition, there was information from various trade associations in the UK on limited sections of the international market. Medlock used these where possible.

RESPONSIBILITY FOR PRICING

The sales manager was responsible for pricing the product in the export market. In this, he was assisted by the quotations manager who did much of the routine work for him and prepared the actual quotation. At intervals, Medlock sent one of these executives, or another senior manager, to visit the countries in which most of Medlock's business was done. The aim was to build up personal contacts with agents and major customers in the country. This was invaluable in setting prices for business in that country.

INFORMATION AVAILABLE

Besides market information, the most important facts that had to be studied when prices were being set were about the cost of manufacturing for each particular contract. With export prices low, some selling had to be done at prices little above marginal cost. To discover costs of manufacture it was vital that they should be correctly identified and analysed. The task of estimating costs was given to the costing section of the Accounting Department. Estimating was done by using a series of formulae, obtained from careful analysis of previous contract costs, and altered to fit the specifications of the contract being priced. At the same time, the costing section also provided the sales manager with details of the lowest price at which he could consider taking the business if he wanted to be certain of making some contribution towards fixed expenses.

A SPECIFIC PRICING DECISION

To show how an actual decision was taken by the sales and quotations managers, we looked at the pricing of a specific contract.

Stage 1
Medlock Engineering was notified by its agent in the country in question that a customer was offering a contract for tender. The agent sent details of the contract to Medlock so that it could decide if it was interested. Medlock decided that it was.

Stage 2
The Design Department drew up a design to match the customer's specifications. This was then sent to the costing section so that an estimate of the cost of manufacture could be made. This was passed to the quotations manager, together with a note of the minimum price at which the sales manager should entertain the business.

Stage 3
The quotations manager studied all available information on previous contracts offered by the particular customer to discover what price was likely to be obtained. If the country had been one which had been the subject of a study by Medlock, then this would have been considered. If Medlock had recently been successful, as it had in this case, in obtaining business from the customer there would be a ready-made guide for pricing the contract. About twelve months previously, Medlock had quoted successfully for a contract from the

customer we were considering. Even though the design specifications were not identical, the quotations manager was able to arrive at a comparable selling price for the contract now being considered, assuming that no changes had occurred in prices in the country.

Stage 4

The sales manager, together with the quotations manager, studied the market situation in the country where the contract was being offered. As the previous quotation had been successful, information about this was used to help in working out plans for the present decision. The Market Research Department also provided information about specific points which needed discussion, such as the competition to be expected and changes in the price level in the country in question.

In this particular case, it was known that the price that Medlock would be able to obtain was likely to be above the minimum acceptable price as calculated by the Costing Department. The minimum price was therefore irrelevant on this particular occasion.

The sales manager decided that Medlock should put in a price which would be the same as it had quoted on the previous contract, allowing for differences in specification. He was fairly confident that the customer would prefer to deal with Medlock again if it could, and this would give some advantage in price as compared with competitors. There was no sign that the price likely to be obtained in the country for the product had risen or fallen to any extent in the most recent business given to competitors. So the quotation was prepared for delivery to the customer on the same lines as the previous one.

The quotation was accepted by the customer and Medlock was awarded the contract. All information obtained on bids from competitors was filed away by the Market Research Department. It would be used in preparing tenders for any future contracts that might be bid for in that country.

CASE STUDY K

Wessex Timber Industries Limited

by R. H. Vause

This case study was concerned with the pricing of a product which was made by Wessex Timber Industries from primary raw materials. It was sold mainly as a raw material which underwent further processing before reaching the final consumer.

THE MARKET SITUATION

The market for the product was a long-established one, with many firms competing in it. During the previous ten years, however, the number of Wessex's competitors had decreased as many of the smaller concerns—mainly family firms—had left the trade, or been merged with, or taken over by, one of the larger organizations. The result was that the trade had come to be dominated by a handful of very large companies of which Wessex was one—but with a considerable number of smaller companies still operating.

The demand for timber is a derived demand depending very directly on the general economic situation. If the building of houses or the purchasing of furniture is restricted, then there is a decline in the demand for timber processed by Wessex. The time lag between a change in the economic climate and its effect on the timber industry is relatively short. This close link with the general state of the economy has, at times, led to severe depression. To overcome this, many of the large companies have diversified into other activities, to provide a cushion against sudden changes in the demand for timber. The average growth rate of the market had been around 5 per cent per annum.

Wessex had to face competition from two sources other than UK competitors. The first, and most important of these, was competition from 'substitutes' for wood. These came predominantly from the plastics industry which had developed a whole range of them over the previous few years. The widespread use of these materials in place of timber could have a big impact on its price, and the demand for it in the UK. To get round this, Wessex Ltd, like many other firms in the industry, entered the plastics industry itself and manufactured several 'substitutes' under a variety of brand names with considerable success.

The second source of competition was from imported, processed timbers. Wessex was mainly processing top-quality imported timbers like mahogany and teak from under-developed countries. It was therefore more susceptible to competition from imported processed timber than firms which traded in such woods as pine coming from areas such as Europe. The under-developed countries found the timber trade particularly attractive because the felling and processing of wood was not highly capital intensive. Nor did it require skilled labour. With their low labour costs, these areas were able to send their timber to the UK at prices which it was difficult for Wessex to match. The import surcharge and import deposit schemes had been quite effective in reducing this threat but Wessex felt that more permanent means would have to be found when the latter was dropped.

Though the market was dominated by a few large companies, no one could be said to control more than a rather small, specialized sector of the market. This was because of the great variety of types and qualities of products which had to be supplied to the customers of the timber industry. The variety made it an uneconomic proposition for one single company to try to provide the entire range of products. Wessex Ltd concentrated on supplying material of high quality and in giving it highly-skilled treatment.

Having been in the timber industry for many years, Wessex had a group of customers for its product which could be regarded as captive: they accounted for roughly 50 per cent of its output. These customers had for a long time been satisfied with the quality of Wessex's service. In turn, Wessex had become used to catering for their idiosyncrasies. The remaining 50 per cent of output had to be sold in an intensively competitive market.

All large buyers of the product were visited regularly—including all of Wessex's customers—by salesmen from all the larger timber processors. If it were possible for a competitor to 'poach' a customer from Wessex by offering more attractive terms, it would do so. This was continually happening.

Obviously, the raw timber used by Wessex was very similar to that used by its competitors, but Wessex did take great care in choosing timber of the highest quality to maintain a constant standard. Some pride was taken in the fact that the company had a good name in the trade for its product. These achievements had helped to shape the company's philosophy.

Wessex marketed its product under its own trade name, and so was well-known both within the industry and by the final consumer. The reputation which Wessex had built up over the years was an advantage in its competitive market.

Wessex tried to work as near 100 per cent capacity as was possible, but was hampered by the difficulty of getting labour to work in the noise and dust produced in converting rough timber into usable sizes and shapes. This problem was most acute in times of full employment. As a result, all processes had been mechanized as far as possible and the industry was rapidly becoming capital intensive and no longer needed to rely on finding large numbers of workers. Large sums had been invested in saw mills, sanding tools and stripping machinery so that to the executives of Wessex the amount of capital employed was one of the main factors considered when they took pricing decisions.

RESPONSIBILITY FOR PRICES

The ultimate responsibility for pricing the products processed by the company lay with the director in charge of the timber side of the business. He worked with a number of his subordinates when deciding what price to charge.

In fact, the actual responsibility lay with the salesman making the sale to the customer, since it was up to him to get the best price he could for the product whilst working within the list price provided for him. The salesman had limited amount of discretion in setting prices for individual orders: this was within ± 1 per cent of the list price. The 'discretion' accounted for a large part of the possible price adjustments open to Wessex. 'A good salesman is seen as one that will turn down business if the price is not good enough', was a statement by one of the directors of the company.

Although salesmen had an ultimate responsibility to the director in charge of timber output, they were expected to work with the manager in charge of their own mill. They could then concentrate on trying to sell the type and quality of wood he was processing.

The organization chart of Wessex Ltd is given below:

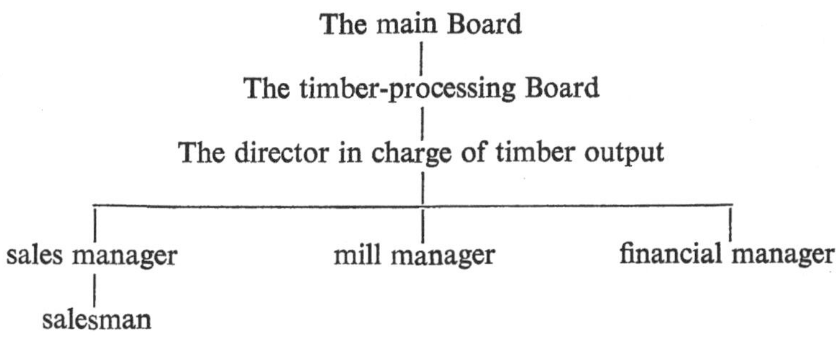

PRICE

The price at which Wessex Ltd could sell its products was largely governed by the current market price. This price traditionally fell within certain generally-accepted price ranges for each type of timber. It was unusual to find business being conducted outside these ranges, except in times of depression.

The trade had certain well-defined centres, mainly historical. Most of them were at the timber ports, or in their hinterlands. Knowledge of the prices being charged spread rapidly between companies and it was very difficult to charge a price out of line with the general level.

The timber industry's salesmen, as well as the buyers of customer firms, congregated in these centres to 'swap' information on various trade topics. There was therefore a highly-effective trade 'grape vine'. Much of the business was conducted in these centres so that buyers had a chance to play one seller off against another so far as prices were concerned. All this tended to keep prices within the ranges mentioned.

Wessex felt that it could usually afford to go slightly above the market price in selling its product, since it had a good name in the trade and used superior quality timber. However, in times of depression the company had to follow the rest of the trade in reducing prices to get enough business.

THE PRICING DECISION

Wessex's pricing procedures could be divided into two distinct stages. These were:

(i) The company's executives held quarterly meetings at which they discussed the previous period's activities to discover how actual performance matched the performance budgeted for that quarter.

Variances were studied to see if they were likely to recur and so to affect the budget for the coming quarter. So, if labour problems were worse than usual, this would be taken into account when fixing the budgeted output for the next quarter. The supply of labour was the chief constraint on Wessex's output.

From these discussions emerged a forecast of output for the following quarter. This was usually expressed in thousands of feet of processed timber.

The executives then looked at the capital employed in the company. The Board had decreed that a return of at least 12½ per cent before tax should be achieved and this was what Wessex's executives had to try to ensure, for the coming period, from selling the budgeted output of processed timber.

The director in charge of output assessed what changes, if any, would occur in such things as the cost of timber, or wages, in the coming period. Any such changes were incorporated into a build-up of anticipated production costs for each type of timber to be processed. These costs were expressed as a cost per foot of timber processed ready for sale, and calculated on the assumption that the output targets would be achieved.

These discussions provided a list price for every type of timber to be processed during the coming quarter. It was this list price which was given to the company's salesmen.

(ii) At the second stage in the pricing decision, the list price provided by Wessex's executives was given to the company salesmen.

These salesmen had the job of selling the entire output of the company by negotiating individual sales with customers. Each salesman had had a long training in all aspects of timber processing, and was fully conversant with all the normal applications of timber, as sold by Wessex.

The salesmen had to be able to judge what their customers' future requirements would be and so needed a detailed knowledge of each customer's business. This was very important. When the customer was a valuable one, hard pressed by business conditions, the salesman could then lower the price to accommodate him.

The salesmen were in constant touch with the executives who set the list price so that they could be told immediately of any changes that were being made. Equally, they could quickly let the executives know of any need to alter prices in the face of competitors' activities or general market conditions.

The salesmen had the discretion to set prices for customers within ±1 per cent of the list price. This discretion had been built into pricing decisions in order to allow the salesmen to meet individual customers' requirements, as well as to allow for small swings in the demand/supply relationship to be met without intervention from Head Office.

With salesmen playing such an important part in pricing decisions, more care was exercised in their appointment than was usual when picking salesmen. For the system to work successfully, there had to be complete confidence in the salesmen. Yet, there was no obvious means by which a mill manager could discover if his salesmen had obtained the best price for any product in any sale.

INFORMATION AVAILABLE FOR DECISIONS

The industry was fortunate in having a number of trade associations which could provide full information on many issues. There were Government-sponsored associations and associations within the industry. Both gave a great deal of information on such matters as the quantity and type of imported products, on domestic production and on the consumption of products by the various trades and industries using them. More specific information was also available to any firm in the trade if it asked for it.

Whilst this information was invaluable for long-term planning and decision-taking of all kinds within Wessex, information of more direct commercial value was more difficult to obtain. Information on the price being quoted by competitors for any type of product could be obtained only by Wessex's own efforts. The chief source of such information was Wessex's salesmen. However, figures giving a general range of prices for each type of product being sold after basic processing, were published in trade journals.

In obtaining market and competitor information the company relied heavily on its salesmen who were in a position to hear what competitors had been offering their customers, or possibly to pick up facts from casual conversations with their opposite numbers in other companies in the industry. There was no formal flow of information on market or competitive situations, but the regular meetings between the salesmen and the company's executives ensured quick reactions to changes in the business climate.

CASE STUDY L

Clean Engineering Limited

by R. H. Vause

This study was of the pricing of water purification equipment which was made by Clean Engineering, in batches, to the specification of local authorities in Great Britain. The product was a highly-technical one, requiring considerable skill in its manufacture. It was well established and sold in a highly competitive market.

THE MARKET SITUATION

The market for water purification equipment was intensively competitive, with over twenty companies manufacturing similar products to meet local authorities needs. The companies were mostly large ones with wide interests in building water purification equipment and in allied manufacturing processes.

The demand for water purification equipment had been steady for some years. Just before our study, the Government had cut back on finance to the local authorities and this had caused a reduction in the amount which they were prepared to spend on water purification. The demand for equipment was closely linked to the size of population; the more people a county had, the bigger was its demand for water, and so for water purification equipment.

As the equipment manufactured by the companies in the industry had to conform to minimum safety requirements of county and national authorities, there was little to distinguish one manufacturer's product from those of his competitors. The manufacturers claimed that there were technical differences in design, running costs and reliability which were emphasized in selling their products to county authorities. Salesmen selling the equipment had to be trained engineers for they were selling to buyers who were also engineers, and had to be able to emphasize the technical superiority of the products of Clean Engineering over competing equipment. For this reason, Clean insisted that all executives must be technically-educated in the design and manufacture of water-purification equipment.

The total value of business in the market was several million pounds sterling per annum. Clean had a relatively steady 15 per cent market share and was one of the larger companies in the industry. All the local authorities had similar, though not identical, minimum specifications for the equipment they used in their water works. Clean had gone some way towards introducing standard, basic equipment which satisfied all these requirements, but could be altered in minor ways to meet the wishes of individual authorities.

PRICE

Clean marketed the equipment through six sales representatives who operated in the main areas where the product was sold. The country was divided into six regions, each of which was the responsibility of a sales representative. The representatives had no authority to agree prices with customers but they were expected to maintain good customer relations and to supply up-to-date and accurate market information. All prices were set by the executives of Clean's head office.

The price which Clean Engineering could obtain for its equipment was largely determined by competition between manufacturers. At the time of our study, the price charged was about 30 per cent of the level five years earlier. This was the result of keen price competition between manufacturers when demand slackened after the slow-down in the British economy and financial stringency, as well as of economies of scale resulting from the introduction of standard, basic designs a few years earlier.

With the drop in price, the only way in which Clean could continue to make a profit from water purification equipment was by obtaining bulk orders. When large numbers of water purification sets could be sold to local authorities, it was reasonably profitable for Clean to make them. Unfortunately, this was also true for Clean's competitors. Competition for bulk orders had forced the price even lower, and when we studied Clean the deciding factor in obtaining contracts was the discount offered to the customer for placing an order for a large number of sets of equipment.

The price for the basic equipment had remained steady at around 50 per cent of the level five years earlier for several months, which suggested that the price had been forced as low as any manufacturer wanted to see it go. Every time the price was reduced for a new contract, the next contract that was offered had to be tendered for at roughly this new price. To avoid a continuing decline of prices in this way, manufacturers were offering discounts for large orders placed with them by customers. While tender prices remained at about half the level five years earlier, the price that the customer actually paid was about 5 per cent below this. With price competition so fierce, it was difficult for Clean Engineering to discover at exactly what price any order had been given to a competitor. It was easy to check that the tender had been taken at the current level of apparent prices, but much harder to be sure whether a discount had been given, and of what size.

THE RESPONSIBLITY FOR PRICING

Every executive in the works producing water purification equipment had some formal training either in production or design. All were fully able to make changes in commercial policy on the basis of changes in the technical design of products or components. The equipment was priced by the commercial manager who was directly responsible to the sales manager for the prices he charged. The sales manager decided the general pricing policy of the company but then left it to the commercial manager to price individual contracts. He took an active part in pricing only when an unusual or important contract was being prepared. The commercial manager had a staff of engineers who prepared quotations for the customer from designs provided by the Design Department.

INFORMATION AVAILABLE

As all, or nearly all, of the customers for water purification plant were local authorities, Clean Engineering obtained large amounts of information from Annual Reports or from answers to parliamentary questions. These helped considerably in planning production or sales. Though information could be obtained about the long-term plans of the various local authorities for increasing their water purification activities, what could not be found was the date on which these schemes would be carried out.

Clean Engineering had a small staff engaged on market research, but quite a large proportion of the time of the head of the Market Research Section was taken up with other work for Clean's management.

Much of the information available to the company's head office came from sales representatives who reported anything of interest they heard as they visited local authorities. They provided information on such matters as the date when the authority would be asking manufacturers to send in quotations for large amounts of water purification equipment in the near future. Apart from this, the area representatives also discovered the prices at which competitors had been selling their equipment. They obtained details of their design specifications and information about how their equipment was operating. All of this information went either directly to the commercial manager or to members of his staff who presented it to him later. He received regular reports from area representatives on the market situation in their areas.

CUSTOMER RELATIONS

As the customers were public authorities, they tended to apply strict rules to be followed in offering business to firms manufacturing water-purification equipment. Their rules not only covered design specifications, which had to match those laid down in Parliament, they also determined how contracts should be awarded. When a county authority called for quotations for making equipment, it would not take seriously tenders from any firm which it felt had enough work of this type already. Authorities could not afford later deliveries of equipment, because this would throw tight investment timetables out of balance. This was very important, because their plans had to fit into the national plan for 'overspill' and for the location of industry.

Several of the local authorities would often band together to obtain even more favourable terms from manufacturers by offering even bigger orders for purification equipment. This presented a problem for each manufacturer. Those who failed to get these very big contracts had to try even harder to obtain business from subsequent tenders or they would be forced out of production. Big discounts were being offered for smallish contracts by the firms who had failed to obtain the really big orders.

Clean Engineering put great emphasis on maintaining personal contact between its staff and the staffs of the local authorities. Such contacts were encouraged at all levels of seniority from the Board downwards. This was seen not only as a way of getting business, but of making satisfactory relationships with customers as well.

THE PRICING DECISION

Once a customer had asked the manufacturers of water-purification equipment to quote for supplying a given amount of equipment, the design staff of Clean Engineering had to work out what was likely to be the most economical and attractive design from the customer's point of view. The design was then passed to the management accountants, who costed it. Together with the estimated production costs, it was then sent to the commercial manager. Given the difficult market conditions faced by Clean Engineering, the accountants provided an estimate of the lowest price at which the commercial manager should contemplate tendering for business.

The commercial manager then had to try to judge what moves his main competitors were likely to make over this contract. Though over twenty firms in the industry were competing for water purification business, eight of these firms accounted for about 70 per cent of the market. The job of watching competitors' action was not quite as hard as might be thought—though this is not to suggest that it was anything but difficult.

The commercial manager would rely on his staff for information about such things as the number of contracts that the main competitors had taken in recent months, and what view the authority now offering business took of Clean Engineering as a supplier. Given the current level of tender prices, he would then have to go on to work out what discounts his main competitors were likely to be offering to the customer. He could then provide at least equally-attractive terms.

Looking at the information the commercial manager had available to make his decision, one soon realized that much of it was intangible rather than precise and quantitative. His skill in pricing depended largely on his 'feel' of the market. Clean Engineering saw this as another reason why it should employ technically-qualified, as well as commercially-qualified, staff.

When we completed our study of Clean Engineering much time was being spent within the firm in trying to discover if it could build up an accurate picture of the discount structure being offered by its main competitors. This would certainly have been invaluable to the commercial manager in deciding what prices to quote. Without it, Clean Engineering could quote an identical price to those of competitors, as well as offering a slightly superior product. Yet it could lose the contract because of a 'hidden' discount offered by a competitor.

The commercial manager looked at all the information that was available and then made his decision about what price to quote. His decision was often a personal one, which then made it very difficult to analyse the way he took his decision, or to find out what weight he gave to any one piece of information, or for how far his own views affected the decision. In one decision we observed, he was helped by two colleagues. As has been mentioned, the commercial manager was unlikely to try to lower the general level of prices. His main decision was on discounts. He would decide on these, though often in consultation with other executives in Clean Engineering. He would be especially likely to consult others if he was changing the policy laid down by the sales manager.

The company's bid would be prepared and passed on to the customer. This case study was interesting because it showed a situation where the price of a product had previously been pushed down to a very low level by strong price competition. Having reached this level, no single manufacturer was willing to take the initiative in lowering it even further. Instead, firms had begun to use an elaborate, and as far as possible secret, discount system. They tried to attract customers and to persuade them to give orders for large amounts of equipment by offering them even lower effective prices in return, but the apparent price remained unchanged.

PRICING OBJECTIVES

The main pricing objective of Clean Engineering was to maintain its present share (about 15 per cent) of a market which was increasing in total value, though slowly during recent years. In the long run, at least, as the market grew it was felt that this business would provide the firm with an adequate profit. The Board was concerned with earning 15–20 per cent on capital employed. This was taken into account in pricing water purification equipment, although existing market conditions made it necessary for the Board to accept a much lower rate of return than this.

CASE STUDY M

Universal Corporation

by R. J. Cripps

This was a study of the pricing of a product made by complex equipment on a large scale to meet demand throughout the country. A price list was produced annually. Our study concentrated on the introduction of a price list drawn up on the basis of marginal analysis.

THE MARKET SITUATION

Universal Corporation's own product was one which accounted for approximately 30 per cent of the total market for this and similar products. Demand for Universal Corporation's own product had grown at an average rate of 7 per cent annually in recent years, while the total market, for all the related products, had grown at only 2 per cent per annum.

The total market was supplied by five firms, all technologically-oriented. The largest firm was highly traditional in its technology, and its output had been declining in absolute terms. So had its market share. Its competitors were all using modern technologies, the smallest one having improved its technology and its marketing activities with some success in previous years. The way the market had changed over ten years is summarized in Table M.1.

TABLE M.1

	Year 1	*Year 10*	*Average Annual Growth*
Total market size	100	120	2%
of which market shares:			
Traditional Company	60%	33%	−4%
Universal Corporation	18%	30%	7%
Company X	7%	10%	5%
Company Y	6%	19%	14%
Company Z	9%	8%	1%

Table M.1 shows that the most vigorous competition to Universal Corporation had come from Company Y. Its product, although different in design and specification, competed directly in many uses with that of Universal Corporation. The forecast was that overall competition would continue to operate in this way during the next few years, though possibly accompanied by a slower growth rate. It also expected that the challenge presented by Company Z would become more serious.

No one knew very much about elasticity of demand. Total demand was thought to be relatively insensitive to price changes, and demand for individual products was believed to be elastic with respect to changes in prices of competing products of more than about 5 per cent. Quantitative data to support these views were not available.

Universal Corporation's product was manufactured in a number of plants, scattered over the country. The product was delivered and

TABLE M.2

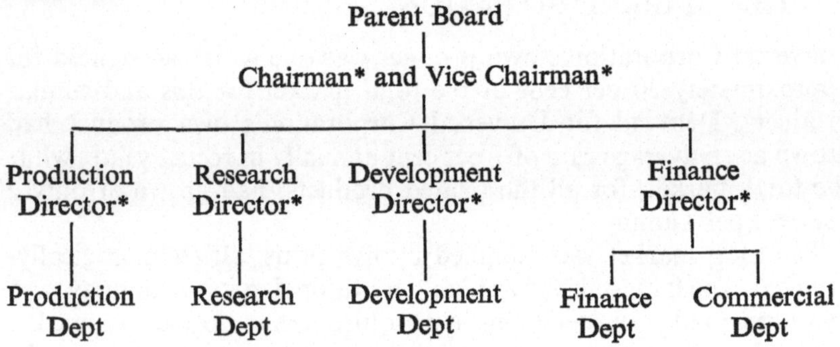

* Members of the Board of Universal Corporation.

sold in bulk to distributors. Distributors did not handle competing products, but had exclusive franchises for Universal Corporation's product in their own areas. Although independent of Universal Corporation, they operated in close conjunction both with Universal Corporation and its parent firm.

Universal Corporation's production methods had been used for a long time, but had recently been extended in scale and improved in efficiency in ways that until recently would have been thought impossible. Traditional raw materials were still used on a wide scale, though recent technological innovations had led to the development of new raw materials, which were being increasingly exploited.

The formal organization of Universal Corporation is shown in Table M.2.

Informal links across the organization, especially between the Production, Finance and Commercial Departments, were vitally important in the pricing process.

PRICING OBJECTIVES

Universal Corporation's objective, laid down by the parent Board, was to earn a specified rate of return on capital employed. The precise way in which profit as a percentage of capital employed should be calculated was laid down by the parent Board.

Universal Corporation's pricing objectives were defined in this way because of two interdependent factors:

(a) the company relied heavily, but not completely, on internal financing of its capital expenditure. An adequate margin of profit was therefore needed;

(b) the plant Universal Corporation used was large and technically-advanced. It was therefore several years before plant currently being planned could be brought into operation.

Because its pricing objective had been set as a return on capital (and to some extent because it was a company tradition) Universal Corporation had based its list price for its product on unit cost. Previously, this had been average cost per unit, at a previously-determined level of output. After debate with the parent Board and with distributors lasting several years, Universal Corporation had recently agreed to base price on marginal cost.

INFORMATION USED FOR PRICE DECISIONS

Because the price list was issued annually in advance, it had to be based on estimates of what demand and costs would be for the following year.

(a) Demand Information

Because its capital assets took so long to build, Universal Corporation required forecasts for a number of years ahead. This provided a basis for plans for developing new types of plant and for determining the amount of capital expenditure to be incurred and serviced financially.

Forecasts of demand for the product in the year ahead were produced annually by Universal Corporation, by its parent firm and by the distributors. These forecasts were discussed at meetings of all three parties. From these discussions emerged an accepted total forecast which was disseminated by the parent group. After further discussion with distributors, the parent firm divided these total forecast sales between distributors, and notified Universal Corporation's

Commercial Department of its forecasts. This analysis was passed to the Production Department, and was the main determinant of Universal Corporation's operating plans; it was also used by the Commercial Department as part of the information going into its simulation programme.

(b) Operational Planning Information

This was information about several fundamental factors. Together with demand forecasts, it made up the data which the Production Department used in planning its operations. The information was also passed to the Commercial Department, which used it in its simulation programme. The main factors about which information was provided were:

Daily and seasonal patterns of demand (based upon experience);
production plant requirements;
costs of individual production plants;
raw material supplies;
plant availability;
distribution problems.

(c) Commercial Department Simulation

This was a computer model of the company's production and distribution system. It was used by the Commercial Department to forecast optimum production for individual plants. Using the model, Universal Corporation worked out optimum production schedules and costs for individual plants. These met the conditions imposed by operational planning and represented the known state of the company's system. The output figures obtained from this simulation tended to be idealized. Although this was an optimum, given the constraints, only a limited number of constraints could be included in the programme, by comparison with the almost infinite number of possible constraints. Nevertheless, it was claimed that the production forecasts produced by the model were more consistent than any produced anywhere else in the company. Moreover, the model was the only means for rapidly linking changes in production costs with changes in the level and pattern of demand.

(d) Basic Cost Data

Information about fixed costs was supplied to the Commercial Department by the Finance Department. The Commercial Department added these costs to those forecast by its simulation programme, after making adjustments for practical operating constraints. These gave a forecast for Universal Corporation's total costs for the year at forecast levels of output. This forecast of total company costs showed the amount which Universal Corporation had to attempt to recover (including the required profit) from the prices established in the price list for the year. In the past, this amount had been divided by total forecast output to obtain the (average) price for a unit of the product.

THE DEVELOPMENT OF MARGINALISM

The crucial factors influencing Universal Corporation's costs were these. First, there was the fact that at no level of output did marginal cost decrease. Second, at all levels of output above the minimum amount it was technically possible to produce (which was much lower than minimum demand), marginal cost always increased; consequently, average cost also increased, though less rapidly than marginal cost.

Universal Corporation's existing procedure, where unit price was linked directly to average unit cost at the forecast level of output, led to a situation where, if sales were in excess of forecast sales, the company made a loss on the extra units sold. The price of those units was not adjusted to take account of their greater unit cost. This situation is illustrated in Figure M.1 where costs have been calculated so as to include the prescribed return on capital.

At this stage, Universal Corporation made a prediction of marginal costs over the next few years. The aim was to estimate their probable behaviour, in view of forecast demand, technological development and planned capital expenditure. The study indicated that, at all likely volumes of output, once current capital investment projects had been completed, marginal costs were unlikely to vary significantly from current average costs.

In view of these facts, it was decided that a system of pricing based upon marginal costs would be desirable and that a smooth transition to such a system was possible. Universal Corporation decided to adapt the average cost basis of its prices by introducing a series of price steps for specified ranges of extra output. These were based on the marginal costs anticipated when current capital investment projects had been completed, along the lines shown in Figure M.2.

Here, the average and marginal cost curves of Figure M.1 have been retained, but output has been divided into two ranges, with a separate price for each. First, for sales within the range O–V_1 units, price per unit is P_1, and is equal to the current average cost for V_1 units. Second, for sales within the range V_1–V_2 units, price per unit is P_2,

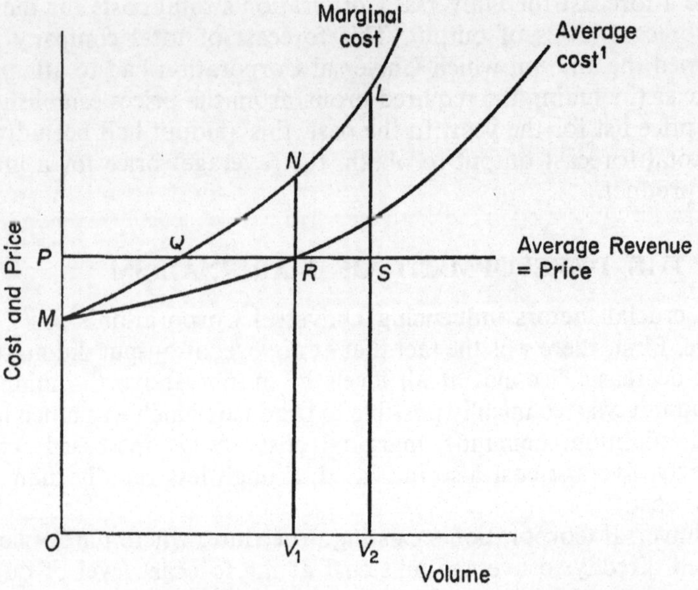

	Forecast Volume (OV_1 Units)	*Actual Volume* (OV_2 Units)
Costs	$O\,M\,N\,V_1$	$O\,M\,L\,V_2$
Revenue	$O\,P\,R\,V_1$	$O\,P\,S\,V_2$
Loss on this range of output	Nil	$N\,L\,S\,R$
	(Profit $P\,Q\,M$ =) (Loss $Q\,N\,R$)	(Gross Loss $Q\,L\,S$) (*less* Profit $P\,Q\,M$)

FIGURE M.1

equal to the current average cost for V_2 units. In fact, three volume ranges and price levels were distinguished, but Figure M.2 has been limited to the two ranges for ease of presentation.

The difficulty in all this was that during the period of transition from average to marginal-cost pricing—i.e. during the period in which the current capital investment programme was being completed—losses would have had to be borne by the company on any output sold at a price below its (current) marginal cost. This was regarded as

[1] Universal Corporation revealed that the average cost curve would slope downwards initially. The reader is asked to accept the illogicality of this diagram. The point being made is a valid one in this firm, and can be shown simply with these curves.

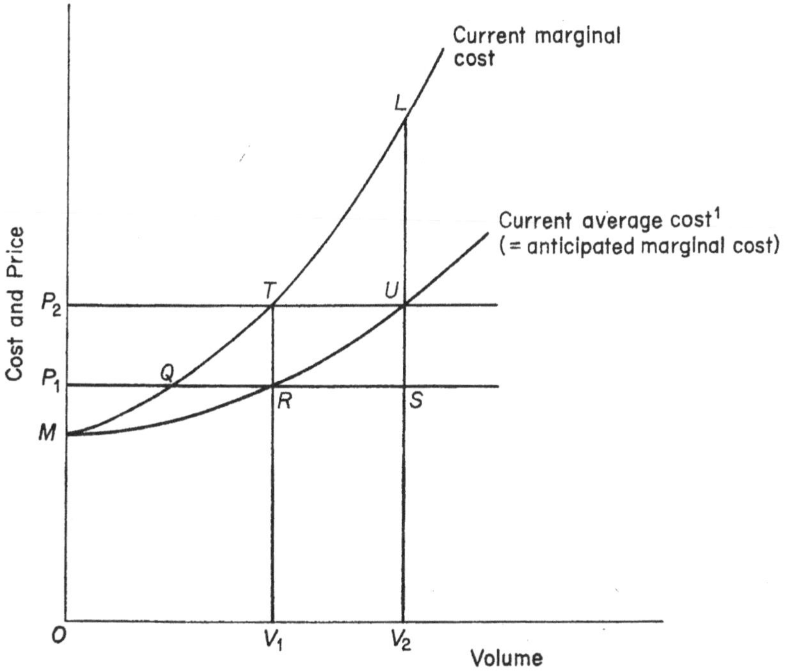

	V_1 *Units*	V_2 *less* V_1 *Units*	*Total* (V_2) *Units*
Price	$O\,P_1$	$O\,P_2$	
Costs	$O\,M\,T\,V_1$	$V_1\,T\,L\,V_2$	$O\,M\,L\,V_2$
Revenue	$O\,P_1\;R\,V_1$	$V_1\,T\,U\,V_2$	$O\,P_1\;R\,T\,U\,V_2$
Loss	Nil	$T\,L\,U$	

{Profit = $P_1\;Q\;M$ Less $Q\;T\;R$}

{Gross Loss = $Q\;L\;S$ *less* Profit $P_1\;Q\;M$ and Revenue $T\;U\;S\;R$}

FIGURE M.2

a transitional difficulty, to be accepted by the company. It was to be resolved partly by introducing new price steps, based on the current average cost of incremental output, and partly by non-price methods. This view was accepted on the ground that it would provide distributors with a comparatively painless movement to an equitable system of charges in the future, whatever volumes distributors purchased; and not only if they bought volumes of output from within the forecast range.

[1] See note to Figure M.1

PRICING DECISION PROCESSES

(a) Preparing the Annual Price List

With this information, the Commercial Department produced an estimate of total costs for the following year. All the later processes of calculating forecast average costs at different volumes of output were carried out by the Commercial Department. They led to the elaboration of proposals for a new price list. No formal set of operational procedures was laid down. The only constraints on the Commercial Department's freedom of operation were the methods used, precedents set and results achieved in the past, as well as the company's objectives, set by the Board.

The Commercial Department's proposals were normally completed some three months before the new price list was due to come into effect. They had to be approved by the company Board, to whom they were presented by the Finance Director. He was the Board's channel of communication with the Commercial Department and informed it of policy changes and of directives about the price list. When prices had been approved, their introduction was the responsibility of the Commercial Department.

Nor was any formal procedure for reviewing the results of pricing decisions built into the sequence for determining prices. However, operating results were monitored continuously through the year for managerial and production control purposes. Factors affecting pricing decisions were taken into account when consideration was being given to the next year's price list. The Board of Universal Corporation expected a review of the year's trading to be provided by the Commercial Department, on each occasion when it produced a price list.

(b) Major Changes to the Price List

When the new price list based on marginal costs was being introduced, these procedures were used, but they were subsidiary to wide discussion and consultation within the company—particularly at Board level—as well as between the Board of Universal Corporation, its parent firm and its distributors. These discussions lasted for a considerable period of time. The experience of an overseas firm with similar experience was also used. The decision to go ahead with marginal pricing was made by the parent Board, in principle, a year before its introduction. Because of the assumption that future marginal costs would not be significantly different from existing average costs, the original price list was based on a refined set of average-cost prices. This was expected to develop, after some years of capital investment, into true marginal-cost prices.

Index